Thorstein Veblen on Culture and Society

Stjepan Mestrovic

SAGE Publications
London • Thousand Oaks • New Delhi

First published 2003

SAGE Publications Ltd
6 Bonhill Street
London EC2A 4PU

SAGE Publications Inc
2455 Teller Road
Thousand Oaks, California 91320

SAGE Publications India Pvt Ltd
B-42 Panchsheel Enclave
Post Box 4109
New Delhi – 100 017

British Library Cataloguing in Publication data

A catalogue record for this book is available from the British Library

ISBN 0 7619 4123 1
ISBN 0 7619 4124 X

Library of Congress Control Number Available

Printed and bound in Great Britain by Athenaeum Press, Gateshead

Theory, Culture & Society

Theory, Culture & Society caters for the resurgence of interest in culture within contemporary social science and the humanities. Building on the heritage of classical social theory, the book series examines ways in which this tradition has been reshaped by a new generation of theorists. It also publishes theoretically informed analyses of everyday life, popular culture, and new intellectual movements.

THE TCS CENTRE
The *Theory, Culture & Society* book series, the journals *Theory, Culture & Society* and *Body & Society*, and related conference, seminar and postgraduate programmes operate from the TCS Centre at Nottingham Trent University. For further details of the TCS Centre's activities please contact:

Centre Administrator
The TCS Centre, Room 175
Faculty of Humanities
Nottingham Trent University
Clifton Lane, Nottingham, NG11 8NS, UK
e-mail: tcs@ntu.ac.uk
web: http://tcs.ntu.ac.uk

Recent volumes include:

The Tourist Gaze
John Urry

Critique of Information
Scott Lash

Liberal Democracy 3.0
Stephen P. Turner

French Social Theory
Mike Gane

Contents

Acknowledgements		vi
Introduction		1
1	The Place of Science in Modern Civilisation	18
2	The Instability of Knowledge and Belief	28
3	The Technology of the Predatory Culture	37
4	The Dynastic State in Germany	41
5	Higher Learning	52
6	Sabotage	85
7	Patriotism	94
8	The Barbarian Status of Women	111
9	The Economic Theory of Women's Dress	120
10	Dementia Praecox	127
11	Manufacture and Salesmanship	133
12	The Larger Uses of Credit	152
Bibliography		192
Index		

Acknowledgements

I am grateful to Chris Rojek and David Riesman for encouragement with this project. I also benefited from discussion at the meeting of the International Veblen Association in New York City in April of 2002. Grateful acknowledgement is made to Penguin Putnam for permission to reproduce the passages from Veblen that are used in this book:

Essays in our Changing Order (1943) New York: Viking, pages 50–64, 65–77, 423–425, 428–435; *Absentee Ownership and Business Enterprise in Recent Times* (1923) New York: Viking, pages 284–288,292–295, 299–323, 326–328, 330–401;*The Place of Science in Modern Civilisation* (1919) New York: Viking, pages 1–17; *Imperial Germany and the Industrial Revolution* (1964) New York: Viking, pages 238–258; *The Vested Interests and the Common Man* (1919) New York: Viking, pages 23–34; *The Higher Learning in America* (1918) New York: Viking, pages 1–30, 161–167, 202–209; *The Engineers and the Price System* (1921) New York: Viking, pages 1–26; *An Inquiry into the Nature of Peace and the Forms of its Perpetuation* (1945) New York: Viking, pages 31–61.

To my daughters, Ivy and Victoria

Introduction

Thorstein Veblen is known primarily as a social critic and economist. He has not been incorporated into mainstream sociology via Talcott Parsons and Anthony Giddens in the way that Marx, Durkheim, and Weber were to form the bedrock for theories of social agency, structural-functionalism, and structuration theory. Veblen's relevance for cultural studies is marginal at best. Certainly, some exceptions to this rule do exist. For example, Jean Baudrillard uses Veblen's ideas concerning conspicuous and vicarious consumption to portray a postmodern world of consuming images in addition to material things. C. Wright Mills makes some use of Veblen with regard to power elites. David Riesman incorporates quite a bit of Veblen's thought into *The Lonely Crowd* (1950), particularly with regard to the concepts of marginal differentiation by the other-directed type and the constant striving for status by the inner-directed type. Riesman also wrote a monograph on Veblen in which he portrays Veblen as a kindred spirit but also in an unsympathetic light as someone who could not grasp the good and kind aspects of vicariously and conspicuously consumptive persons, whom Riesman renamed the other-directed.[1] Chris Rojek (1994) makes complicated use of Veblen with regard to leisure studies by arguing, for example, that the rich are not as idle as Veblen made them out to be and that leisure often takes on the organized characteristics of work. Theodor Adorno took Veblen seriously but criticized him for his obsessive, one-sided assault on wealth and power, and inability to appreciate the aesthetics that lie beneath ostentatious display. Interestingly, the intellectuals who make use of Veblen are themselves often regarded as social critics.

But so-called mainstream social and cultural theorists do *not* make use of Veblen and include: Talcott Parsons, Jürgen Habermas, Anthony Giddens, Zygmunt Bauman, even Robert Park and Everett Burgess, among others. It is safe to say that Veblen is a problematic figure in social theory and has been neglected in cultural studies. Most people know Veblen because of his book, *The Theory of the Leisure Class*, but they do not connect this work to Veblen's other writings on war and peace, women, advertising, and economics, among other cultural phenomena. And they do not connect him to central issues and theories in social theory and cultural studies such as social agency, the problem of social order, modernity, and postmodernity.

Yet this is a curious neglect, worth pursuing further. The homage paid to Veblen is unusual: he is typically hailed as one of the greatest American social critics. His basic ideas have become the staple of everyday culture: "conspicuous consumption" is a term bantered about in editorials and in ordinary conversation. Most people believe they can imagine examples of what Veblen termed "conspicuous waste." Veblen's concept of "conspicuous leisure" is accepted by many writers in the field of leisure studies. Even among academics, it is well known that Veblen posited irreconcilable conflict between the "business enterprise" and the "common man," the "instinct for workmanship" and the "pecuniary instincts," modernity and barbarism. But the truly fascinating aspect of Veblen's fame is the ease with which he is dismissed as a satirist, as being silly for positing the need for a soviet of engineers, as being irrelevant to modern economics, obsolete, inconsistent, and as hopelessly ambiguous.[2] He was criticized during his lifetime as well as after his death by liberals, conservatives, and radicals (Tilman, 1992). The strong passions shown by his admirers as well as detractors lead one to believe that there is more to Veblen than meets the eye.

Consider, for example, Veblen's scattered references to advertising. In the new millennium, he seems more correct than ever before in stating that most advertising is "wasteful" in the sense that it does less to convey information about a product and more to convey an "honorific value" — and added costs — to the product. He notes also that advertising is competitive, hence barbaric, because it involves the victory of one corporation at the expense of another making a similar product. He depicts advertising as a contemporary form of medieval warfare. The motto seems to be, "kill or be killed." The recent controversy surrounding Nike tennis shoes, which compete with other high-status tennis shoes, and which are manufactured in sweatshops in the Far East but are advertised for millions of dollars by cultural "superstars" such as Michael Jordan, seems to illustrate Veblen's point very well. Veblen correctly prophesied that more than half of newspaper space would be devoted to advertising, not the news. He was correct to observe that the packaging of a product is far more important than the actual qualities of the product. Veblen was invoking a widespread *culture* of barbarism and envy that erupts in and through phenomena that one would not normally consider barbaric. Or consider, as one more example, Veblen's many references to the "machine" and "machine culture" as *the* exemplars of modernity. Veblen is clearly discussing more than the assembly line and the Ford system: he is discussing a *cultural* move toward standardization at the expense of spontaneous human emotions. In other words, Veblen argues that mechanization moves out of the factory and takes over a culture's laws, customs, norms, universities, and minute aspects of everyday life. Yet he is not invoked by theorists who have pursued a similar line of inquiry *vis-à-vis* Max Weber, such as George Ritzer in *The McDonaldization of Society* (1992). Despite nearly a century of commentary, theorists have not linked his discussion of mechanized culture with similar discussions by George Orwell in *The Road to Wigan Pier* ([1937] 1958) or Henry Adams in "The Dynamo and the Virgin" ([1900] 1983) or other reactions to the Gilded Age in the humanities and social sciences. These are several examples among many, but they suggest that Veblen's relevance has not been exhausted despite a mountain of commentary and analysis.[3]

Veblen and the Culture of Narcissism

In this edited volume, I propose to demonstrate Veblen's relevance to the topics that concern Anthony Giddens and other leading cultural theorists, namely, Westernization, modernity, globalization, postmodernity, and other topics in cultural studies. Rather than treat Veblen as he has been approached in the past, as an economist, social critic, and problematic sociologist, I offer a new vision of him as a cultural theorist. This is because he obviously made the transmission of culture *vis-à-vis* "habits" central to all of his writings. In Veblen's words, culture is "the organised complex of habits and thought and of conduct by which [a society's] own routine of life is regulated." Readers of Veblen seem to overlook the fact that he approached all the concepts for which he has become famous in the light of this definition of culture, and that a unifying theme can be found for the manner in which he approached these concepts. He concerned himself with topics that concern students of culture: fashion, leisure, work, education, the status of women, and other topics. I offer a selection of Veblen's works whose importance has still not been appreciated. I do *not* offer selections from Veblen's best-known work, *The Theory of the Leisure Class* ([1899] 1969) yet I refer to this work occasionally in order to demonstrate the cohesiveness in Veblen's style which many critics find scattered. In summary, unlike most of the literature on Veblen, this book treats Veblen as a cultural social theorist, not exclusively as an economist or social critic. In other words, Veblen's roles as economist and social critic are subsumed under the rubric of theorist of culture. Moreover, I use narcissism and its derivatives as the unique and unifying strand to Veblen's cultural approach.

It is important to seek a unifying strand in Veblen's apparently ambiguous and ambivalent works *vis-à-vis* current debates in cultural studies, including debates concerning modernity and postmodernity. Specifically, I argue that Veblen was foreshadowing the coming of a strange new culture of narcissism characterized by widespread use of the psychological mechanism that psychologists call "splitting" or dissociation. It is a culture in which emotions are cut off from the intellect, things and people are idealized at the same time that they are devalued, and in general, barbarism co-exists with what Veblen called peaceable cultural traits. The narcissistic type is split psychologically and socially. One side of him or her is obsessed with status-consciousness and displays lack of empathy, envy, and self-absorption. One finds the narcissist in the rich details that go into Veblen's searing portraits of the consumer, the self-made man or woman, the patriot, the follower of fashion, and other social types. But the other side of the narcissist is the hidden self that feels worthless and injured, and therefore seeks the admiration, even affection, of others. Hence, Veblen emphasizes the *conspicuous* nature of waste, leisure, and consumption, or what Riesman termed other-directedness. Veblen's narcissist does not simply waste — he or she seeks to be liked by others through various refractions of waste.

Veblen's readers and critics have noticed that he was obsessed with affluence, but not that he was more specifically obsessed with various refractions of envy. Christopher Lasch has argued in *The Culture of Narcissism* (1975) that narcissism becomes an increasingly common cultural trait for some individuals in upwardly mobile societies such as the United States, Great Britain, and other Western societies. Veblen not only preceded Lasch in making this argument, albeit not in the modernist sense used by Lasch (namely, that the USA began to produce more narcissists in the 1960s as a result of widespread hedonism), but Veblen implicitly decenters this concept into a discussion of cultural realms neglected by Lasch, such as science, the conduct of warfare, advertising, fashion, the institution of higher learning, and other cultural phenomena. These and other cultural phenomena become arenas for various refractions of envy, and envy is one of the major components of narcissism. A cultural, decentered understanding of narcissism is the key for unlocking the unity and relevance of Veblen's works.

Psychiatrists seem to believe that they have established the existence of a common psychological disorder in late Western societies, the narcissistic personality disorder. In the present study, I am not interested in the "reality" of narcissism *vis-à-vis* psychiatrically disturbed individuals or cultures of narcissism in the manner described by Lasch. I approach narcissism as a text, and argue that Veblen was writing narratives about narcissism as text when he wrote about leisure, war, advertising, fashion, and other cultural phenomena. A postmodern or deconstructionist approach to this psychiatric approach to narcissism is beyond the scope of the present study. Suffice it to say that psychiatrists do not seem able to agree on the differences between healthy versus unhealthy narcissism, nor its cultural ramifications. Nevertheless, it is helpful to examine briefly the criteria set forth by psychiatrists for establishing the narcissistic personality disorder in order to appreciate Veblen's neglected contribution of uncovering a widespread culture of narcissism in late Western societies. According to the *Diagnostic and Statistical Manual-IV*, seven of the following nine traits qualify an individual as suffering from narcissistic personality disorder (Widiger et al., 1995: 134):

1. has a grandiose sense of self-importance;
2. is preoccupied with fantasies of unlimited success, power, brilliance, beauty, or ideal love;
3. believes that he or she is special and unique and can only be understood by, or should associate with other special or high-status people;
4. requires excessive admiration;
5. has a sense of entitlement;
6. is interpersonally exploitative;
7. lacks empathy;
8. is often envious of others or believes that others are envious of him or her;
9. shows arrogant, haughty behaviors or attitudes.

The relevance of the concept of narcissism as a text for the present study is that it exposes aspects of Veblen's approach to topics that some readers have found baffling. He was not merely mocking the "captains of industry," government leaders, religious leaders, and other cultural representatives of latter-day barbarism. He was exposing narcissistic aspects of some ordinary activities on the part of ordinary persons. In this sense, he was offering a genuinely sociological and cultural explanation that is often disturbing. For example, many readers are offended by his peculiar verbal attack on the ownership of dogs (found in *The Theory of the Leisure Class*) as representing predatory and barbaric values because dogs are allegedly "useless" and therefore, in Veblen's view, are kept primarily as a sign of status. Some of my students have remarked, and I think rightly, that Veblen overlooks the fact that some people keep dogs for the very useful purpose of companionship. The more important point seems to be that perceiving dogs as useful is a common rationalization, whereas Veblen continues to offend many people because he exposed the narcissistic element in one of the most common cultural habits in the West, ownership of dogs. He is not saying that dog-owners are narcissistic, but that a culture of narcissism impels ordinary persons toward status-seeking in arenas which one would not ordinarily notice status-seeking. He makes similar implicit accusations of narcissism in his detailed but one-sided descriptions of the lawn, smoking cigarettes, going to the horse races, attending church, shopping and so on – over and over again he finds envy and its derivatives.

Towards a Sociology of Narcissism

Far more significant is the observation that Veblen describes wholesale cultures and aspects of culture as narcissistic. He was using a mode of enquiry quite different from that of Christopher Lasch and most psychiatrists who are interested in how a culture of narcissism produces upwardly mobile individual narcissists. For example, Veblen's once celebrated essays on barbaric tendencies in Japan and Germany are basically descriptions of pre-war Japan and Germany as primarily narcissistic collective entities or collective political actors on the world stage. In other words, Veblen was describing Japan and Germany in a Durkheimian mode, as arenas of collective consciousness, and describing a particular collective consciousness as behaving in a narcissistic fashion in addition to how some individuals in those societies behaved. Thus, pre-World War I Germany is described by Veblen as behaving in an arrogant fashion toward its neighbors, as causing envy in other nations, as filled with an inflated sense of self-importance, as seeking unlimited power, as fostering the illusion that Germany is unique and special, as exploiting other nations and as possessing a collective sense of privilege and entitlement. Veblen was making a bold statement about war and peace in the modern era: much like an individual narcissist will start fights with an individual partner in his or her relationship due to a grandiose self-image, an entire nation will resort to war and start fights with other nations due to a collective sense of grandiosity and other dynamics pertaining to narcissism. If, once appreciated, Veblen's insight holds merit, it is an important contribution to the literature on war and peace. It could be the case that contemporary Germany and Japan are peaceful nations because their collective narcissism was deliberately cut down to size by organized programs of collective self-reflection, guilt, and atonement.

Riesman has already noted Veblen's inconsistency in condemning war as barbaric and as being an ardent supporter of American involvement in World War I. But as the selection from Veblen in Chapter 10 shows, there is still more to Veblen's apparent inconsistency. He criticizes the United States for not achieving the total defeat of Germany once it entered the war, and speculates that the United States and its allies did not finish the job because of vested business interests — which is to say, because of collective narcissism. Whether he criticizes war or peace, he cannot seem to escape his suspicion that vested, predatory, and barbaric goals are involved. Yet, despite his disturbing suspiciousness, his observations concerning World War I seem to apply to recent American wars against Iraq, Serbia, and the Taliban. America and its allies still do not seem to finish the job in the sense of achieving their stated goals of vanquishing a demonized enemy, and the layperson does suspect that vested interests are involved in both the waging of war and the negotiation of peace. War and peace are linked to business. In addition, Veblen describes the post-World War I mood of victory as "schizophrenic," wherein Americans were not quite sure what was won or lost. This sense of ambivalence can also be linked to narcissism, as I will demonstrate later.

In general, Veblen seems to have abhorred patriotism. He curtly dismisses any possibility that patriotism can promote peaceful, cooperative, or otherwise socially beneficial ends. For Veblen, patriotism serves only the ends of competition that often lead to death and destruction. Patriotism is a derivative of what he called "the instinct for sportsmanship" (of course, none of the "instincts" that Veblen describes are real, biological instincts), hence barbaric and predatory. While his argument is extreme in its one-sidedness, it is also useful for exposing what many contemporary persons refuse to admit, namely, that even supposedly peace-loving nations will often go to war because of patriotic fervor even though these warlike aims are rationalized as being in the name of civilization, justice, and morality. Veblen makes a useful and significant point. A missile launched by a nation such as the United States or Great Britain that perceives itself as moral and therefore superior to its enemy, and that ends up killing women and children, is used for barbaric purposes even if the death is rationalized away as unavoidable "collateral damage."

Similarly, Veblen's stereotypes of the businessman and the lawyer as modern predators bent upon their own sense of entitlement and upon ruthless exploitation of the weak are basically refractions of the contemporary psychiatric images of the narcissist. It is beside the point that kind, nonpredatory businessmen and lawyers do exist and did exist in Veblen's time. Veblen's view was definitely one-sided. Yet he was making an argument akin to Max Weber's ideal-type depiction of the Puritan and Simmel's descriptions of social types such as the adventurer, the miser, and the poor, among others. It is not the exceptions to the rule that count, but the cultural basis for the stereotype. Veblen argued that modern social institutions rest upon modern, predatory and barbaric business principles. Hence, scientists, artists, educators, the clergy and other representatives of social institutions must make money in order to pursue their humanitarian objectives. And they must make or obtain money in predatory, competitive, and often exploitative ways, much like the stereotypical businessman makes money. It is easy to find illustrations of this neglected and offensive insight by Veblen. University professors in the West are rated on the basis of how much research money they bring to their universities, on the number of publications they produce, and on the general sense of honor and prestige they bring to their departments. Lip service is paid to quality of teaching (but teaching, too, is measured on the basis of businesslike criteria such as quantifiable ratings by students, size of classes, grade point averages and other ratings that are not much different from how businesses are rated) and the pursuit of knowledge for its own sake, but everyone at the university knows that what really counts for tenure and promotion is quantity of publications and research money. Lecturers and graduate students are exploited by the university to teach courses on extremely low pay if tenured faculty cannot be found to teach these courses. In a real sense, the modern, Western university professor is an entrepreneur in business for him or herself. He or she is forced to become a narcissist because of cultural forces toward narcissism that have transformed most social institutions into business enterprises. Contemporary churches, schools, art museums, and other social institutions must also act like businesses.

Veblen made the image of the "self-made man" central to his depictions of the leisure class, the businessman, the lawyer, other predators, and American culture as a whole. He claimed that America is the native habitat of the self-made man, but the self-made man is a pecuniary organism. Of course, Veblen's descriptions of the self-made man must be extrapolated to include the self-made woman. Translated into the vocabulary of contemporary psychiatry, Veblen was claiming that the self-made man (or woman) is a narcissist, and is compelled to become a narcissist by institutional forces beyond his or her control. He or she is a narcissist in arenas of cultural life other than just work, and this is what makes Veblen's argument unique.

For example, Veblen's writings on fashion are different from those of Simmel. Simmel felt that following fashion was a way to achieve a sense of personal uniqueness at the same time that one tried to conform to fashion trends: fashion is simultaneously an act of individuation and association. But for Veblen, fashion is described as a narcissistic activity that involves status, waste, self-aggrandizement, a desire for admiration, envy, and other narcissistic goals. Thus, fashion is an extension of traditional adornment, and involves causing a sense of envy in others. Fashion, for Veblen, must involve conspicuously unproductive expenditure. It must display novelty and taste, but taste requires time to acquire, so that the display of taste in fashion is a sign to others that one has the time to waste to engage in self-absorption.

Convenience, comfort, and health are not the central goals of fashion. Veblen also foresaw that not only women but men and children would increasingly become entwined in the inexorable cultural forces that drive fashion. Again, to illustrate Veblen's point, one has only to consider the recent trends in Western countries for infants, toddlers, and small children to display fashionable clothing. What possible use can a toddler have for clothing that is fashionable (uncomfortable, impractical, expensive, and designed to cause envy in others)? Clearly, adults dress their children in fashionable clothing in order to evoke envy in others and in order to make a statement about the grandiosity of an entire family, not just the adult members in it. In these and other ways, Veblen's arguments are offensive and disturbing, yet they expose aspects of contemporary Western culture that few are willing to admit. Yet Veblen seems completely unable to find the advantages of following fashion: that people are drawn to beauty, that they want to be liked by others, that they want to feel as if they are a part of trends. He could not empathize with the human elements of fashion. He could not see that an expensive dress is not "wasteful" if it makes one feel that the end result of such a beautiful, expensive dress is romance or a dream evening.

The Other Side of Narcissism

A thinker as hyper-vigilant as Veblen to the vicissitudes of narcissism would be compelled to be just as hyper-vigilant about cultural states that are the opposite of narcissism. In fact, one of the peculiarities of the narcissistic personality is that he or she over-idealizes the self at the same time that he or she devalues others as well as one's self. If one is deemed beautiful, others are ugly. If one is grandiose, others are common. If one is constantly seeking status, one is keenly aware of those who are immune to status and can be exploited. Moreover, deep down, narcissists consider their true selves to be ugly, common, and worthless, which is the reason why they project grandiose visions of themselves onto the world. Psychiatrists call this psychological defense "splitting." Small children use splitting as a matter of course: they frequently say "I love you" and "I hate you" to the same parent in the space of a few minutes. In this sense, narcissists are childish: they over-utilize a defense mechanism that is normal for children but problematic for adults. Veblen's cultural analysis exposes these and other split nuances of conspicuous leisure, waste, and consumption. In this sense, Riesman completed Veblen's descriptions of the actor bent upon leisure, waste, and consumption as also seeking to be liked and appreciated by others, as feeling very insecure, and as seeking conformity even as he or she sought marginal differentiation from others — hence, the other-directed type.

Using these insights, perhaps one is able to appreciate in a new way Veblen's neglected and misunderstood discussions of "idle curiosity," "the instinct for workmanship," "peaceable traits," and the good qualities of matriarchal culture that he over-idealized. In fact, most if not all of

Veblen's writings can be reduced to the simple dualism of barbaric versus non-barbaric and communal cultural forces. He depicts these cultural forces as social atmospheres or outlooks on the world. Thus, the barbaric part of the split narcissist is basically competitive, warlike, wasteful, and oriented toward personal rather than communal achievements. His or her nemesis is the peaceful, cooperative, frugal, and communal social type engaged in the "instinct for workmanship." But what is peculiar about cultural tendencies to engage in splitting is that the human agent keeps these contradictory cultural world-views in separate, logic-tight compartments.

For example, because Veblen exposed the university system as being bent upon honor, status, prestige, and money, he had to posit a mysterious state of being that he called idle curiosity as one in which one learned things for no perceived motive at all. He felt that idle curiosity was common in traditional cultures and to some extent in modern cultures prior to the cultural invention of the machine system. The machine system was designed to mass-produce goods for the sake of profit — a narcissistic goal — not necessarily quality of workmanship. For Veblen, the machine system has to battle with and eventually conquer the "instinct for workmanship," which is a more humane goal of wanting to produce quality for its own sake, and not for the sake of honor, status, and pecuniary reward. This is an extreme assessment by Veblen and assumes that the grandiose aspects of the split narcissistic personality will conquer the humble aspects. It is probably more realistic to suppose that both traditional and modern cultures exhibited and still do exhibit both barbaric and what he calls peaceable traits.

In his discussion of narcissistic traits that lead to war, he also discusses peaceable traits such as cooperation with other nations, discussion, and negotiation to offset the fervent patriotism bent upon death and destruction. But he is unable to find anything benign about patriotism (such as paying taxes for the common welfare, the desire for self-defense, a love for one's country that is as natural as the love for one's family, and so on). For Veblen, patriotism is the negative, split aspect of the narcissist. There is a strong tendency in all of Veblen's writings to regard women as the bearers of some mysterious matriarchal culture from the past based upon caring, a concern for others, and communication which is being gradually replaced by masculine, patriarchal traits of narcissism. In general, Veblen idealized women and devalued men. But against Veblen, it is more realistic to assume that narcissism and barbarism are gender-blind: both sexes can be and are barbaric as well as charitable albeit in different ways. He is a pessimist with regard to short-term trends in modernity: he felt that the machine system, pecuniary values, and the desire for honor were steadily replacing the non-narcissistic cultural values that he felt characterized traditional societies, and he felt that some remnants of these good values still survived in the ways that women behaved in societies. In terms of long-term development, he could be construed as an optimist, in that he held open the possibility that the barbaric, predatory, self-absorbed values might eventually collapse and be replaced by cultural values pertaining to peace, cooperation, idle curiosity, and the instinct for workmanship. But this argument assumes splitting, the total victory of one set of idealized cultural traits and the total annihilation of one set of devalued traits.

Finding Veblen's Place in Social Theory

In these regards, Veblen was carving out a unique sociological niche. His thinking is somewhat similar to Durkheim's condemnation of egoism and anomie as collective, modern sicknesses similar to narcissism. But Durkheim felt that all societies at all times must find a balance between egoism and anomie on the one hand and altruism and fatalism on the other, even though he felt that the latter characterized traditional societies and the former characterized modern societies for the most part. Using psychiatric jargon, one could say that Durkheim made use of dualisms, but did not explore cultural splitting. In contradistinction to Durkheim, Veblen felt that in modernity, narcissistic traits were steadily winning the battle, and no balance with contrary cultural forces was possible. Veblen's thought is inimical to that of Herbert Spencer, who glorified egoism on the basis of some peculiar understanding of Darwin and Lamarck that resulted in the doctrine of social Darwinism or what is commonly known as "the survival of the fittest." Yet Veblen also seems to have subscribed to some curious blend of Darwinism and Lamarckianism, often writing that some cultural traits are transmitted not only through learning but also through heredity. This is yet another instance of Veblen's maddening inconsistency. Like Marx, Veblen condemned the predatory practices of modern business. But unlike Marx and the Marxists, Veblen thought that even communist or socialist systems that used the machine system as the basis of cultural life would be subjected to the same predatory tendencies found in capitalist cultures. Unlike Marx, Veblen could not find anything benign in the machine system. In addition, Marx condemned the backwardness of traditional, pre-capitalist societies whereas Veblen idealized them. Like Max Weber, Veblen was sensitive to the intrusion of machine-like rationality into all social institutions. But Weber tried to be value-neutral and tried to find good as well as bad aspects to the rationality that results in bureaucracy and formal organizations. Unlike Weber, Veblen clearly condemns the machine system. Whereas Simmel tried to find a balance between "life" and "forms," the tendency toward individuation and association in most of his writings, Veblen finds no place for balance in his writings. Like Durkheim, Simmel made use of dualisms, but avoided splitting.

One can see how both Parsons and Giddens could draw upon Durkheim, Weber, Marx, and other classical theorists apart from Veblen in order to derive some variation of what is known as social action theory. Both Parsons and Giddens seek to portray the modern individual as one who is capable of the self-reflexivity necessary to make a rational decision concerning the choice of means to achieve a desired goal. More than Parsons, Giddens is concerned with making the human agent seem like more than a cultural dupe, more than the victim of cultural forces beyond his or her control. In other words, Parsons and Giddens assume an integrated personality and an integrated social system. Veblen was ignored by Parsons, Giddens, and other social action theorists for the obvious reason that Veblen assumed a split personality and a split social system. In very complicated ways, Veblen depicts the modern individual as well as modernist types (the businessman, the lawyer, the predator, etc.) as being active agents and passive child-like persons simultaneously. Veblen's position is not fundamentally different from Freud's and other psychiatric depictions of narcissism as an involuntary response to extreme narcissistic injuries in childhood: the adult narcissist develops a grandiose self because he or she felt too vulnerable and insignificant as a child. Therapy can offer insight and some control into the narcissistic process, but can never provide a wholesale "cure." Similarly, for Veblen, the machine system was the equivalent of the primary narcissistic injury to world cultures: it first threatened and later came to progressively destroy the idealized, small-minded, family-oriented cultures that fostered idle curiosity, the instinct for workmanship, and other traditional values that he considers good. Traditional societies seek to emulate the success of modern Western societies due to envy, yet seek to maintain cultural traits that are non-predatory and non-barbaric. Hence, the push and pull, acceptance and rejection, idealization and devaluation characteristic of cultural interaction between the West and the non-West.

If Veblen's writings in these regards seem disturbing and overly pessimistic, one could argue that Parsons (1937) and Giddens (1990) fail to appreciate the perceived helplessness and feelings of insignificance in non-Western cultures *vis-à-vis* modernity. Akbar Ahmed's (1992) writings on the conflicts within Islamic cultures as they seek to emulate the West are particularly helpful in appreciating what Parsons and Giddens omitted, although, Ahmed also ignores Veblen.

Veblen on Postmodernism

Veblen uses the term, "postmodern," in one specific passage that is included in Chapter 2 of this collection of essays:

> But it has been only during the later decades of the modern era — during that time interval that might fairly be called the post-modern era — that this mechanistic conception of things has begun seriously to affect the current system of knowledge and belief . . . So that it has not hitherto seriously invaded the established scheme of institutional arrangements, the system of law and custom, which governs the relations of men to one another and defines their mutual rights, obligations, advantages and disabilities. . . . It should seem reasonable to expect, therefore, that the scheme of law and custom will also fall into line with this mechanistic conception that appears to mark the apex of growth in modern intellectual life.

Of course, the literature on postmodernism is so vast that one cannot argue that Veblen's understanding of postmodernism is similar to usages of this term by Baudrillard, Bauman, Giddens, and other contemporary social theorists. One could also make the point that Veblen used the term only once (to the best of my knowledge) so that it is not relevant for understanding the rest of his writings. One could make other objections to taking seriously Veblen's understanding of postmodernity. But in the end, objections of this sort are purely academic. This is because there does not exist a single, unifying understanding of postmodernism in contemporary sociological thought or in cultural studies, so that Veblen's perspective can only help clarify what exists in the literature. Furthermore, the one passage in which Veblen uses the term postmodern is so clear, and so relevant to this discussion, that I will argue that it is important for comprehending the unity in Veblen's entire thought as well as his relevance to current debates in cultural studies.

As noted by Chris Rojek, many of these debates center on the issue of whether modernity produces order or chaos. Rojek argues that there exist two forms of modernity, and that one is associated with order while the other is associated with chaos. In a sense, Rojek exposes a "split personality" to modernity. Academics also debate whether postmodernity is an extension of modernity or a rebellion against modernity. This, in itself, constitutes a form of splitting. But if there exist two forms of modernity, then it may follow that there exist two forms of postmodernity. One form extols ambiguity and chaos, while the other follows a deadening formula of postmodern style that is every bit as controlling as the ordering form of modernity.

In the context of the preceding discussion, one can appreciate that Veblen was claiming that postmodernism is the extension of the machine system into customs, laws, and social institutions other than just business. But because he regards the machine system as fundamentally split off from the instinct for workmanship, he regards postmodernism as fundamentally unintegrated. As I have mentioned previously, this is somewhat similar to George Ritzer's (1992) thesis in *The McDonaldization of Society*, but without the theoretical assumptions of Max Weber that Ritzer uses in his analysis. Following Weber, Ritzer cannot seem to decide if the trends toward efficiency, calculability, and predictability found in the fast-food restaurant, and now extended to other domains in social life, are good or bad or both, modernist or postmodernist, and he feels that the individual can take steps to fight the negative aspects of McDonaldization. Ritzer offers a list of options for the individual to take in this battle, such as, eat at a Mom and Pop restaurant, return unwanted junk mail, get to know your professors, and so on. I have already indicated that Veblen finds these Weberian assumptions completely impossible. Veblen eschews any semblance of social agency. In summary, following Weber, Ritzer offers a balanced assessment of the extreme rationality that results in McDonaldization, whereas Veblen's assessment is literally unbalanced and split.

Veblen regarded postmodernity as an inexorable tendency toward cultural narcissism in which the barbaric, pecuniary, and predatory values associated with the machine system will do battle with their split opposites even as they take over law, religion, education, the family, and other societal institutions in Western societies. As such, postmodernity, for Veblen, does not constitute a radical break with modernity, as it does for Giddens. Rather, postmodernity is both a break with and a continuation of modernity simultaneously. Contrary to Baudrillard's depiction of postmodernism as a chaotic sea of circulating simulacra, Veblen seems to imply that postmodernity is the carefully constructed production of fictions with the aim of honor, status, prestige, waste, envy, and pecuniary reward. For example, I have included in this collection of essays Veblen's long diatribe on credit, the investment banker, salesmanship, and absentee ownership despite the fact that his illustrations of these tendencies are dated. More important is the fact that Veblen wisely foresaw the institutionalization of credit as the creation of fictionalized money, or in Baudrillard's vocabulary, as the simulacra of money. But far from understanding the use and misuse of credit by corporations as well as individuals as a circulating fiction, he understands credit as an organized and deliberate creation of fiction by postmodern culture. Against Ritzer's (1995) balanced understanding of credit as a rational as well as an irrational phenomenon, and in some ways a benign process — an extension of the sort of rationality found in McDonaldization — Veblen argues predictably that credit is part of the barbaric, predatory, and what I have called narcissistic tendency in postmodern cultures. In summary, for Veblen, individuals and corporations resort to the simulacra of money as part of the self-absorbed pursuit of prestige, honor, and status.

In contradistinction to Bauman's (1992) advice that the postmodern individual should be comfortable in the postmodern social world of moral and social ambiguity, Veblen's contribution seems to be that the postmodern individual is a narcissist, and narcissism offers no comfort. Narcissism is the domain of envy. Whether one is envious of others or tries to make others envious of one's self, envy is exhausting. This is because envy automatically presupposes extreme humility and a sense of helplessness in the social world that is compensated for by a split, grandiose image. The narcissist suffers from narcissistic injury, and compensates for this injury with grandiosity, but this ambivalent reaction is not comforting. Giddens (1990) soothes the reader by claiming that for all the disembeddedness, dislocations, and ruptures caused by what he calls "high modernity," one can always be re-embedded, re-located, and globalized. Giddens seems to imply that modernity conceived as a juggernaut that disrupts everything in its path will cause narcissistic injuries (dislocation, disembedding, and so on) on a widespread social scale, but that these injuries are rather easily remedied. Veblen's vision is more scathing: postmodernism destroys the sense of home, family, community and other non-narcissistic domains that would have made becoming re-embedded possible. In Veblen's dark vision, there is nothing left to which one can become re-embedded. In addition, the narcissist is too scarred emotionally to seek re-embeddedness.

I have also included an essay by Veblen on what he calls sabotage, the deliberate withholding or obstruction of benign, cooperative, and other good tendencies derived from the instinct for workmanship that lead to genuine efficiency and globalism. Veblen moves from obvious examples of sabotage such as the shutdown of factories in order to prevent output that would lower prices to less obvious examples such as the protective tariff and the censorship of information. Interestingly, he sees even democratic nations such as the United States as exhibiting censorship, which leads to sabotage in the sense of preventing genuine cosmopolitanism. In the context of the preceding discussion, one may link his observations on cultural sabotage to narcissism and predatory values: elites seek to control or create bias in the flow of information in order to pursue their selfish goals of pecuniary gain. Even if Veblen could have foreseen the development of the Internet, he most likely would not have seen its democratic uses for putting individuals and nations on an equal footing with regard to information. He probably would have pointed out that the Internet is most available in Western nations that exhibit the culture of narcissism that he sought to unmask. In an ironic sort of way, the Internet becomes a tool for cultural sabotage. Yet it cannot be doubted that despite these and other objections to the Internet, it offers individuals throughout the world an opportunity to bypass the sabotage of information to some extent.

Veblen links the concept of sabotage to salesmanship and advertising. If industry can produce only as much as the market can withstand, argues Veblen, then it must turn to advertising with the aim of taking over a disproportionate share of the run of sales. Industry will make use of advertising in a systematic, machine-like way, hiring consultants and public relations experts, emphasizing the packaging and presentation of products, and devoting an ever-increasing portion of its budget to salesmanship. In the end, he sees in advertising and salesmanship nothing more than the predatory aim of putting something over on the consumer. But what is postmodern about this, in Veblen's view, is that the culture of advertising is a subdomain of the culture of narcissism, and is linked to the machine system. What he cannot appreciate is that some consumers are able to use advertising to act as human agents, to eventually find what they desire in the marketplace.

Veblen does not spare the university in his understanding of narcissistic postmodernism. According to Veblen, the university pretends that it supports idle curiosity, which is non-barbaric and good. In fact, the university is run like a corporation. Increasingly, the university becomes the arena of machine system business innovations: standardization, gradation, accounting, classification, credit, and penalties. It seeks more and more undergraduates who are themselves bent upon pecuniary aims, not learning for its own sake. Higher enrollment means more money, while the undergraduates come to see education as a marketable commodity. The end result is that the university becomes a pecuniary institution that has been overtaken by businesslike aims and values, chiefly self-aggrandizement and envy. Again, the postmodern element in all this is the intrusion of the machine system and of values pertaining to envy into the domain of idle curiosity. The narcissistic element is that the university becomes the cultural arena of conspicuous status-seeking, not idle curiosity. Yet, against Veblen, one can easily imagine that religious and other cultural forces worked against idle curiosity in traditional societies, and that despite the bureaucracy of the modern university, more knowledge than ever before is available to the curious investigator.

In a sense, Veblen is the Dostoevsky of cultural studies. Veblen is dark and pessimistic in his existential analysis of postmodern culture because he exposes the futility of unceasing status-seeking, envy, exploitation, and self-absorption. It is important to verify whether Veblen's disturbing vision captures a collective sociological disturbance in late Western societies. If it does, perhaps one can seek collective remedies to cultural narcissism through the kind of self-reflexivity described by Giddens. If it does not, one is right to dismiss Veblen. However, as mentioned from the outset, it is difficult to dismiss Veblen because it is easy for the reader to identify with many of Veblen's points, even if his observations are haughty, offensive, one-sided and often sarcastic. Some of the specific questions, issues, and debates that flow from the present reading and discussion of Veblen include, but are not limited to, the following.

First, *who is the real barbarian?* Veblen argued that the USA, Germany, and Japan exhibited the most predatory and wasteful cultural values and therefore barbarism.[4] That these provocative claims are still relevant is illustrated by often repeated claims in Great Britain that contemporary Germany is still dangerous to the European Union, and that one should never fully trust the Germans. Japan's economic miracle following World War II has not diminished its fearful image in Korea, the Philippines, China and other Pacific Rim countries. And of course, the US effort to export capitalism to former Communist nations (Veblen thought of capitalism as latter-day barbarism), which has largely failed so far, raises anew the old issues that Veblen raised concerning capitalism. The status of capitalism in the contemporary world-order is not a settled matter, as so many analysts have assumed, and Veblen's observations are still relevant. Is the exportation of capitalism to developing countries really the cultural exportation of narcissism?

Second, *nationalism: the fewer governments the better*. Veblen thought of nationalism as honorific, hence wasteful and barbaric, a phenomenon that was inconsistent with a world economy. Nationalism may be re-conceptualized as a kind of collective narcissism. Social theorists debate whether nationalism is a modern or a pre-modern phenomenon. In either case, the twentieth century as a whole, and especially the years since the end of the Cold War, have witnessed a proliferation of new nations (the nations of the former Soviet Union and Yugoslavia), the potential for still further secession (Quebec in Canada, Scotland in the United Kingdom), and the rise of nationalism as arguably the most powerful social force in the world. The current debates that center on the "politics of meaning" (communitarianism, the emphasis on caring as an alternative to the selfishness fostered by capitalism, etc.) could profit from Veblen's writings on nationalism. Was Veblen wrong or right about nationalism? Does the increase in contemporary nationalism indicate a further descent into barbarism? Nationalism has not disappeared into the neat and tidy idea of the nation-state, as so many contemporary analysts had predicted, but seems to have degenerated into nations in search of states, a veritable "pandemonium" (as argued by Senator Daniel Patrick Moynihan [1993]). Again, Veblen seems fresh and vibrant in this regard. It may be helpful to recast this debate in the context of cultural narcissism. In order to realize the dream of a truly global culture, the grandiose illusions of many nations will have to be cut down to size. On the other hand, the idea of a global culture easily provokes ethnocentrism, nationalism, and collective narcissism in many places in the world today.

Third, *feminism*. Veblen was an early feminist who thought of women as the bearers of civilization in the sense that they, much more than men, were attuned to non-barbaric values that he termed "the instinct for workmanship."[5] Veblen thought that women were more caring than men. Since he wrote, have women started to emulate male barbarism and narcissism or have men started to emulate female civilization? Veblen really seems to have distinguished between a "male voice" and a "female voice" (extrapolating from Carol Gilligan's *In a Different Voice* [1982]) and their roles in culture. Contemporary feminism has not decided the debate as to whether emancipation from male domination will occur along the lines of the male or the female voice, and Veblen seems to assume (like Jung with his distinction between the anima and the animus as existing in both males and females) that both cultural voices can exist or can be used in/by both males and females.

Fourth, *the professions*. Veblen thought of law as the most barbaric profession, one geared almost exclusively to predatory values. Conversely, he thought of engineers as the profession that was most likely to produce a non-barbaric culture.[6] Perhaps few would disagree with his assessment of lawyers today, yet his writings on engineers come across as a technocratic illusion. He seems really to have thought that engineers build things mainly from a desire to help people, not from narcissism. He could not foresee that many engineers would make a living from designing Star Wars weapons and other machines aimed at war. In addition, he denigrated higher education as wasteful, honorific, inimical to change, and otherwise barbaric because it was increasingly being run as a business enterprise.[7] As mentioned previously, it seems that the contemporary university is run like a corporation. On the other hand, much of the Western public sees the life of the typical university professor as offering much time for idle curiosity. Yet despite his feminism, Veblen paid no attention to the predominantly female elementary school teacher as an important conduit for civilization. Women dominate the ranks of many of the helping professions, from nursing to kindergarten teaching, and they continue to resist the narcissistic tendencies that Veblen foresaw.

Finally, *postmodernism*. Contrary to the postmodern vision of the world as a sea of rootless, circulating fictions that center on consumerism and are themselves consumed, Veblen thought of these fictions or simulacra as being rooted in the machine system. If the machine system could be humanized or even tempered *vis-à-vis* narcissistic values, so-called postmodernism would crumble as a cultural system. There would be less waste in the world, less grandiosity, less exploitation, and more empathy. Veblen's contributions to the postmodernist debate are manifold and include the following: he casts postmodernism in a decidedly negative light, as the culmination of narcissistic cultural values. He implies that 'progress' to postmodernism is not necessarily linear, but could be reversed if anti-narcissistic tendencies could gain strength. Veblen eschews essentialism, and implies that the machine system is a cultural system of habits that can and eventually will be replaced by different cultural systems of habits. An important implication that may be drawn from Veblen's thought is that two sorts of postmodernism co-exist. One is in the service of narcissistic, predatory, and barbaric values. The other is in the service of communal, cooperative, and global values. Perhaps an important addition to current debates concerning postmodernism would be to distinguish between the two types of postmodernism and reflexively to foster the benign form and control the destructive form. Of course, such reflexivity and social agency are inimical to Veblen's thought, but if drawn from Parsons and Giddens, and grafted onto Veblen artificially, the intellectual result would be interesting.

Notes

1 David Riesman, *Thorstein Veblen* (New Brunswick, NJ: Transaction, [1953] 1995).

2 See, for example, Mark Blaug, *Thorstein Veblen (1857—1929)* (Brookfield, VT: Edward Elgar Publishing, 1992).

3 See, for example, the comprehensive guide to this mountain of secondary sources in Rick Tilman, *Thorstein Veblen: A Reference Guide* (Boston: G.K. Hall and Co., 1985).

4 See especially Veblen's *Imperial Germany and the Industrial Revolution* (1939).

5 See especially Veblen's *The Instinct of Workmanship* (1914).

6 See Veblen's *The Engineers and the Price System* (1921).

7 See Veblen's *Higher Learning in America* (1918).

1

The Place of Science in Modern Civilisation

It is commonly held that modern Christendom is superior to any and all other systems of civilised life. Other ages and other cultural regions are by contrast spoken of as lower, or more archaic, or less mature. The claim is that the modern culture is superior on the whole, not that it is the best or highest in all respects and at every point. It has, in fact, not an all-around superiority, but a superiority within a closely limited range of intellectual activities, while outside this range many other civilisations surpass that of the modern occidental peoples. But the peculiar excellence of the modern culture is of such a nature as to give it a decisive practical advantage over all other cultural schemes that have gone before or that have come into competition with it. It has proved itself fit to survive in a struggle for existence as against those civilisations which differ from it in respect of its distinctive traits.

Modern civilisation is peculiarly matter-of-fact. It contains many elements that are not of this character, but these other elements do not belong exclusively or characteristically to it. The modern civilised peoples are in a peculiar degree capable of an impersonal, dispassionate insight into the material facts with which mankind has to deal. The apex of cultural growth is at this point. Compared with this trait the rest of what is comprised in the cultural scheme is adventitious, or at best it is a by-product of this hard-headed apprehension of facts. This quality may be a matter of habit or of racial endowment, or it may be an outcome of both; but whatever be the explanation of its prevalence, the immediate consequence is much the same for the growth of civilisation. A civilisation which is dominated by this matter-of-fact insight must prevail against any cultural scheme that lacks this element. This characteristic of western civilisation comes to a head in modern science, and it finds its highest material expression in the technology of the machine industry. In these things modern culture is creative and self-sufficient; and these being given, the rest of what may seem characteristic in western civilisation follows by easy consequence. The cultural structure clusters about this body of matter-of-fact knowledge as its substantial core. Whatever is not consonant with these opaque creations of science is an intrusive feature in the modern scheme, borrowed or standing over from the barbarian past.

Other ages and other peoples excel in other things and are known by other virtues. In creative art, as well as in critical taste, the faltering talent of Christendom can at the best follow the lead of the ancient Greeks and the Chinese. In deft workmanship the handicraftsmen of the middle Orient, as well as the Far East, stand on a level securely above the highest European achievement, old or new. In myth-making, folklore, and occult symbolism many of the lower barbarians have achieved things beyond what the latter-day priests and poets know how to propose. In metaphysical insight and dialectical versatility many orientals, as well as the Schoolmen of the Middle Ages, easily surpass the highest reaches of the New Thought and the Higher Criticism. In a shrewd sense of the religious verities, as well as in an unsparing faith in devout observances, the people of India or Tibet, or even the mediaeval Christians, are past-masters in comparison even with the select of the faith of modern times. In political finesse, as well as in unreasoning, brute loyalty, more than one of the ancient peoples give evidence of a capacity to which no modern civilised nation may aspire. In warlike malevolence and abandon, the hosts of Islam, the Sioux Indian, and the "heathen of the northern sea" have set the mark above the reach of the most strenuous civilised warlord.

To modern civilised men, especially in their intervals of sober reflection, all these things that distinguish the barbarian civilisations seem of dubious value and are required to show cause why they should not be slighted. It is not so with the knowledge of facts. The making of states and dynasties, the founding of families, the prosecution of feuds, the propagation of creeds and the creation of sects, the accumulation of fortunes, the consumption of superfluities – these have all in their time been felt to justify themselves as an end of endeavor; but in the eyes of modern civilised men all these things seem futile in comparison with the achievements of science. They dwindle in men's esteem as time passes, while the achievements of science are held higher as time passes. This is the one secure holding-ground of latter-day conviction, that "the increase and diffusion of knowledge among men" are indefeasibly right and good. When seen in such perspective as will clear it of the trivial perplexities of workday life, this proposition is not questioned within the horizon of the western culture, and no other cultural ideal holds a similar unquestioned place in the convictions of civilised mankind.

On any large question which is to be disposed of for good and all the final appeal is by common consent taken to the scientist. The solution offered in the name of science is decisive so long as it is not set aside by a still more searching scientific inquiry. This state of things may not be altogether fortunate, but such is the fact. There are other, older grounds of finality that may conceivably be better, nobler, worthier, more profound, more beautiful. It might conceivably be preferable, as a matter of cultural ideals, to leave the last word with the lawyer, the duelist, the priest, the moralist, or the college of heraldry. In past times people have been content to leave their weightiest questions to the decision of some one or other of these tribunals, and, it cannot be denied, with very happy results in those respects that were then looked to with the greatest solicitude. But whatever the common-sense of earlier generations may have held in this respect, modern common-sense holds that the scientist's answer is the only ultimately true one. In the last resort enlightened common-sense sticks by the opaque truth and refuses to go behind the returns given by the tangible facts.

Quasi lignum vitae in paradiso Dei, et quasi lucerna fulgoris in domo Domini, such is the place of science in modern civilisation. This latterday faith in manner-of-fact knowledge may be well grounded or it may not. It has come about that men assign it its high place, perhaps idolatrously, perhaps to the detriment of the best and most intimate interests of the race. There is room for much more than a vague doubt that this cult of science is not altogether a wholesome growth — that the unmitigated quest of knowledge, of this matter-of-fact kind, makes for race-deterioration and discomfort on the whole, both in its immediate effects upon the spiritual life of mankind, and in the material consequences that follow from a great advance in matter-of-fact knowledge.

But we are not here concerned with the merits of the case. The question here is: How has this cult of science arisen? What are its cultural antecedents? How far is it in consonance with hereditary human nature? And, What is the nature of its hold on the convictions of civilised men?

In dealing with pedagogical problems and the theory of education, current psychology is nearly at one in saying that all learning is of a "pragmatic" character; that knowledge is inchoate action inchoately directed to an end; that all knowledge is "functional"; that it is of the nature of use. This, of course, is only a corollary under the main postulate of the latter-day psychologists, whose catchword is that The Idea is essentially active. There is no need of quarreling with this "pragmatic" school of psychologists. Their aphorism may not contain the whole truth, perhaps, but at least it goes nearer to the heart of the epistemological problem than any earlier formulation. It may confidently be said to do so because, for one thing, its argument meets the requirements of modern science. It is such a concept as matter-of-fact science can make effective use of it is drawn in terms which are, in the last analysis, of an impersonal, not to say tropismatic, character; such as is demanded by science, with its insistence on opaque cause and effect. While knowledge is construed in teleological perms, in terms of personal interest and attention, this teleological attitude is itself reducible to a product of unteleological natural selection. The teleological bent of intelligence is an hereditary trait settled upon the race by the selective action of forces that look to no end. The foundations of pragmatic intelligence are not pragmatic, nor even personal or sensible.

This impersonal character of intelligence is, of course, most evident on the lower levels of life. If we follow Mr. Loeb, e. g., in his inquiries into the psychology of that life that lies below the threshold of intelligence, what we meet with is an aimless but unwavering motor response to stimulus.[ii] The response is of the nature of motor impulse, and in so far it is "pragmatic," if that term may fairly be applied to so rudimentary a whose of sensibility. The responding organism may be called an "agent" in so far. It is only by a figure of speech that these terms are made to apply to tropismatic reactions. Higher in the scale of sensibility and nervous complication instincts work to a somewhat similar outcome. On the human plane, intelligence (the selective effect of inhibitive complication) may throw the response into the form of a reasoned line of conduct looking to an outcome that shall be expedient for the agent. This is naïve pragmatism of the developed kind. There is no longer a question but that the responding organism is an "agent" and that his intelligent response to stimulus is of a teleological character. But that is not all. The inhibitive nervous complication may also detach another chain of response to the given stimulus, which does not spend itself in a line of motor conduct and does not fall into a system of uses. Pragmatically speaking, this outlying chain of response is unintended and irrelevant. Except in urgent cases, such an idle response seems commonly to be present as a subsidiary phenomenon. If credence is given to the view that intelligence is, in its elements, of the nature of an inhibitive selection, it seems necessary to assume some such chain of idle and irrelevant response to account for the further course of the elements eliminated in giving the motor response the character of a reasoned line of conduct. So that associated with the pragmatic attention there is found more or less of an irrelevant attention, or idle curiosity. This is more particularly the case where a higher range of intelligence is present. This idle curiosity is, perhaps, closely related to the aptitude for play, observed both in man and in the lower animals.[iii] The aptitude for play, as well as the functioning of idle curiosity seems peculiarly lively in the young, whose aptitude for sustained pragmatism is at the same time relatively vague and unreliable.

This idle curiosity formulates its response to stimulus, not in terms of an expedient line of conduct, nor even necessarily in a chain of motor activity but in terms of the sequence of activities going on in the observed phenomena. The "interpretation" of the facts under the guidance of this idle curiosity may take the form of anthropomorphic or animistic explanations of the "conduct" of the objects observed. The interpretation of the facts takes a dramatic form. The facts are conceived in an animistic way, and a pragmatic animus is imputed to them. Their behavior is construed as a reasoned procedure on their part looking to the advantage of these animistically conceived objects, or looking to the achievement of some end which these objects are conceived to have at heart for reasons of their own.

Among the savage and lower barbarian peoples there is commonly current a large body of knowledge organised in this way into myths and legends, which need have no pragmatic value for the learner of them and no intended bearing on his conduct of practical affairs. They may come to have a practical value imputed to them as a ground of superstitious observances, but they may also not.[iv] All students of the lower cultures are aware of the dramatic character of the myths current among these peoples, and they are also aware that, particularly among the peaceable communities, the great body of mythical lore is of an idle kind, as having very little intended bearing on the practical conduct of those who believe in these myth-dramas. The myths on the one hand, may be nearly independent of one another. Such is the case in an especial degree among those peoples who are prevailingly of a peaceable habit of life, among whom the myths have not in any great measure been canonised into precedents of divine malevolence.

The lower barbarian's knowledge of the phenomena of nature, in so far as they are made the subject of deliberate speculation and are organised into a consistent body, is of the nature of life-histories. This body of knowledge is in the main organised under the guidance of an idle curiosity. In so far as it is systematised under the canons of curiosity rather than of expediency, the test of truth applied throughout this body of barbarian knowledge is the test of dramatic consistency. In addition to their dramatic cosmology and folk legends, it is needless to say, these peoples have also a considerable body of worldly wisdom in a more or less systematic form. In this the test of validity is usefulness.[v]

The pragmatic knowledge of the early days differs scarcely at all in character from that of the maturest phases of culture. Its highest achievements in the direction of systematic formulation consist of didactic exhortations to thrift, prudence, equanimity, and shrewd management — a body of maxims of expedient conduct. In this field there is scarcely a degree of advance from Confucius to Samuel Smiles. Under the guidance of the idle curiosity, on the other hand, there has been a continued advance toward a more and more comprehensive system of knowledge. With the advance in intelligence and experience there come closer observation and more detailed analysis of facts.[vi] The dramatisation of the sequence of phenomena may then fall into somewhat less personal, less anthropomorphic formulations of the processes observed; but at no stage of its growth — at least at no stage hitherto reached — does the output of this work of the idle curiosity lose its dramatic character. Comprehensive generalisations are made and cosmologies are built up, but always in dramatic form. General principles of explanation are settled on, which in the earlier days of theoretical speculation seem invariably to run back to the broad vital principle of generation. Procreation, birth, growth, and decay constitute the cycle of postulates within which the dramatised processes of natural phenomena run their course. Creation is procreation in these archaic theoretical systems, and causation is gestation and birth. The archaic cosmological schemes of Greece, India, Japan, China, Polynesia, and America, all run to the same general effect on this head.[vii] The like seems true for the Elohistic elements in the Hebrew scriptures.

Throughout this biological speculation there is present, obscurely in the background, the tacit recognition of a material causation, such as conditions the vulgar operations of workday life from hour to hour. But this causal relation between vulgar work and product is vaguely taken for granted and not made a principle for comprehensive generalisations. It is overlooked as a trivial matter of course. The higher generalisations take their color from the broader features of the current scheme of life. The habits of thought that rule in the working-out of a system of knowledge are such as are fostered by the more impressive affairs of life, by the institutional structure under which the community lives. So long as the ruling institutions are those of blood-relationship, descent, and clannish discrimination, so long the canons of knowledge are of the same complexion.

When presently a transformation is made in the scheme of culture from peaceable life with sporadic predation to a settled scheme of predaceous life, involving mastery and servitude, gradations of privilege and honor, coercion and personal dependence, then the scheme of knowledge undergoes an analogous change. The predaceous, or higher barbarian, culture is, for the present purpose, peculiar in that it is ruled by an accentuated pragmatism. The institutions of this cultural phase are conventionalised relations of force and fraud. The questions of life are questions of expedient conduct as carried on under the current relations of mastery and subservience. The habitual distinctions are distinctions of personal force, advantage, precedence, and authority. A shrewd adaptation to this system of graded dignity and servitude becomes a matter of life and death, and men learn to think in these terms as ultimate and definitive. The system of knowledge, even in so far as its motives are of a dispassionate or idle kind, falls into the like terms, because such are the habits of thought and the standards of discrimination enforced by daily life.[viii]

The theoretical work of such a cultural era, as, for instance, the Middle Ages, still takes the general shape of dramatisation, but the postulates of the dramaturgic theories and the tests of theoretic validity are no longer the same as before the scheme of graded servitude came to occupy the field. The canons which guide the work of the idle curiosity are no longer those of generation, blood-relationship, and homely life, but rather those of graded dignity, authenticity, and dependence. The higher generalisations take on a new complexion, it may be without formally discarding the older articles of relief. The cosmologies of these higher barbarians are cast in terms of a feudalistic hierarchy of agents and elements, and the causal nexus between phenomena is conceived animistically after the manner of sympathetic magic. The laws that are sought to be discovered in the natural universe are sought in terms of authoritative enactment. The relation in which the deity, or deities, are conceived to stand to facts is no longer the relation of progenitor, so much as that of suzerainty. Natural laws are corollaries under the arbitrary rules of status imposed on the natural universe by an all-powerful Providence with a view to the maintenance of his own prestige. The science that grows in such a spiritual environment is of the class represented by alchemy and astrology, in which the imputed degree of nobility and prepotency of the objects and the symbolic force of their names are looked to for an explanation of what takes place.

The theoretical output of the Schoolmen has necessarily an accentuated pragmatic complexion, since the whole cultural scheme under which they lived and worked was of a strenuously pragmatic character. The current concepts of things were then drawn in terms of expediency, personal force, exploit, prescriptive authority, and the like, and this range of concepts was by force of habit employed in the correlation of facts for purposes of knowledge even where no immediate practical use of the knowledge so gained was had in view. At the same time a very large proportion of the scholastic researches and speculations aimed directly at rules of expedient conduct, whether it took the form of a philosophy of life under temporal law and custom or of a scheme of salvation under the decrees of an autocratic Providence. A naïve apprehension of the dictum that all knowledge is pragmatic should find more satisfactory corroboration in the intellectual output of scholasticism that in any system of knowledge of an older or a later date.

With the advent of modern times a change comes over the nature of the inquiries and formulations worked out under the guidance of the idle curiosity — which from this epoch is often spoken of as the scientific spirit. The change in question is closely correlated with an analogous change in institutions and habits of life, particularly with the changes which the modern era brings in industry and in the economic organisation of society. It is doubtful whether the characteristic intellectual interests and teachings of the new era can properly be spoken of as less "pragmatic," as that term is sometimes understood, than those of the scholastic times; but they are of another kind, being conditioned by a different cultural and industrial situation.[ix] In the life of the new era conceptions of authentic rank and differential dignity have grown weaker in practical affairs, and notions of preferential reality and authentic tradition similarly count for less in the new science. The forces at work in the external world are conceived in less animistic manner although anthropomorphism still prevails, at least to the degree required in order to give a dramatic interpretation of the sequence of phenomena.

The changes in the cultural situation which seem to have had the most serious consequences for the methods and animus of scientific inquiry are those changes that took place in the field of industry. Industry in early modern time is a fact of relatively greater preponderance, more of a tone-giving factor, that it was under the régime of feudal status. It is the characteristic trait of the modern culture, very much as exploit and fealty were the characteristic cultural traits of the earlier time. This early-modern industry is, in an obvious and convincing degree, a matter of workmanship. The same has not been true in the same degree either before or since. The workman, more or less skilled and with more or less specialised efficiency, was the central figure in the cultural situation of the time; and so the concepts of the scientists came to be drawn in the image of the workman. The dramatisations of the sequence of external phenomena worked out under the impulse of the idle curiosity were then conceived in terms of workmanship. Workmanship gradually supplanted differential dignity as the authoritative canon of scientific truth, even on the higher levels of speculation and research. This, of course, amounts to saying in other words that the law of cause and effect was given the first place, as contrasted with dialectical consistency and authentic tradition. But this early-modern law of cause and effect — the law of efficient causes — is of an anthropomorphic kind. "Like causes produce like effects," in much the same sense as the skilled workman's product is like the workman; "nothing is found in the effect that was not contained in the cause," in much the same manner.

These dicta are, of course, older than modern science, but it is only in the early days of modern science that they come to rule the field with an unquestioned sway and to push the higher grounds of dialectical validity to one side. They invade even the highest and most recondite fields of speculation, so that at the approach to the transition from the early-modern to the late-modern period, in the eighteenth century, they determine the outcome even in the counsels of the theologians. The deity, from having been in mediaeval times primarily a suzerain concerned with the maintenance of his own prestige, becomes primarily a creator engaged in the workmanlike occupation of making things useful for man. His relation to man and the natural universe is no longer primarily that of a progenitor, as it is in the lower barbarian culture, but rather that of a talented mechanic. The "natural laws" which the scientists of that era make so much of are no longer decrees of a preternatural legislative authority, but rather details of the workshop specifications handed down by the master-craftsman for the guidance of handicraftsmen working out his designs. In the eighteenth-century science these natural laws are laws specifying the sequence of cause and effect, and will bear characterisation as a dramatic interpretation of the activity of the causes at work, and these causes are conceived in a quasi-personal manner. In later modern times the formulations of causal sequence grow more impersonal and more objective, more matter-of-fact; but the imputation of activity to the observed objects never ceases, and even in the latest and maturest formulations of scientific research the dramatic tone is not wholly lost. The causes at work are conceived in a highly impersonal way, but hitherto no science (except ostensibly mathematics) has been content to do its theoretical work in terms of inert magnitude alone. Activity continues to be imputed to the phenomena with which science deals; and activity is, of course, not a fact of observation, but is imputed to the phenomena by the observer.[x] This is, also of course, denied by those who insist on a purely mathematical formulation of scientific theories, but the denial is maintained only at the cost of consistency. Those eminent authorities who speak for colorless mathematical formulation invariably and necessarily fall back on the (essentially metaphysical) preconception of causation as soon as they go into the actual work of scientific inquiry.[xi]

Since the machine technology has made great advances, during the nineteenth century, and has become a cultural force of wide-reaching consequence, the formulations of science have made another move in the direction of impersonal matter-of-fact. The machine process has displaced the workman as the archetype in whose image causation is conceived by the scientific investigators. The dramatic interpretation of natural phenomena has thereby become less anthropomorphic; it no longer constructs the life-history of a cause working to produce a given effect — after the manner of a skilled workman producing a piece of wrought goods — but it constructs the life-history of a process in which the distinction between cause and effect need scarcely be observed in an itemised and specific way, but in which the run of causation unfolds itself in an unbroken sequence of cumulative change. By contrast with the pragmatic formulations of worldly wisdom these latter-day theories of the scientists appear highly opaque, impersonal, and matter-of-fact; but taken by themselves they must be admitted still to show the constraint of the dramatic prepossessions that once guided the savage myths-makers.

In so far as touches the aims and animus of scientific inquiry, as seen from the point of view of the scientist, it is a wholly fortuitous and insubstantial coincidence that much of the knowledge gained under machine-made canons of research can be turned to practical account. Much of this knowledge is useful, or may be made so, by applying it to the processes in which natural forces are engaged. This employment of scientific knowledge for useful ends is technology, in the broad sense in which the term includes, besides the machine industry proper, such branches of practice as engineering, agriculture, medicine, sanitation, and economic reforms. The reason why scientific theories can be turned to account for these practical ends is not that these ends are included in the scope of scientific inquiry. These useful purposes lie outside the scientist's interest. It is not that he aims, or can aim, at technological improvements. His inquiry is as "idle" as that of the Pueblo myth-maker. But the canons of validity under whose guidance he works are those imposed by the modern technology, through habituation to its requirements; and therefore his results are available for the technological purpose. His canons of validity are made for him by the cultural situation; they are habits of thought imposed on him by the scheme of life current in the community in which he lives; and under modern conditions this scheme of life is largely machine-made. In the modern culture, industry, industrial processes, and industrial product have progressively gained upon humanity, until these creations of man's ingenuity have latterly come to take the dominant place in the cultural scheme; and it is not too much to say that they have become the chief force in shaping men's daily life, and therefore the chief factor in shaping men's habits of thought. Hence men have learned to think in the terms in which the technological processes act. This is particularly true of those men who by virtue of a peculiarly strong susceptibility in this direction become addicted to that habit of matter-of-fact inquiry that constitutes scientific research.

Modern technology makes use of the same range of concepts, thinks in the same terms, and applies the same tests of validity as modern science. In both, the terms of standardisation, validity, and finality are always terms of impersonal sequence, not terms of human nature or of preternatural agencies. Hence the easy copartnership between the two. Science and technology play into one another's hands.

Notes

i Reprinted by permission from *The American Journal of Sociology*, Vol. XI, March, 1906.

ii Jacques Loeb, *Heliotropismus der Thiere*, and *Comparative Psychology* and *Physiology of the Brain*.

iii Cf. Gross, *Spiele der Thiere*, chap. 2 (esp. pp. 65-76), and chap. 5; *The Play of Man*, Part III, sec 3; Spencer, *Principles of Psychology*, sects. 533—35.

iv The myths and legendary lore of the Eskimo, the Pueblo Indians, and some tribes of the northwest coast afford good instances of such idle creations. Cf. Various *Reports* of the Bureau of American Ethnology; also, e.g., Tylor, *Primitive Culture*, esp. the chapters on "Mythology" and "Animism."

v "Pragmatic" is here used in a more restricted sense than the distinctively pragmatic school of modern psychologists would commonly assign the term. "Pragmatic," "teleological," and the like terms have been extended to cover imputation of purpose as well as conversion to use. It is not intended to criticise this ambiguous use of terms, nor to correct it; but the terms are here used only in the latter sense, which alone belongs to them by force of early usage and etymology. "Pragmatic" knowledge, therefore, is such as is designed to serve an expedient end for the knower, and is here contrasted with the imputation of expedient conduct to the facts observed. The reason for preserving this distinction is simply the present need of a simple term by which to mark the distinction between worldly wisdom and idle learning.

vi Cf. Ward, *Pure Sociology*, esp. pp. 437—48.

vii Cf., e.g., Tylor, *Primitive Culture*, chap. 8.

viii Cf. James, *Psychology*, chap. 9, esp. sec. 5.

ix As currently employed, the term "pragmatic" is made to cover both conduct looking to the agent's preferential advantage, expedient conduct, and workmanship directed to the production of things that may or may not be of advantage to the agent. If the term be taken in the latter meaning, the culture of modern times is no less "pragmatic" than that of the Middle Ages. It is here intended to be used in the former sense.

x Epistemologically speaking, activity is imputed to phenomena for the purpose of organising them into a dramatically consistent system.

xi Cf., e.g., Karl Pearson,*Grammar of Science*, and compare his ideal of inert magnitudes as set forth in his exposition with his actual work as shown in chaps. 9, 10, and 12, and more particularly in his discussions of "Mother Right" and related topics in *The Chances of Death*.

2

The Instability of Knowledge and Belief

As is true of any other point of view that may be characteristic of any other period of history, so also the modern point of view is a matter of habit. It is common to the modern civilised peoples only in so far as these peoples have come through substantially the same historical experience and have thereby acquired substantially the same habits of thought and have fallen into somewhat the same prevalent frame of mind. This modern point of view, therefore, is limited both in time and space. It is characteristic of the modern historical era and of such peoples as lie within the range of that peculiar civilisation which marks off the modern world from what has gone before and from what still prevails outside of its range. In other words, it is a trait of modern Christendom, of Occidental civilisation as it has run within the past few centuries. This general statement is not vitiated by the fact that there has been some slight diffusion of these modern and Western ideas outside of this range in recent times.

By historical accident it happens that the modern point of view has reached its maturest formulation and prevails with the least faltering among the French and English-speaking peoples; so that these peoples may be said to constitute the center of diffusion for that system of ideas which is called the modern point of view. Outward from this broad center the same range of ideas prevail throughout Christendom, but they prevail with less singleness of conviction among the peoples who are culturally more remote from this center; increasingly so with each farther remove. These others have carried over a larger remainder of the habits of thought of an earlier age, and have carried them over in a better state of preservation. It may also be that these others, or some of them, have acquired habits of thought of a new order which do not altogether fit into that system of ideas that is commonly spoken of as the modern point of view. That such is the case need imply neither praise nor blame. It is only that, by common usage, these remainders of ancient habits of thought and these newer preconceptions that do not fit into the framework of West-European conventional thinking are not ordinarily rated as intrinsic to the modern point of view. They need not therefore be less to the purpose as a guide and criterion of human living; it is only that they are alien to those purposes which are considered to be of prime consequences in civilised life as it is guided and tested by the constituent principles of the modern point of view.

What is spoken of as a point of view is always a composite affair; some sort of a rounded and balanced system of principles and standards, which are taken for granted, at least provisionally, and which serve as a base of reference and legitimisation in all questions of deliberate opinion. So when any given usage or any line of conduct or belief is seen and approved from the modern point of view, it comes to the same as saying that these things are seen and accepted in the light of those principles which modern men habitually consider to be final and sufficient. They are principles of right, equity, propriety, duty, perhaps of knowledge, belief, and taste.

It is evident that these principles and standards of what is right, good, true, and beautiful, will vary from one age to another and from one people to another, in response to the varying conditions of life; inasmuch as these principles are always of the nature of habit; although variation will of course range only within the limits of that human nature that finds expression in these same principles of right, good, truth, and beauty. So also, it will be found that something in the way of a common measure of truth and sufficiency runs through any such body of principles that are accepted as final and self-evident at any given time and place — in case this habitual body of principles has reached such a degree of poise and consistency that they can fairly be said to constitute a stable point of view. It is only because there is such a degree of consistency and such a common measure of validity among the commonly accepted principles of conduct and belief today, that it is possible to speak intelligently of the modern point of view, and to contrast it with any other point of view which may have prevailed earlier or elsewhere, as, e.g., in the Middle Ages or in Pagan Antiquity.

The Romans were given to saying, Tempera mutantur, and the Spanish have learned to speak indulgently in the name of Costumbres del país. The common law of the English-speaking peoples does not coincide at all points with what was indefeasibly right and good in the eyes of the Romans; and still less do its principles countenance all the vagaries of the Mosaic code. Yet, each and several, in their due time and institutional setting, these have all been tried and found valid and have approved themselves as securely and eternally right and good in principle.

Evidently these principles, which are so made to serve as standards of validity in law and custom, knowledge and belief, are of the nature of canons, established rules, and have the authority of precedent, prescription. They have been defined by the attrition of use and wont and disputation, and they are accepted in a somewhat deliberate manner by common consent, and are upheld by a deliberate manner by common consent, and are upheld by a deliberate public opinion as to what is right and seemly. In the popular apprehension of the trained jurists and scholars for the time being, these constituent principles of the accepted point of view are "fundamentally and eternally right and good." But this perpetuity with which they are so habitually invested in the popular apprehension, in their time, is evidently such a qualified perpetuity only as belongs to any settled outgrowth of use and wont. They are of an institutional character and they are endowed with that degree of perpetuity only that belongs to any institution. So soon as a marked change of circumstances comes on — a change of a sufficiently profound, enduring and comprehensive character, such as persistently to cross or to go beyond those lines of use and wont out of which these settled principles have emerged — then these principles and their standards of validity and finality must presently undergo a revision, such as to bring on a new balance of principles, embodying the habits of thought enforced by a new situation, and expressing itself in a revised scheme of authoritative use and wont, law and custom. In the transition from the medieval to the modern point of view, e.g., there is to be seen such a pervasive change in men's habitual outlook, answering to the compulsion of a new range of circumstances which then came to condition the daily life of the peoples of Christendom.

In this mutation of the habitual outlook, between medieval and modern times, the contrast is perhaps most neatly shown in the altered standards of knowledge and belief, rather than in the settled domain of law and morals. Not that the mutation of habits which then overtook the Western world need have been less wide or less effectual in matters of conduct; but the change which has taken effect in science and philosophy, between the fourteenth century and the nineteenth, e.g., appears to have been of a more recognizable character, more easily defined in succinct and convincing terms. It has also quite generally attracted the attention of those men who have interested themselves in the course of historical events, and it has therefore become something of a commonplace in any historical survey of modern civilisation to say that the scheme of knowledge and belief underwent a visible change between the Middle Ages and modern times.

It will also be found true that the canons of knowledge and belief, the principles governing what is fact and what is credible, are more intimately and intrinsically involved in the habitual behavior of the human spirit than any factors of human habit in other bearings. Such is necessarily the case, because the principles which guide and limit knowledge and belief are the ways and means by which men take stock of what is to be done and by which they take thought of how it is to be done. It is by the use of their habitual canons of knowledge and belief, that men construct those canons of conduct which serve as guide and standards in practical life. Men do not pass appraisal on matters which lie beyond the reach of their knowledge and belief, nor do they formulate rules to govern the game of life beyond that limit.

So, congenitally blind persons do not build color schemes; nor will a man without an "ear for music" become a master of musical composition. So also, "the medieval mind" took no thought and made no provision for those later-arisen exigencies of life and those later-known facts of material science which lay yet beyond the bounds of its medieval knowledge and belief; but this "medieval mind" at the same time spent much thought and took many excellent precautions about things which have now come to be accounted altogether fanciful — things which the maturer insight, or perhaps the less fertile conceit, of a more experienced age has disowned as being palpably not in accord with fact.

That is to say, things which once were convincingly substantial and demonstrable, according to the best knowledge and belief of the medieval mind, can now no longer be discerned as facts, according to those canons of knowledge and belief that are now doing duty among modern men as conclusive standards of reality. Not that all persons who are born within modern times are thereby rendered unable to know and to believe in such medieval facts, e.g., as horoscopes, or witchcraft, or gentle birth, of the efficacy of prayer, or the divine right of kings; but, taken by and large, and in so far as it falls under the control of the modern point of view, the deliberate consensus of knowledge and belief now runs to the effect that these and other imponderables like them no longer belong among ascertained or ascertainable facts; but that they are on the other hand wholly illusory conceits, traceable to a mistaken point of view prevalent in that earlier and cruder age.

The principles governing knowledge and belief at any given time are primary and pervasive, beyond any others, in that they underlie all human deliberation and comprise the necessary elements of all human logic. But it is also to be noted that these canons of knowledge and belief are more immediately exposed to revision and correction by experience than the principles of law and morals. So soon as the conditions of life shift and change in any appreciable degree, experience will enforce a revision of the habitual and increasingly obvious failure of what has before habitually been regarded as an ascertained fact. Things which, under the ancient canons of knowledge, have habitually been regarded as known facts — as, e.g., witchcraft or the action of bodies at a distance — will under altered circumstances prove themselves by experience to have only a suppositious reality.

Any knowledge that run in such out-worn terms turns out to be futile, misleading, meaningless; and the habit of imputing qualities and behavior of this kind to everyday facts will then fall into disuse, progressively as experience continues to bring home the futility of all that kind of imputation. And presently the habit of perceiving that class of qualities and behavior in the known facts is therefore gradually lost. So also, in due time the observances of and the precautions and provisions embodied in law and custom of the preservation or the control of these lost imponderables will also fall into disuse and disappear out of the scheme of institutions, by way of becoming a dead letter by abrogation. Particularly will such a loss of belief and insight, and the consequent loss of those imponderables whose ground has thereby gone out from under them, take effect with the passing of generations.

An Imponderable is an article of make-believe which has become axiomatic by force of settled habit. It can accordingly cease to be an Imponderable by a course of unsettling habit. Those elders in whom the ancient habits of faith and insight have been ingrained, and in whose knowledge and belief the imponderables in question have therefore had a vital reality, will presently fall away; and the new generation whose experience has run on other lines are in a fair way to lose these articles of faith and insight, by disuse. It is a case of obsolescence by habitual disuse. And the habitual disuse which so allows the ancient canons of knowledge and belief to fall away, and which thereby cuts the ground from under the traditional system of law and custom, is reinforced by the advancing discipline of a new order of experience, which exacts an habitual apprehension of workday facts in terms of a different kind and thereby brings on a revaluation and revision of the traditional rules governing human relations. The new terms of workday knowledge and belief, which do not conform to the ancient canons, go to enforce and stabilise new canons and standards, of a character alien to the traditional point of view. It is, in other words, a case of obsolescence by displacement as well as by habitual disuse.

This unsettling discipline that is brought to bear by workday experience is chiefly and most immediately the discipline exercised by the material conditions of life, the exigencies that beset men in their everyday dealings with the material means of life; inasmuch as these material facts are insistent and uncompromising. And the scope and method of knowledge and belief which is forced on men in their everyday material concerns will unavoidably, by habitual use, extend to other matters as well; so as also to affect the scope and method of knowledge and belief in all that concerns those imponderable facts which lie outside the immediate range of material experience. It results that, in the further course of changing habituation, those imponderable relations, conventions, claims and prerequisites, that make up the time-worn system of law and custom will unavoidably also be brought under review and will be revised and reorganised in the light of the same new principles of validity that are found to be sufficient in dealing with material facts.

Given time and a sufficiently exacting run of experience, and it will follow necessarily that much the same standards of truth and finality will come to govern men's knowledge and valuation of facts throughout; whether the facts in question lie in the domain of material things or in the domain of those imponderable conventions and preconceptions that decide what is right and proper in human intercourse. It follows necessarily, because the same persons, bent by the same discipline and habituation, take stock of both and are required to get along with both during the same lifetime. More or less rigorously the same scope and method of knowledge and valuation will control the thinking of the same individuals throughout; at least to the extent that any given article of faith and usage which is palpably at cross-purposes with this main intellectual bent will soon begin to seem immaterial and irrelevant and will tend to become obsolete by neglect.

Such has always been the fate which overtakes any notable articles of faith and usage that belong to a bygone point of view. Any established system of law and order will remain securely stable only on condition that it be kept in line or brought into line to conform with those canons of validity that have the vogue for the time being; and the vogue is a matter of habits of thought ingrained by everyday experience. And the moral is that any established system of law and custom is due to undergo a revision of its constituent principles so soon as a new order of economic life has had time materially to affect the community's habits of thought. But all the while the changeless native proclivities of the race will assert themselves in some measure in any eventual revision of the received institutional system; and always they will stand ready eventually to break the ordered scheme of things into a paralytic mass of confusion if it cannot be bent into some passable degree of congruity with the paramount native needs of life.

What is likely to arrest the attention of any student of the modern era from the outset is the peculiar character of its industry and of its intellectual outlook; particularly the scope and method of modern science and technology. The intellectual life of modern Europe and its cultural dependencies differs notably from what has gone before. There is all about it an air of matter-of-fact both in its technology and in its science which culminates in a mechanistic conception of all those things with which scientific inquiry is concerned and in the light of which many of the dread realities of the Middle Ages look like superfluous make-believe.

But it has been only during the later decades of the modern era — during that time interval that might fairly be called the post-modern era — that this mechanistic conception of things has begun seriously to affect the current system of knowledge and belief; and it has not hitherto seriously taken effect except in technology and in the material sciences. So that it has not hitherto seriously invaded the established scheme of institutional arrangements, the system of law and custom, which governs the relations of men to one another and defines their mutual rights, obligations, advantages and disabilities. But it should reasonably be expected that this established system of rights, duties, proprieties and disabilities will also in due time come in for something in the way of a revision, to bring it all more nearly into congruity with the matter-of-fact conceptions of things that lie at the root of the late-modern civilisation.

The constituent principles of the established system of law and custom are of the nature of imponderables, of course; but they are imponderables which have been conceived and formulated in terms of a different order from those that are convincing to the twentieth-century scientists and engineers. Whereas the line of advance of the scientists and engineers, dominated by their mechanistic conception of things, appears to be the main line of march for modern civilisation. It should seem reasonable to expect, therefore, that the scheme of law and custom will also fall into line with this mechanistic conception that appears to mark the apex of growth in modern intellectual life. But hitherto the "due time" needed for the adjustment has apparently not been had, or perhaps the experience which drives men in the direction of a mechanistic conception of all things has not hitherto been driving them hard enough or unremittingly enough to carry such a revision of ideas out in the system of law and custom. The modern point of view in matters of law and custom appears to be somewhat in arrears, as measured by the later advance in science and technology.

But just now the attention of thoughtful men centers on questions of practical concern, questions of law and usage, brought to a focus by the flagrant miscarriages of that organisation of Christendom that has brought the War upon the civilised nations. The paramount question just now is, what to do to save the civilised nations from irretrievable disaster, and what further may be accomplished by taking thought so that no similar epoch of calamities shall be put in train for the next generation. It is realised that there must be something in the way of a "reconstruction" of the scheme of things; and it is also realised, though more dimly, that the reconstruction must be carried out with a view to the security of life under such conditions as men will put up with, rather than with a view to the impeccable preservation of the received scheme of law and custom. All of which is only saying that the constituent principles of the modern point of view are to be taken under advisement, reviewed and — conceivably — revised and brought into line, in so far as these principles are constituent elements of that received scheme of law and custom that is spoken of as the *status quo*. It is the *status quo* in respect of law and custom, not in respect of science and technology or of knowledge and belief; but no man of sound mind hopes to revise the modern system of knowledge and belief so as to bring it all into conformity with the time-worn scheme of law and custom of the *status quo*.

Therefore the bearing of this stabilised modern point of view, stabilised in the eighteenth century, on these questions of practical concern is of present interest — its practical value as ground for a reasonably hopeful reconstruction of the war-shattered scheme of use and wont; its possible serviceability as a basis of enduring settlement; as well as the share which its constituent principles have had in the creation of that *status quo* out of which this epoch of calamities has been precipitated. The *status quo ante*, in which the roots of this growth of misfortunes and impossibilities are to be found, lies within the modern era, of course, and it is nowise to be decried as an alien, or even as an unforeseen, outgrowth of this modern era. By and large, this eighteenth-century stabilised modern point of view has governed men's dealings within this era, and its constituent principles of right and honest living must therefore, presumptively, be held answerable for the disastrous event of it all — at least to the extent that they have permissively countenanced the growth of those sinister conditions which have now ripened into a state of world-wide shame and confusion.

How and how far is this modern point of view, this body of legal and moral principles established in the eighteenth century, to be accounted an accessory to this crime? And if it be argued that this complication of atrocities has come on, not because of these principles of conduct which are so dear to civilised men and so blameless in their sight, but only in spite of them, then, what is the particular weakness or shortcoming inherent in this body of principles which has allowed such a growth of malignant conditions to go on and gather head? If the modern point of view, these settled principles of conduct by which modern men collectively are actuated in what they will do and in what they will permit — if these canons and standards of clean and honest living have proved to be a fatal snare, then it becomes an urgent question: Is it safe, or sane to go into the future by the light of these same established canons of right, equity, and propriety that so have been tried and found wanting?

Perhaps the question should rather take the less didactic form: Will the present experience of calamities induce men to revise these established principles of conduct, and the specifications of the code based on them, so effectually as to guard against any chance of return to the same desperate situation in the calculable future? Can the discipline of recent experience and the insight bred by the new order of knowledge and belief, reinforced by the shock of the present miscarriage, be counted on to bring such a revision of these principles of law and custom as will preclude a return to that *status quo ante* from which the miscarriage of civilisation has resulted? The latter question is more to the point. History teaches that men, taken collectively, learn by habituation rather than by precept and reflection; particularly as touches those underlying principles of truth and validity on which the effectual scheme of law and custom finally rests.

In the last analysis it resolves itself into a question as to how and how far the habituation of the recent past, mobilised by the shock of the present conjecture, will have affected the frame of mind of the common man in these civilised countries; for in the last analysis and with due allowance for a margin of tolerance it is the frame of mind of the common man that makes the foundation of society in the modern world; even though the elder statesmen continue to direct its motions from day to day by the light of those principles that were found good some time before yesterday. And the fortunes of the civilised world, for good or ill, have come to turn on the deeds of commission and of omission of these advanced peoples among whom the frame of mind of the common run is the finally conditioning circumstance in what may safely be done or left undone. The advice and consent of the common man have lately come to be indispensable to the conduct of affairs among civilised men, somewhat in the same degree in which the community is to be accounted a civilised people. It is indispensable at least in a permissive way, at least to the extent that no line of policy can long be pursued successfully without the permissive tolerance of the common run; and the margin of tolerance in the case appears to be narrower the more alert and the more matter-of-fact the frame of mind of the common man.

In so far as concerns the present question, that is to say as regards those standards and principles which underlie the established system of law and custom, the modern point of view was stabilised and given a definitive formulation in the eighteenth century; and in so far as concerns the subsequent conduct of practical affairs, its constituent principles have stood over without material change or revision since that time. So that for practical purposes it is fair to say that the modern point of view is now some one hundred and fifty years old.

It will not do to say that it is that much behind the times; because its time-worn standards of truth and validity are a very material factor in the makeup of "our time." That such is the case is due in great part to the fact that this body of principles was stabilised at that time and that they have therefore stood over intact, in spite of other changes that have taken place. It is only that the principles which had been tested and found good under the conditions of life in the modern era up to that time were at that time held fast, canvassed, defined, approved, and stabilised by being reduced to documentary form.

3

The Technology of the Predatory Culture

The scheme of technological insight and proficiency current in any given culture is manifestly a product of group life and is held as a common stock, and as manifestly the individual workman is helpless without access to it. It is none too broad to say that he is a workman only because and so far as he effectually shares in this common stock of technological equipment. He may be gifted in a special degree with workmanlike aptitudes, may by nature be stout or dextrous or keen-sighted or quick-witted or sagacious or industrious beyond his fellows; but with all these gifts, so long as he has assimilated none of this common stock of workmanlike knowledge he remains simply an admirable parcel of human raw material; he is of no effect in industry. With such special gifts or with special training based on this common stock an individual may stand out among his fellows as a workman of exceptional merit and value, and without the common run of workmanlike aptitudes he may come to nothing worth while as a workman even with the largest opportunities and most sedulous training. It is the two together that make the working force of the community; and in both respects, both in his inherited and in his acquired traits, the individual is a product of group life.

Using the term in a sufficiently free sense, pedigree is no less and no more requisite to the workman's effectual equipment than the common stock of technological mastery which the community offers him. But his pedigree is a group pedigree, just as his technology is a group technology. As is sometimes said to the same effect, the individual is a creature of heredity and circumstance. And heredity is always group heredity, Perhaps peculiarly so in the human species.

The promptings of invidious self-respect commonly lead men to evade or deny something to the breadth of their inheritance in respect to human nature. "I am not as the publican yonder, 'whether I have the grace to thank god for this invidious distinction or more simply charge it to the account of my reputable ancestors in the male line'". With a change of venue by which the cause is taken out of the jurisdiction of interested parties, its complexion changes. So evident is the fact of group heredity in the lower animals, for instance, that biologists have no inclination to deny its pervading force, apart from any conceivably parthenogenetic lines of descent, — and, to the inconvenience of the eugenic pharisee, parthenogenetic descent never runs in the male line, besides being of extremely rare occurrence in the human species. As a matter of course the Darwinian biologists have the habit of appealing to group heredity as the main factor in the stability of species, and they are very curious about the special circumstances of any given case in which it may appear not to be fully operative: and they have, on the other hand, even looked hopefully to a fortuitous isolation of particular lines of descent as a possible factor in the differentiation and fixation of specific types, being at a loss to account for such differentiation or fixation so long as no insuperable mechanical obstacle stands in the way of persistent crossing. The like force of group heredity is visible in the characteristic differences of race. The heredity of any given race of mankind is always sufficiently homogeneous to allow all its individuals to be classed under the race. And when an individual comes to light in a fairly pure-bred community who shows physical traits that vary obviously from the common racial type of the community, the question which suggests itself to the anthropologists is not, How does this individual differ from others of the same breed? but, What is the alien strain, and how has it come in? And what is true of the physical characters of the race in this respect is only less obviously true of its spiritual traits.

In a culture where all individuals are hybrids, in point of pedigree, as is the case with all the leading peoples of Christendom, the ways of this group heredity are particularly devious, and the fortunes of the individual in this respect are in a peculiar degree exposed to the caprice of Mendelian contingencies; so that his make-up, physical and spiritual, is, humanly speaking, in the main a chapter of accidents. Where each individual draws for his hereditary traits on a wide ancestry of unstable hybrids, as all civilised men do, his chances are always those of the common lot, with some slight antecedent probably of his resembling the nearer ones among his variegated ancestry. But he has also and everywhere in this hybrid panmixis an excellent chance of being allotted something more accentuated, for good or ill, in the way of hereditary traits than anything shown by his varied assortment of ancestors. It commonly happens in such a hybrid community that takes place at every marriage, some new idiosyncrasy, slight or considerable, comes to light in the offspring, beyond anything visible in the parents of the remoter pedigree; for in the crossing of what may be called multiple-hybrid parents, complementary characters that may have been dormant or recessive in the parents will come in from both sides, combine, re-inforce one another, and cumulatively give an unlooked-for result. So that in a hybrid community the fortunes of all individuals are somewhat precarious in respect of heredity.

Such are the conditions which have prevailed among the peoples of Europe since the first beginnings of that culture that has led up to the Western civilisation as known to history. In these circumstances any individual, therefore, owes to the group not only his share of that certain typical complement of traits that characterise the common run, but usually something more that is coming to him in the way of individual qualities and infirmities if he is in any way distinguishable from the common run, as well as a blind chance of transmitting almost any traits that he is not possessed of.

In the lower cultures, where the division of labour is slight and the diversity of occupations is mainly such as marks the changes of the seasons, the common stock of technological knowledge and proficiency is not so extensive or so recondite but that the common man may compass it in some fashion, and in its essentials it is accessible to all members of the community by common notoriety, and the training required by the state of the industrial arts comes to everyone as a matter of course in the routine of daily life. The necessary material equipment of tools and appliances is slight and the acquisition of it is a simple matter that also arranges itself as an incident in the routine of daily life. Given the common run of aptitude for the industrial pursuits incumbent on the members of such a community, the material equipment needful to find a livelihood or to put forth the ordinary productive effort and turn out the ordinary industrial output can be compassed without strain by an individual in the course of his work as he goes along. The material equipment, the tools, implements, contrivances necessary and conductive to productive industry, is incidental to the day's work; in much the same way but in a more unqualified degree than the like is true as to the technological knowledge and skill required to make use of this equipment.

As determined by the state of the industrial arts in such a culture, the members of the community co-operate in much of their work, to the common gain and to no one's detriment, since there is substantially no individual, or private, gain to be sought. There is substantially no bartering or hiring, though there is a recognised obligation in all members to lend a hand; and there is of course no price, as there is no property and no ownership, for the sufficient reason that the habits of life under these circumstances do not provoke such a habit of thought. Doubtless, it is a matter of course that articles of use and adornment pertain to their makers or users in an intimate and personal way; which will come to be construed into ownership when in the experience of the community an occasion for such a concept as ownership arises and persists in sufficient force to shape the current habits of thought to that effect. There is also more or less of reciprocal service and assistance, with a sufficient sense of mutuality to establish a customary scheme of claims and obligations in that respect. So it is also true that such a community holds certain lands and customary usufructs and that any trespass on these customary holdings is resented. But it would be a vicious misapprehension to read ideas and rights of ownership into these practices, although where civilised men have come to deal with instances of the kind, they have commonly been unable to put any other construction on the customs governing the case; for the reason that civilised men's relations with these peoples of the lower culture have been of a pecuniary kind and for a pecuniary purpose, and they have brought no other than pecuniary conceptions from home. There being little in hand worth owning and little purpose to be served by its ownership, the habits of thought which go to make the institution of ownership and property rights have not taken shape. The slight facts which would lend themselves to ownership are not of sufficient magnitude or urgency to call the institution into effect and are better handled under customs which do not yet take cognisance of property rights. Naturally, in such a cultural situation there is no appreciable accumulation of wealth and no inducement to it; the nearest approach being an accumulation of trinkets and personal belongings, among which should, at least in some cases, be included certain weapons and perhaps tools. These things belong to their owner or bearer in much the same sense as his name, which was not held on tenure of ownership or as a pecuniary asset before the use of trade-marks and merchantable good-will.

4

The Dynastic State in Germany

[...] it has appeared that any project for transfusing the characteristic elements of the current German culture abroad among the other nations of Christendom would be nugatory, owing to the fact that, however intrinsically desirable it may be, what the Fatherland has to offer in this way is, in its elements, out of date and therefore out of touch with the habits of thought in such communities of a maturer culture as, e.g., the French or the English. The chief distinctive characteristic of the German culture being a retarded adherence to certain mediaeval or sub-mediaeval habits of thought, the equivalents of which belong farther back than the historic present in the experience of these others. It is further argued, on similar ground, that any endeavor to hold fast the main body of this peculiarly German culture *in statu quo* within the confines of the Fatherland would similarly be nugatory, because as a cultural scheme it is out of date and touch with itself, in that it is in part archaic and in part quite new. All this, of course, does not bear on the intrinsic merits of this body of culture or on the question of its desirability. It is also, of course, intended only to describe the facts in the case and the effective practicability of such conceivable endeavor, and it is by no means intended to set forth the run of convictions current on this head among loyal German subjects.

So seen in its historical setting and in the light of the circumstances that have shaped it and that will continue to determine its further life-history — that is to say, considered genetically — this variant of the Western civilisation is evidently an exceptionally unstable, transitory, and in a sense unripe phase. Comprising, rather than combining, certain archaic elements — as, e.g., its traditional penchant for Romantic metaphysics and feudalistic loyalty — together with some of the latest ramifications of mechanistic science and an untempered application of the machine industry, it necessarily lacks that degree of homogeneity in its logic orientation that would characterise a maturer cultural complex. The resulting want of poise is not to be accounted an infirmity, perhaps; it makes for versatility and acceleration of change; but it is also a clear warrant that the existing congeries of cultural elements does not constitute a stable compound.

Such is, of course, not the appraisal of the spokesmen of this culture, in whose apprehension it necessarily stands as a finality, since it is all their own. And doubtless, sound and kindly men as they are, they are sincerely concerned to benefit mankind at large by its extension over the civilised world. Indeed, in their appraisal, as it abundantly comes into view, much is made of the stability, poise, deliberation and "profundity" of the national character in which this culture is conceived to be imbedded. Doubtless, a penchant for profundity and deliberation bulks large among the habits of those who cultivate this culture. But nothing can be more profoundly and meticulously deliberate than the measured footsteps of the man who no longer knows where he is going, though he is on his way.

Now, to carry out this benevolent design of extending the dominion of the culture of the Fatherland it is indispensable that the Prussian-Imperial State should extend its dominion; inasmuch as the prime postulate of the faith that moves these its spokesmen runs to the effect that the State is the first need of any cultured community; and as the Prussian-Imperial State is central and intrinsic to the German cultural scheme, it follows that this State will necessarily be the indispensable prime mover and chief end in the regeneration of humanity that so is to be effectuated. Whoever wills the end must make his peace with the means. So it has come about that the higher fortunes of humanity are conceived to be bound up indissolubly with the paramount dominion of the Prussian-Imperial State; which in its turn, in concrete fact, is identified with the suzerainty of the Hohenzollern dynasty. All of which greatly simplifies the plan of cultural salvation, at the same time that it brings the clear call of human duty to accord with the sportsmanlike impulsion of patriotic sentiment.

It is true, the run of the reasoning by which such a patriotic conclusion is reached may in fact be the reverse of that here given. The initiative and point of departure may in effect lodge in the patriotic sentiment, from which the analysis may then be run back into these profounder grounds of human duty and high intent, which so come to authenticate and sanctify the sportsmanlike zeal of the patriotic devotee. But the policy to be pursued is more commonly justified on some such moral grounds as indicated, rather than as an impulsive onset of sportsmanlike patriotism. And the outcome is the same in either case; it is an admirably single-minded devotion to the ascendancy of the Imperial State.

Something has already been said of the economic policy pursued by the Imperial government. This policy has been much commended for the benefits it has conferred on the German people. No doubt, much of this commendation is an uncritical laudation of success; and earlier passages of this inquiry have shown reasons for believing that this industrial success has in part been due to circumstances not connected with the state or its policy. But after all due allowance for adventitious circumstances there doubtless remains much to be credited to the government's policy. A critical scrutiny will probably bring into relief the meritorious deeds of omission and riddance that should be credited to the Empire, but the Imperial policy is by no means without merit on the side of its deeds of commission also.

The economic policy of the Empire has not run the same throughout its course, although it has consistently aimed at warlike power throughout. In its earlier period, the administration of Bismarck, the aim seems to have been warlike security rather than Imperial expansion; since the present reign it has, with fairly consistency, been the latter. But throughout the Imperial era the material fortunes of the nation have consistently been furthered and conserved for the ulterior end of warlike power. To this end it has been sought to make the Fatherland, as near as practicably may be, a self-contained industrial community, — a policy which conduces to no other end, and which, incidentally but unavoidably, lowers the industrial efficiency of the nation.

A policy directed to making a nation industrially self-contained or self-sufficient necessarily depends on measures of inhibition. It is only by obstructing the free ramification of the industrial system across the national frontiers that such self-sufficiency can be achieved. A self-contained industrial community is one whose industry draws for its raw materials only on the natural resources comprised within the national frontiers, whose population draws its subsistence from the soil of the country, and which exports only superfluities, or at the most, articles of consumption that can readily be dispensed with. On the other hand the modern state of the industrial arts is drawn on an international scale, in that it works to the best, that is to say the most productive, effect by the free use of materials drawn from many sources, far and near, and by such free local specialisation of industry as will permit the supply of any given line of goods, finished or half-wrought, to be turned out wherever the facilities for their production are at their best. This is the chief service of the modern means of transport and communication.

Illustrations of this point should seem needless, yet an illustrative instance or two drawn from the German situation may not be out of place. So, it is evident that German industry would better depend on outside sources for its necessary supply of copper and petroleum, as well as for the precious metals, and it is only a degree less evident that the industrial community at large, as distinct from special interests, would profit by free access to outside supplies of iron, coal and lumber. With modern means of transportation, the economy of such free access is sufficiently evident. So, again, it is evident that the German population can find their needed supply of fruits, grain, meat and fish at less cost by drawing a large proportion of it from outside, in exchange for their wrought goods, rather than from the soil of the Fatherland.

It is only by putting obstacles in the way, or — what comes to the same thing — by offering special inducements to special interests, that the ramifications of the industrial system can be prevented from extending across the national frontiers; which comes to saying that that end can be achieved only by hindering the industrial community from taking full advantage of the modern state of the industrial arts, and so lowering its industrial efficiency below what it could be in the absence of such hindrance. This, of course, is commonplace. In the German case as in others elsewhere, the chief instrument of this obstructive nationalist policy has been the national tariff. The results achieved have, of course, fallen far short of the desired self-sufficiency on the part of the German nation. To set aside the effects of modern technology to that extent has not been feasible.

Doubtless the Imperial endeavors to create such a self-contained war power in the Fatherland have materially abated the net industrial efficiency of the German community; but the effects of the control and inhibition exercised with this end in view have after all not been so serious, nor has the net waste involved in armament and warlike preparation been nearly so grave a matter, as the mere *prima facie* statistical computations in the case would tend to show. The effects of this government management are not exhausted if the first incidence of the measures is taken; in effect there is involved something like that "repercussion" of which the theories of taxation take account. Most obvious among such secondary effects, after the analogy of "repercussion," would be the effect intended by the Imperial tariff system. It has diverted industry to less productive channels, but it has also had much of its intended effect in making the nation self-dependent in the material respect and has bred an enhanced attitude of national animosity toward foreign nationalities. These are valuable assets for the Imperial purpose. It has also had the further intended effect of holding the loyal affections of the Agrarians and maintaining them in their position of preponderance. These are obvious matters, and notorious.

Less obvious are certain secondary consequences and circumstances due to this Imperial war policy. In earlier passages of this inquiry attention has been directed to the cumulative growth of wasteful expenditures, euphemistically spoken of as a rising standard of living, in the British community in modern time. Enforced by a sense of conventional propriety, this wasteful consumption has been institutionalised and so has taken on a character of moral necessity As has also been noted, the German population brought relatively little of this line of conventions with them when they came into the modern industrial world, half-a-century ago, having been trained in a school of penurious frugality under the earlier régime of small means and princely rapacity. Now, the Imperial drought on current resources, while it has not fallen directly and formally on such wasteful expenditures, has after all acted to reduce the margin of surplus available for such wasteful consumption; so that it has in part, to that extent, merely diverted to warlike waste what would otherwise have gone into conspicuously wasteful living at the hands of its recipients. In the measure in which the resulting drought on the nation's income for warlike expenditure has so constituted a deduction from expenditures on conspicuous waste, it may on a large view fairly be said to have cost the country nothing. It may perhaps safely be taken as a matter of course that the cost of the warlike establishment is not all to be checked off in this way against bootless private waste foregone; but it is equally a matter of course that under the peculiar circumstances affecting the life of the German population during this period a very appreciable compensatory effect of this kind will have been had.

Yet, while warlike expenditures have in the aggregate undoubtedly exceeded what any reasonable allowance for conspicuous waste in the service of gentility might amount to, and while the drain of military and Imperial needs has doubtless reduced and retarded the growth of wasteful standards of living, still such a growth has by no means been altogether wanting. The decencies — mostly pecuniary and emulative — cannot be denied their equitable claim, and the German people have after all done something appreciable toward bringing their standards of decent expenditure into line with those of their neighbors. The disposable margin of output above (conventionally) necessary consumption has doubtless been narrowed appreciably by this means. And still, to the extent to which this policy of warlike expenditure has reduced the conventionally necessary waste, it has not only not impoverished the community (directly, at least) but has also left the country by so much the more capable to bear any sudden strain put on it by warlike enterprise in the event of actual hostilities.

There is another count of the same general bearing that similarly comes into view on contrasting the German case with the English. Distinguishable from, but inextricably woven into the broad web of wastefully respectable living in the United Kingdom, is the addiction to sports. Taken merely as a matter of wasteful consumption — which means in statistical terms approximately one hundred per cent — this cultivation of sports will count up simply as a wasteful dissipation of time and substance, of course; but it has its value also as a staple means of diverting the energies and attention, and therefore the acquired proficiencies and the further habituation, of a large section of the community into this, economically speaking, arid channel of dissipation; whereby the time, use and effect of this fraction of the population are diverted from useful ends to the production of a moderate output of mischief.

When the modern era set in Germany that country was not possessed of anything like a full complement of these genteel and manly dissipations, and what there was to carry over of a home-bred equivalent was largely jettisoned in the trans-shipment, so as to leave something of a margin of energy, intelligence and manly conceit free to be taken up by any reputable interest that might offer. Such an outlet, reputable, sensational and conspicuous was found for the Fatherland's sporting blood in drafting this susceptible element of the idle classes into the service; with no loss to the community in any visible respect and with great gain to the warlike preparations of the State. All this has in some measure hindered the free development of sportsmanship in Germany and has also doubtless contributed materially to the growth of an aggressive war spirit.

The comprehensive and exacting demands of universal military service as it applies to the population at large have had a somewhat similar effect on the common man, by diverting interest from the make-believe of sports to that of war; and it is not at all certain that the loss to industry from the cause, considerable as it has unquestionably been, has not been fully offset by the greater docility of the working classes resulting from their experience of surveillance and subjection in the army. A military organisation is necessarily a servile organisation, and the discipline of servile obedience will always have its effect.[i]

Running to the same general effect, and working in harmonious concert with the servile discipline of the army, is the government policy of tutelage for the working class, in the way of hospital service, insurance and pension arrangements, and the like. In this, again, there is no visible economic loss, perhaps, even a visible economic gain, in that it offsets some of the untoward effects of a businesslike quest of profits on the part of capitalist-employers gifted with a scant regard for the long-term welfare of the community. What will be the ulterior consequences of such a policy of tutelage cannot well be surmised, but among these consequences should come a more passive dependence of the common man on the directive authority of the government and its bureaucratic machinery, together with a slackening of initiative and of the spirit of autonomy, and the growth of a certain partisan loyalty to the reigning house. Past experience and discipline, it should be remarked, predispose the workmen for this tutelage and its effects. As is well known, though not always avowed, under the circumstances of the large-scale industry as managed for business ends, the indigent workmen are helpless while acting in severalty, and no effectual remedy for this individual helplessness has yet been found in any form of self-directed collective action. The economic value, and the political expediency, of the crown's tutelage are all the more evident, and the ulterior consequences of this tutelage may accordingly be expected to be all the more far-reaching. But such ulterior consequences are chiefly to be looked for among the effects of habit, and in the main they are yet in the future.

It will be seen, then, that both in its cultural antecedents and in the current circumstances there are several factors of considerable scope peculiar to this German case and converging to an outcome different from what has resulted, so far, among the English-speaking peoples as a consequence of their taking over the modern industrial arts, — different, indeed, in a very appreciable degree from what can by any dispassionate line of reasoning be looked for among the English-speaking peoples within the calculable future.

Germany carried over from a recent and retarded past a State, of the dynastic order, with a scheme of detail institutions and a popular habit of mind suitable to a coercive, centralised, and irresponsible control and to the pursuit of dynastic dominion. Quite unavoidably, the united Fatherland came under the hegemony of the most aggressive and most irresponsible — substantially the most archaic — of the several states that coalesced in its formation; and quite as a matter of course the dynastic spirit of the Prussian state has permeated the rest of the federated people, until the whole is now very appreciably nearer the spiritual bent of the militant Prussian State of a hundred years ago than they have been at any time since the movement for German Union began in the nineteenth century.

This united German community, at the same time, took over from their (industrially) more advanced neighbors the latest and highly efficient state of the industrial arts, — wholly out of consonance with their institutional scheme, but highly productive, and so affording a large margin disposable for the uses of the dynastic State. Being taken over ready-made and in the shortest practicable time, this new technology brought with it virtually none of its inherent drawbacks, in the way of conventional waste, obsolescent usage and equipment, or class animosities; and as it has been brought into full bearing within an unexampled short time, none of these drawbacks or handicaps have yet had time to grow to formidable dimensions.

Owing in part to the same unprecedentedly short period of its acquirement and installation, and in part to the nearly unbroken mediaevalism of the institutional scheme into which the new technology has been intruded, it has hitherto had but a slight effect in the way of inducing new habits of thought on institutional matters among the German population, such as have formed the institutional counterpart of its gradual development among the English-speaking peoples. Such institutional consequences of a workday habituation to any given state of the industrial arts will necessarily come on by slow degrees and be worked out only in the course of generations.

In the English case, as has been indicated in earlier passages, such growth of popular institutions and ideals of autonomy and initiative as may be observed in modern times has not placed popular autonomy in anything like a position of unqualified domination in any of the collective concerns of life. There is much standing over from the earlier, feudalistic and dynastic, régime, as, e.g., the crown, the nobility with its house of lords, and the established church; although these remains so left over are in a visibly infirm state and have something of an air of incongruity and anachronism in their modern setting. "Dead letter" and "legal fiction" have a large place in English conceptions, and these archaic strands in the institutional fabric are in great part to be viewed in that light. At the same time, while the modern institutional notions of popular autonomy have been encroaching on the domain once held by feudalism and the State, there have, along with this growth, also grown into the scheme a new range of customary conceptions and usages that greatly circumscribe the *de facto* supremacy of popular institutions in the British commonwealth.

Any English-speaking community is a commonwealth rather than a State; but none of these communities, for all that, is a commonwealth of free, equal, and ungraded men; their citizens are not "masterless men," except in the cognizance of the law. Discrepancies of wealth have grown great and found secure lodgment in the institutional scheme at the same time that these modern communities have been falling back on those ancient ideals of personal insubordination that make the substance of their free institutions. And serious discrepancies of wealth are a matter not provided for in that ancient hereditary bent that once made the petty anarchistic groups of the Baltic culture a practicable engine of social control, and that is now reasserting itself in democratic discontent. While property rights work no *de jure* disturbance of the democratic scheme, their *de facto* consequences are sufficiently grave, so that it is doubtful if a free but indigent workman in a modern industrial community is at all better off in point of material circumstances than the workmen on a servile tenure under feudalism. Indeed, so grave and perplexing has the situation in the English-speaking countries become, in respect of the *de facto* control of the community's material fortunes by the owners of large property, that none but a graceless "pessimist" is conceived to be capable of calling attention to so sore a difficulty for which no remedy can be discovered. Yet, while the current administration of affairs may be carried on by bailiffs of the wealthy and well-to-do, and primarily in their interest, it remains true that in point of popular sentiment the sovereignty vests collectively in the common man; and it will scarcely be questioned that if brought to a test, this popular sentiment would stubbornly assert its paramount dominion.

Partial and incomplete as this shift to popular autonomy proves to have been in the English-speaking nations, it has taken some centuries of experience to carry the community from a position comparable to that occupied by the Germans at the formation of the empire to the compromise in force among these peoples today. This growth of free institutions and insubordination, such as it is, has apparently come partly of the positive discipline in mechanistic habits of thought given by the modern industrial arts, but partly also as a reassertion of the hereditary anarchistic bent of this population in the absence of duly rigorous circumstance going to enforce a scheme of coercion and loyalty. The net outcome may be rated as a gain or loss, according as one is inclined to see it. But it is an outcome of the working of the modern industrial system, and if it is to be accepted as one of the concomitants of that system, inseparable from it in the long run because it is made of the same substance as this technological system.

It is this "long run" that is still wanting in the German case, and it must necessarily be all the longer a run for the care taken by the Imperial State to prevent such an outcome. Meantime the Imperial State has come into the usufruct of this state of the industrial arts without being hampered with its long-term institutional consequences. Carrying over a traditional bias of Romantic loyalty, infused anew with a militant patriotism by several successful wars, and irritably conscious of national power in their new-found economic efficiency, the feudalistic spirit of the population has yet suffered little if any abatement from their brief experience as a modern industrial community. And borne up by its ancient tradition of prowess and dynastic aggression, the Prussian-Imperial State has faithfully fostered this militant spirit and cultivated in the people the animus of a solidarity of prowess. Hence a pronounced retardation in the movement toward popular autonomy, due to follow from habituation to the mechanistic logic of the modern technology and industrial organisation.

In this work of retarding the new and conserving the old the Imperial State has been greatly furthered by finding ready at hand a large and serviceable body of men, useless for industrial purposes by force of conventional and temperamental disabilities, who have eagerly entered the career of prowess opened to them by the warlike enterprise of the Empire and have zealously fallen in with the spirit of that policy, — such being the run of traditions out of which they have come in the recent past. Indeed, so large, so strongly biased, and so well entrenched in the use and wont of the Fatherland, have this contingent of specialists in prowess been, that even with a very moderate degree of moral support from the constituted authorities, perhaps even on a footing of tolerance — if such a footing were conceivable under the Imperial auspices — their organisation into a specialised corps of war-leaders should have followed as a matter of course; and the presence of such a body of professional military men, pervaded with a headlong enthusiasm for warlike enterprise, would of itself have had the effect of heightening the war spirit abroad in the community at large and inducing a steady drift of sentiment leading to a warlike climax.

It has been the usual fortune of military establishments and warlike class organisations presently to fall into a certain state of moral decay, whereby rank, routine, perquisites and intemperate dissipation come to engage the best attention of the specialists in war. Like other works of use and wont this maturing of the warlike establishment takes time, and the corps of war specialists under the Imperial auspices has not yet had time to work out the manifest destiny of warlike establishments in this respect; although it may be admitted that "irregularities" of the kind alluded to have by no means been altogether wanting. The corrosion of military use and wont, in the way of routine, subordination, arrogance, indolence and dissipation, has perhaps gone so far as would unfit this picked body of men for the duties of citizenship under any but an autocratic government, but they have probably suffered no appreciable impairment in respect of their serviceability for war and its advocacy.

In the same connection, it is also credibly reported, though not officially confirmed, that the highly efficient school system of the empire, perhaps especially of Prussia, is, under Imperial auspices, made a vehicle for propaganda of the same patriotism of prowess that pervades the body of officers. Something of the kind is known to be true of the Prussian universities. Much can of course be done toward giving a bent of this kind to the incoming generation by well-directed inculcation during the impressionable period of schoolboy life.

One further item should be included in any recital of the special circumstances that go to make Imperial Germany and shape its destiny. Among the gains that have come to the Imperial State, and by no means least among these gains if one is to judge by the solicitous attention given it, is the use of the modern technology for warlike equipment and strategy. It has already been noted that the railway system, as also the merchant marine and its harbor equipment, has been developed under surveillance, with a view to its serviceability in war; in part this transportation system has been projected and built avowedly for strategic use, in part under specifications and with subventions designed to make it an auxiliary arm. The importance of such a competently organised transportation system in modern strategy needs no argument; its bearing on the animus of the statesmen at whose disposal so efficient a factor of warlike equipment is held, as well as on that of the people at large, should also not be overlooked.[ii] But beyond this, and doubtless of graver import, is the direct service rendered by the modern technology and applied science to the art of war. Since the modern technology fell into the hands of the Germans they have taken the lead in the application of this technological knowledge to what may be called the industrial arts of war, with at least no less zeal and no less effect than in its utilisation in the arts of peace. In the "armed peace" of Europe, Imperial Germany has consistently aimed to be the most heavily armed and the readiest for any eventual breach of the peace. These preparations, it has been usual to declare, to have been made with a view to keeping the peace. Some weight may perhaps attach to these declarations. They have been made by statesmen of the school of Frederick the Great. The run of the facts in the case is that throughout the forty-four years of its life-history hitherto, and more particularly through the latter quarter of a century, preparation for war on a large scale has been going forward uninterruptedly, and at a constantly accelerating rate, whether as measured in terms of absolute magnitude or as measured in terms of expenditure per capita of the population, or of percentages of current income or of accumulated wealth, or as compared with the corresponding efforts of neighboring states.

This drift toward a warlike fatality has been facilitated by subsidiary consequences that should, in their immediate incidence, seem to have no bearing of the kind. So, e.g., their great success in business and industry has inspired the commonplace German subjects with a degree of confidence and self-complacency that impresses their neighbors as conceit and braggadocio. Human nature being what it is, it is unavoidable that German subjects should take the German successes to heart in this way and that they should fall into something of an overbearing attitude toward other nationalities, and on similarly sufficient grounds it follows that those who are brought in contact with this very natural magisterial swagger find it insufferable. All of which engenders a resentful animosity, such as will place all international relations on a precarious footing. So, by force of circumstances over which no control could be had, and which it must be admitted have not been sought to be controlled, it has come about that their economic success has brought the German people an abundance of ill-will; not unmixed with envy, but good and competent ill-will for all that.

It may be worth noting that something of the same sense of estrangement is visible in the attitude of the continental peoples toward the English of the swaggering Elizabethan times, and after. But the resulting animosity in that case appears not to have reached so high a pitch, and the insular position of the English served in any case to prevent any such animosity from becoming a menace to the public peace.

Notes

i So, universal military service has proved the most effectual corrective yet brought to bear on the socialistic propaganda and similar movements of discontent and insubordination; and the discipline of servility, or of servitude, enforced in the service is probably to be accounted the chief agency in bringing about the definitive collapse of socialism in Germany, — definitive, that is, for the present and the calculable future, and in all respects but the name, the ritual and the offices. The concomitant warlike propaganda and unstinted dynastic magniloquence have contributed their share to this consummation, but except for the positive training in subjection to personal authority given by universal military service it is at least very doubtful if the German socialist movement could by this date have fallen into its present state of "innocuous desuetude."

ii "There is something in the possession of superior strength most dangerous, in a moral view, to its possessor. Brought in contact with semi-civilised man, the European, with his endowments and effective force so immeasurably superior, holds him as little higher than the brute, and as born equally for his service. He feels that he has a natural right, as it were, to his obedience, and that this obedience is to be measured, not by the powers of the barbarian, but by the will of his conqueror. Resistance becomes a crime to be washed out only in the blood of the victim. The tale of such atrocities is not confined to the Spaniard." —Prescott, *Conquest of Peru*, bk. iv.

Such loss of moral perspective through an overweening sense of power appears to follow equally whether the stronger is or is not superior in another respect, — perhaps even more pronouncedly in the latter case. The Huns and Turks show it in their dealings with the Romanised Europeans, just as the Children of Israel show it on contact with Canaanites and Philistines, and as it appears again in the animus of Gauls, Goths, Visigoths, and Vandals, in their time. So also the swaggering Elizabethan "gentleman adventurer" in his degree as well as the Spanish conquistador or the Prussian-Imperial statesman. It is the moral attitude of the pot-hunter towards the fur-bearing animals. One does not keep faith with the fur-bearing animals.

5

Higher Learning

In any known civilization there will be found something in the way of esoteric knowledge. This body of knowledge will vary characteristically from one culture to another, differing both in content and in respect of the canons of truth and reality relied on by its adepts. But there is this common trait running through all civilizations, as touches this range of esoteric knowledge, that it is in all cases held, more or less closely, in the keeping of a select body of adepts or specialists — scientists, scholars, savants, clerks, priests, shamans, medicine men — whatever designation may best fit the given case.

In the apprehension of the given society within which any such body of knowledge is found, it will also be found that the knowledge in question is related as an article of great intrinsic value, in some way a matter of more substantial consequence than any or all of the material achievements of possessions of the community. It may take shape as a system of magic or of religious beliefs, of mythology, theology, philosophy or science. But whatever shape it falls into the given case, it makes up the substantial core of the civilization in which it is found, and it is felt to give characters and distinction to that civilization.

In the apprehension of the group in whose life and esteem it lives and takes effect, this esoteric knowledge is taken to embody a systematization of fundamental and eternal truth; although it is evident to any outsider that it will take its character and its scope and method from the habits of life of the group, from the institutions with which it is bound in a web of give and take. Such is manifestly the case in all the historic phases of civilization, as well as in all those contemporary cultures that are sufficiently remote from our everyday interests to admit of their being seen in adequate perspective. A passably dispassionate inquiry into the place which modern learning holds in modern civilization will show that such is also the case of this latest, and in the mind of its keepers the most mature, system of knowledge. It should by no means be an insuperably difficult matter to show that this "higher learning" of the modern world, the current body of science and scholarship, also holds its place on such a tenure of use and wont, that it has grown and shifted in point of content, aims and methods in response to the changes in habits of life that have passed over the Western peoples during the period of its growth and ascendancy. Nor should it be embarrassingly difficult to reach the persuasion that this process of change and supersession in the scope and method of knowledge is still effectually at work, in a like response to institutional changes that still are incontinently going forward.[i]

To the adepts who are occupied with this esoteric knowledge, the scientists and scholars on whom its keeping devolves, the matter will of course not appear in just that light; more particularly so far as regards that special segment of the field of knowledge with the keeping and cultivation of which they may, each and several, be occupied. They are, each and several, engaged on the perfecting and conservation of a special line of inquiry, the objective end of which, in the view of its adepts, will necessarily be the final and irreducible truth as touches matters within its scope. But, seen in perspective, these adepts are themselves to be taken as creatures of habit, creatures of that particular manner of group life out of which their preconceptions in matters of knowledge, and the manner of their interest in the run of inquiry, have sprung. So that the terms of finality that will satisfy the adepts are also a consequence of habituation, and they are to be taken as conclusive only because and in so far as they are consonant with the discipline of habituation enforced by that manner of group life that has induced in these adepts their particular frame of mind.

Perhaps at a farther remove than many other current phenomena, but none the less effectually for that, the higher learning takes its character from the manner of life enforced on the group by the circumstances that so condition the scope and method of learning that are primarily, and perhaps most cogently, the conditions imposed by the state of the industrial arts, the technological situation; but in the second place, and scarcely less exacting in detail, the received scheme of use and wont in its other bearings has its effect in shaping the scheme of knowledge, both as to its content and as touches the norms and methods of its organization. Distinctive and dominant among the constituent factors of this current scheme of use and wont is in the pursuit of business, with the outlook and predilections which that pursuit implies. Therefore any inquiry into the effect which recent institutional changes may have upon the pursuit of the higher learning will necessarily be taken up in a peculiar degree with the consequences which an habitual pursuit of business in modern times has had for the ideals, aims and methods of the scholars and schools devoted to the higher learning.

The higher learning as currently cultivated by the scholars and scientists of the Western civilization differs not generically from the esoteric knowledge purveyed by specialists in other civilizations, elsewhere and in other times. It engages the same general range of aptitudes and capacities, meets the same range of human wants, and grows out of the same impulsive propensities of human nature. Its scope and method are different from what has seemed good in other cultural situations, and its tenets and canons are so far peculiar as to give it a specific character different from these others; but in the main this specific character is due to a different distribution of emphasis among the same general range of native gifts that have always driven men to the pursuit of knowledge. The stress falls in a somewhat obviously different way among the canons of reality by recourse to which men systematize and verify the knowledge gained; which is in its turn due to the different habituation to which civilized men are subjected, as contrasted with the discipline exercised by other and earlier cultures.

In point of its genesis and growth any system of knowledge may confidently be run back, in the main, to the initiative and bias afforded by two certain impulsive traits of human nature; an Idle Curiosity, and the Instinct of Workmanship.[ii]

In this generic trait the modern learning does not depart from the rule that holds for the common run. Men instinctively seek knowledge, and value it. The fact of this proclivity is well summed up in saying that men are by native gift actuated with an idle curiosity, — "idle" in the sense that a knowledge of things is sought, apart from any ulterior use of the knowledge so gained.[iii] This, of course, does not imply that the knowledge so gained will not be turned to practical account. In point of fact, although the fact is not greatly relevant to the inquiry here in hand, the native proclivity here spoken of as the instinct of workmanship will unavoidably incline men to turn to account, in a system of ways and means, whatever knowledge so becomes available. But the instinct of workmanship has also another and more pertinent bearing in these premises, in that it affords the norms, or the scheme of criteria and canons of verity, according to which the ascertained facts will be construed and connected up in a body of systematic knowledge. Yet the sense of workmanship takes effect by recourse to divers expedients and reaches its ends by recourse to varying principles, according as the habituation of workday life has enforced one or another scheme of interpretation for the facts with which it has to deal.

The habits of thought induced by workday life impose themselves as ruling principles that govern the quest of knowledge; it will therefore be the habits of thought enforced by the current technological scheme that will have most (or most immediately) to say in the current systematization of facts. The working logic of the current state of the industrial arts will necessarily insinuate itself as the logical scheme which must, of course, effectually govern the interpretation and generalizations of fact in all their commonplace relations. But the current state of the industrial arts is not all that conditions workmanship. Under any given institutional situation, — and the modern scheme of use and wont, law and order, is no exception, — workmanship is held to a more or less exacting conformity to several tests and standards that are not intrinsic to the state of the industrial arts, even if they are not alien to it; such as the requirements imposed by the current system of ownership and pecuniary values. These pecuniary conditions that impose themselves on the processes of industry and on the conduct of life, together with the pecuniary accountancy that goes with them — the price system — have much to say in the guidance and limitations of workmanship. And when and in so far as the habituation so enforced in the traffic of workday life goes in to effect a scheme of logic governing the quest of knowledge, such principles as have by habit found acceptance as being conventionally salutary and conclusive in the pecuniary conduct of affairs will necessarily leave their mark on the ideals, aims, methods and standards of science and scholarship. More particularly, those principles and standards of organization, control and achievement, that have been accepted as an habitual matter of course in the conduct of business will, by force of habit, in good part reassert themselves as indispensable and conclusive in the conduct of the affairs of learning. While it remains true that the bias of workmanship continues to guide the quest of knowledge, under the conditions imposed by modern institutions it will not be the naïve conceptions of primitive workmanship that will shape the framework of the modern system of learning; but rather the preconceptions of that disciplined workmanship that has been instructed in the logic of the modern technology and sophisticated with much experience in a civilization in whose scheme of life pecuniary canons are definitive.

The modern technology is of an impersonal, matter-of-fact character in an unexampled degree, and the accountancy of modern business management is also of an extremely dispassionate and impartially exacting nature. It results that the modern learning is of a similarly matter-of-fact, mechanistic complexion, and that it similarly leans on statistically dispassionate tests and formulations. Whereas it may fairly be said that the personal equation once — in the days of scholastic learning — was the central and decisive factor in the systematization of knowledge, it is equally fair to say that in later time no effort is spared to eliminate all bias of personality from the technique or the results of science or scholarship. It is the "dry light of science" that is always in request, and great pains are taken to exclude all color of sentimentality.

Yet this highly sterilized, germ-proof system of knowledge, kept in a cool, dry place, commands the affection of modern civilized mankind no less unconditionally, with no more afterthought of an extraneous sanction, than once did the highly personalized mythological and philosophical constructions and interpretations that had the vogue in the days of schoolmen.

Through all the mutations that have passed over this quest of knowledge, from its beginnings in puerile myth and magic to its (provisional) consummation in the "exact" sciences of the current fashion, any attentive scrutiny will find that the driving force has consistently been of the same kind, traceable to the same proclivity of human nature. In so far as it may fairly be accounted esoteric knowledge, or a "higher learning," all this enterprise is actuated by an idle curiosity, a disinterested proclivity to gain a knowledge of things and to reduce this knowledge to a comprehensible system. The objective end is a theoretical organization, a logical articulation of things known, the lines of which must not be deflected by any consideration of expediency or convenience, but must turn true to the canons of reality accepted at the time. These canons of reality, or of verity, have varied from time to time, have in fact varied incontinently with the passage of time and the mutations of experience. As the fashions of modern time have come on, particularly the later phases of modern life, the experience that so has shaped and reshaped the canons of verity for the use of inquiring minds has fallen more and more into the lines of mechanical articulation and has expressed itself ever more unreservedly in terms of mechanical stress. Concomitantly the canons of reality have taken on a mechanistic complexion, to the neglect and progressive disuse of all tests and standards of a more genial sort; until in the off-hand apprehension of modern men, "reality" comes near being identified with mechanical fact, and "verification" is taken to mean a formulation in mechanical terms. But the final test of this reality about which the inquiries of modern men so turn is not the test of mechanical serviceability for human use, but only of mechanistically effectual matter-of-fact.

So it has come about that modern civilization is in a very special degree a culture of the intellectual powers, in the narrower sense of the term, as contrasted with the emotional traits of human nature. Its achievements and chief merits are found in this field of learning, and its chief defects elsewhere. And it is on its achievements in this domain of detached and dispassionate knowledge that modern civilized mankind most ingenuously plumes itself and confidently rests its hopes. The more emotional and spiritual virtues that once held the first place have been overshadowed by the increasing consideration given to proficiency in matter-of-fact knowledge. As prime movers in the tide of civilized life, these sentimental movements of the human spirit belong in the past, — at least such is the self-complacent avowal of the modern spokesmen of culture. The modern technology, and the mechanistic conception of things that goes with that technology, are alien to the spirit of the "Old Order." The Church, the court, the camp, the drawing-room, where these elder and perhaps nobler virtues had their laboratory and playground, have grown weedy and gone to seed. Much of the apparatus of the old order, with the good old way, still stands over in a state of decent repair, and the sentimentally reminiscent endeavors of certain spiritual "hold-overs" still lend this apparatus of archaism something of a galvanic life. But that power of aspiration that once surged full and hot in the cults of faith, fashion, sentiment, exploit, and honor, now at its best comes to such a head as it may in the concerted adulation of matter-of-fact.

This esoteric knowledge of matter-of-fact has come to be accepted as something worth while in its own right, a self-legitimating end of endeavor in itself, apart from any bearing it may have on the glory of God or the good of man. Men have, no doubt, always been possessed of a more or less urgent propensity to inquire into the nature of things, beyond the serviceability of any knowledge so gained, and have always been given to seeking curious explanations of things at large. The idle curiosity is a native trait of the race. But in past times such a disinterested pursuit of unprofitable knowledge has, by and large, not been freely avowed as a legitimate end of endeavor; or such has at any rate been the state of the case through that later segment of history which students commonly take account of. A quest of knowledge has overtly been rated as meritorious, or even blameless, only in so far as it has appeared to serve the ends of one or another of the practical interests that have from time to time occupied men's attention. But latterly, during the past few generations, this learning has so far become an avowed "end in itself" that "the increase and diffusion of knowledge among men" is now freely rated as the most humane and meritorious work to be taken care of by any enlightened community or any public-spirited friend of civilization.

The expediency of such "increase and diffusion" is no longer held in doubt, because it has ceased to be a question of expediency among the enlightened nations, being itself the consummation upon which, in the apprehension of civilized men, the advance of culture must converge. Such has come to be the long-term commonsense judgement of enlightened public opinion. A settled presumption to some such effect has found lodgement as a commonplace conviction in the popular mind, in much the same measure and in much the same period of time as the current body of systematic knowledge has taken on the character of matter-of-fact. For good or ill, civilized men have come to hold that this matter-of-fact knowledge of things is the only end in life that indubitably justifies itself. So that nothing more irretrievably shameful could overtake modern civilization than the miscarriage of this modern learning, which is the most valued spiritual asset of civilized mankind.

The truth of this view is borne out by the professions even of those lieutenants of the powers of darkness who are straining to lay waste and debauch the peoples of Christendom. In high-pitched concert they all swear by the name of a "culture" whose sole inalienable asset is this same intellectual mastery of matters of fact. At the same time it is only by drawing on the resources of this matter-of-fact knowledge that the protagonists of reaction are able to carry on their campaign of debauchery and desolation.

Other interests that have once been held in higher esteem appear by comparison to have fallen into abeyance, — religious devotion, political prestige, fighting capacity, gentility, pecuniary distinction, profuse consumption of goods. But it is only by comparison with the higher value given to this enterprise of the intellect that such other interests appear to have lost ground. These and the like have fallen into relative disesteem, as being sordid and insubstantial by comparison. Not that these "lower" human interests, answering to the "lower" ranges of human intellect, have fallen into neglect; it is only that they have come to be accounted "lower," as contrasted with the quest of knowledge; and it is only on sober second thought, and perhaps only for the ephemeral present, that they are so accounted by the common run of civilized mankind. Men still are in sufficiently hot pursuit of all these time-worn amenities, and each for himself is, in point of fact, more than likely to make the pursuit of such self-seeking ends the burden of his life; but on a dispassionate rating, and under the corrective of deliberate avowal, it will appear that none of these commend themselves as intrinsically worth while at large. At the best they are rated as expedient concessions to human infirmity or as measures of defense against human perversity and the outrages of fortune. The last resort of the apologists of these more sordid endeavors is the plea that only by these means can the ulterior ends of a civilization of intelligence be served. The argument may fairly be paraphrased to the effect that in order to serve God in the end, we must all be ready, to serve the Devil in the meantime.

It is always possible, of course, that this pre-eminence of intellectual enterprise in the civilization of the Western peoples is a transient episode; that it may eventually — perhaps even precipitately, with the next impending turn in the fortunes of this civilization — again be relegated to a secondary place in the scheme of things and become only an instrumentality in the service of some dominant aim or impulse, such as a vainglorious patriotism, or dynastic politics, or the breeding of a commercial aristocracy. More than one of the nations of Europe have moved so far in this matter already as to place the primacy of science and scholarship in doubt as against warlike ambitions; the aspirations of the American community appear to be divided — between patriotism in the service of the captains of war, and commerce in the service of the captains of finance. But hitherto the spokesmen of any such cultural reversion are careful to declare a perfunctory faith in that civilization of disinterested intellectual achievement which they are endeavouring to suborn to their several ends. That such pro forma declarations are found necessary argues that the faith in a civilization of intelligence is still so far intact as to require all reactionaries to make their peace with it.

Meantime the easy matter-of-course presumption that such a civilization of intelligence justifies itself goes to argue that the current bias which so comes to expression will be the outcome of a secure and protracted experience. What underlies and has brought on this bent in the temper of the civilized peoples is a somewhat intricate question of institutional growth, and cannot be gone into here; but the gradual shifting of this matter-of-fact outlook into the primacy among the ideals of modern Christendom is sufficiently evident in point of fact, to any attentive student of modern times. Conceivably, there may come an abrupt term to its paramount vogue, through some precipitate sweep of circumstances; but it did not come in by anything like the sudden intrusion of a new invention in deals — after the fashion of a religious conversion — nor by the incursion of a hitherto alien element into the current scheme of life, but rather by force of a gradual and unintended, scarcely perceptible, shifting of emphasis between the several cultural factors that conjointly go to make up the working scheme of things.

Along with this shifting of matter-of-fact knowledge into the foreground among the ideals of civilized life, there has also gone on a similarly unpremeditated change in the attitude of those persons and establishments that have to do with this learning, as well as in the rating accorded them by the community at large. Again it is a matter of institutional growth, of self-wrought changes in the scheme of use and wont; and here as in other cases of institutional growth and displacement, the changes have gone forward for the most part blindly, by impulse, without much foreknowledge of any ulterior consequences to which such a sequence of change might be said to tend.

It is true, many other lines of work, and of endeavor that may not fairly be called work, are undertaken by schools of university grade; and also, many other schools that call themselves "universities" will have substantially nothing to do with the higher learning. But each and several of these other lines of endeavor, into which the universities allow themselves to be drawn, are open to question. Their legitimacy remains an open question in spite of the interested arguments of their spokesman, who advocate the partial submergence of the university in such enterprises as professional training, undergraduate instruction, supervision and guidance of the secondary school system, edification of the unlearned by "university extension" and similar excursions into the field of public amusement, training of secondary school teachers, encouragement of amateurs by "correspondence," etc. What and how much of these extraneous activities that university should allow itself is a matter on which there is no general agreement even among those whose inclinations go far in that direction; but what is taken for granted throughout all this advocacy of outlying detail is the secure premise that the university is in the first place a seminary of the higher learning, and that no school can make good its pretensions to university standing except by proving its fitness in this respect.[iv]

The conservation and advancement of the higher learning involve two lines of work, distant but closely bound together: (a) scientific and scholarly inquiry, and (b) the instruction of students.[v] The former of these is primary and indispensable. It is this work of intellectual enterprise that gives its character to the university and marks it off from the lower schools. The work of teaching properly belongs in the university only because and in so far as it incites and facilitates the university man's work of inquiry, — and the extent to which such teaching furthers the work of inquiry is scarcely to be appreciated without a somewhat extended experience. By and large, there are but few and inconsequential exceptions to the rule that teaching, as a concomitant of investigation, is distinctly advantageous to the investigator; particularly in so far as his work is of the nature of theoretical inquiry. The instruction necessarily involved in university work, therefore, is only such as can readily be combined with the work of inquiry, at the same time that it goes directly to further the higher learning in that it trains the incoming generation of scholars and scientists for the further pursuit of knowledge. Training for other purposes is necessarily of a different kind and is best done elsewhere; and it does not become university work by calling it so and imposing its burden on the men and equipment whose only concern should be the higher learning.

University teaching, having a particular and special purpose — the pursuit of knowledge — has also a particular and special character, such as to differentiate it from other teaching and at the same time leave it relatively ineffective for other purposes. Its aim is to equip the student for the work of inquiry, not to give him facility in that conduct of affairs that turns such knowledge to "practical account." Hence the instruction that falls legitimately under the hand of the university man is necessarily subsidiary and incidental to the work of inquiry, and it can effectually be carried on only by such a teacher as is himself occupied with the scrutiny of what knowledge is already in hand and with pushing the inquiry to further gains. And it can be carried on by such a teacher only by drawing his students into his own work of inquiry. The student's relation to his teacher necessarily becomes that of an apprentice to his master, rather than that of a pupil to his schoolmaster.

A university is a body of mature scholars and scientists, the "faculty," —

with whatever plant and other equipment may incidentally serve as appliances for their work in any given case. The necessary material equipment may under modern conditions be very considerable, as may also the number of caretakers, assistants, etc.; but all that is not the university, but merely its equipment. And the university man's work is the pursuit of knowledge, together with whatever advisory surveillance and guidance he may consistently afford such students as are entering on the career of learning at a point where his outlook and methods of work may be of effect for them. No man whose energies are not habitually bent on increasing and proving up the domain of learning belongs legitimately on the university staff. The university man is, properly, a student, not a schoolmaster. Such is the unmistakable drift of sentiment and professed endeavour, in so far as it is guided by the cultural aspirations of civilized mankind rather than by the emulative strategy of individuals seeking their own preferment.[vi]

All this, of course, implies no undervaluing of the work of those men who aim to prepare the youth for citizenship and a practical career. It is only a question of distinguishing between the university man, on the one hand, and the schoolmaster on the other hand, both belong within the later growth of civilization; but a differentiation of the two classes, and a division of their work, is indispensable if they are to do their work as it should be done, and as the modern community thoughtfully intends that it should be done. And while such a division of labor has hitherto not been carried through with any degree of consistency, it is at least under way, and there is nothing but the presumption of outworn usage that continues to hold the two lines of work, to the detriment of both; backed, it is true, by ambitions of self-aggrandizement on the part of many schools and many of their directorates.

The schoolmaster and his work may be equally, or more, valuable to the community at large — presumably more rather than less — but in so far as his chief interest is of the pedagogical sort, his place is not in the university. Exposition, instruction and drill belong in the secondary and professional schools. The consistent aim there is, and should be, to instruct, to inculcate a knowledge of results, and to give the pupil a working facility in applying it. On the university level such information and training is (should be) incidental to the work of research. The university man is almost unavoidably a teacher, by precept and example, but he cannot without detriment to his work as scientist or scholar serve as a taskmaster or a vehicle of indoctrination. The student who comes up to the university for the pursuit of knowledge is expected to know what he wants and to want it, without compulsion. If he falls short in these respects, if he has not the requisite interest and initiative, it is his own misfortune, not the fault of his teacher. What he has a legitimate claim to is an opportunity for such personal contact and guidance as will give him familiarity with the ways and means of the higher learning, — any information imparted to him being incidental to this main work of habituation. He gets a chance to make himself a scholar, and what he will do with his opportunities in this way lies in his own discretion.

The difference between the modern university and the lower and professional schools is broad and simple; not so much a difference of degree as of kind. There is no difficulty about appreciating this difference; the dispute turns not on the practicability of distinguishing between the two, but on the desirability of letting such a distinction go into effect. It is a controversy between those who wish to hold fast that which once was good and those who look to make use of the means in hand for new ends and meet new exigencies.

The lower schools (including the professional schools) are, in the ideal scheme, designed to fit the incoming generation for civil life; they are therefore occupied with instilling such knowledge and habits as will make their pupils fit citizens of the world in whatever position in the fabric of workday life they may fall. The university on the other hand is specialized to fit men for a life of science and scholarship and it is accordingly concerned with such discipline only as will give efficiency in the pursuit of knowledge and fit its students for the increase and diffusion of learning. It follows that while the lower schools necessarily take over the surveillance of their pupils' everyday life, and exercise a large measure of authority and responsible interference in that behalf, the university assumes (or should assume) no responsibility for its students' fortunes in the moral, religious, pecuniary, domestic, or hygienic respect.

Doubtless the larger and more serious responsibility in the educational system belongs not to the university but to the lower and professional schools. Citizenship is a larger and more substantial category than scholarship; and the furtherance of civilized life is a larger and more serious interest than the pursuit of knowledge for its own idle sake. But the proportions which the quest of knowledge is latterly assuming in the scheme of civilized life require that the establishments to which this interest is committed should not be charged with extraneous duties particularly not with extraneous matters that are themselves of such grave consequence as this training for citizenship and practical affairs. These are too serious a range of duties to be taken care of as a side issue, by a seminary of learning, the members of whose faculty, if they are fit for their own special work, are not men of affairs or adepts in worldly wisdom.

In point of historical pedigree the American universities are of another derivation than their European counterpart; although the difference in this respect is not so sharp a matter of contrast as might be assumed at first sight. The European (Continental) universities appear to have been founded, originally, to meet the needs of professional training, more particularly theological (and philosophical) training in the earlier times. The American universities are, historically, an outgrowth of the American college; and the latter was installed, in its beginnings, largely as a means of professional training; chiefly training for Divinity, secondarily for the calling of the schoolmaster. But in neither case, neither in that of the European university nor in that of the American College, was this early vocational aim of the schools allowed to decide their character in the long run, nor to circumscribe the lines of their later growth. In both cases, somewhat alike, the two groups of schools came to their mature development, in the nineteenth century, as establishments occupied with disinterested learning, given over to the pursuit of intellectual enterprise, rather than as seminaries for training of a vocational kind. They still had a vocational value, no doubt, and the vocational needs of their students need not have been absent from the considerations that guided their directorates. It would particularly be found that the (clerical) directorates of the American colleges had more than half an eye to the needs of Divinity even at so late a date as when, in the third quarter of the century, the complexion of the American college situation began seriously to change. It is from this period — from the era of the Civil War and the Reconstruction — that the changes set in which have reshaped the academic situation in America.

At this era, some half a century ago, the American college was, or was at least presumed to be, given over to disinterested instruction, not specialized with a vocational, or even a denominational, bias. It was coming to take its place as the superior or crowning member, a sort of capstone, of the system of public instruction. The life-history of any one of the state universities whose early period of growth runs across this era will readily show the effectual guidance of such an ideal of a college, as a superior and definitive member in a school system designed to afford an extended course of instruction looking to an unbiased increase and diffusion of knowledge. Other interests, of a professional or vocational kind, were also entrusted to the keeping of these new-found schools; but with a conclusive generality the rule holds that in these academic creations a college establishment of a disinterested, non-vocational character is counted in as the indispensable nucleus, — that much was at that time a matter of course.

The further development shows two marked features: The American university has come into bearing; and the college has become an intermediate rather than a terminal link in the conventional scheme of education. Under the names "undergraduate" and "graduate," the college and the university are still commonly coupled together as subdivisions of a complex whole; but this holding together of the two disparate schools is at the best a freak of aimless survival. At the worst, and more commonly, it is the result of a gross ambition for magnitude on the part of the joint directorate. Whether the college lives by itself as an independent establishment on a foundation of its own, or is in point of legal formality a subdivision of the university establishment, it takes its place in the educational scheme as senior member of the secondary school system and it bears no peculiarly close relation to the university as a seat of learning. At the closest it stands to the university in the relation of a fitting school; more commonly its relations are closer with the ordinary professional and vocational schools; and for the most part it stands in no relation, beyond that of juxtaposition, with the one or the other.

The attempt to hold the college and the university together in bonds of ostensible solidarity is by no means an advisedly concerted adjustment to the needs of scholarship as they run today. By historical accident the older American universities have grown into bearing on the ground of an underlying college, and the external connection so inherited has not usually been severed; and by ill-advised, or perhaps unadvised, imitation the younger universities have blundered into encumbering themselves with an undergraduate department to simulate this presumptively honorable pedigree, to the detriment both of the university and of the college so bound up with it. By this arrangement the college — undergraduate department — falls into the position of an appendage, a side issue, to be taken care of by afterthought on the part of a body of men whose chief legitimate interest runs — should run — on the other things than the efficient management of such an undergraduate training-school, — provided always that they are a bona fide university faculty, and not a body of secondary-school teachers masquerading under the assumed name of a university.

The motive to this inclusion of an undergraduate department in the newer universities appears commonly to have been a headlong eagerness on the part of the corporate authorities to show a complete establishment of the conventionally accepted pattern, and to enroll as many students as possible.

Whatever may have been true for the earlier time, when the American college first grew up and flourished, it is beyond question that the undergraduate department which takes the place of the college today cannot be rated as an institution of the higher learning. At the best it is now a school for preliminary training, preparatory to entering on the career of learning, or in preparation for the further training required for the profession; but it is also, and chiefly, an establishment designed to give the concluding touches to the education of young men who have no designs on learning, beyond the close of the college curriculum. It aims to afford a rounded discipline to those whose goal is the life of fashion or of affairs. How well, or how ill, the college may combine these two unrelated purposes is a question that does not immediately concern the present inquiry. It is touched on here only to point the contrast between the American college and the university.

It follows from the character of their work that while the university should offer no set curriculum, the college has, properly, nothing else to offer. But the retention or inclusion of the college and its aims within the university corporation has necessarily led to the retention of college standards and methods of control even in what is or purports to be university work; so that it is by no means unusual to find university (graduate) work scheduled in the form of a curriculum, with all that boarding-school circumstance and apparatus that is so unavoidable an evil in all undergraduate training. In effect, the outcome of these short-sighted attempts to take care of the higher learning by the means and method of the boys' school, commonly is to eliminate the higher learning from the case and substitute the aims and results of a boys' training-school.

Undergraduate work being task work, it is possible, without fatal effect, to reduce it to standard units of time and volume, and so control and enforce it by a system of accountancy and surveillance; the methods of control, accountancy and coercion that so come to be worked out have all that convincing appearance of tangible efficiency that belongs to any mechanically defiant and statistically accountable routine, such as will always commend itself to the spirit of the schoolmaster; the temptation to apply such methods of standardized routine wherever it is at all feasible is always present, and it is cogently spoken for by all those to whom drill is a more intelligible conception than scholarship. The work of learning, which distinctively belongs in the university, on the other hand, is a matter of personal contact and co-operation between teacher and student, and is not measurable in statistical units or amenable to mechanical tests; the men engaged in this work can accordingly offer nothing of the same definite character in place of the rigid routine and accountancy advocated by the schoolmasters; and the outcome in nearly all cases where the control of both departments vests in one composite corporate body, as it usually does, is the gradual insinuation of undergraduate methods and standards in the graduate school; until what is nominally university work settles down, in effect, into nothing more than an extension of the undergraduate curriculum. This effect is had partly by reducing such of the graduate courses as are found amenable to the formalities of the undergraduate routine, and partly by dispensing with such graduate work as will not lend itself, even ostensibly, to the schoolmaster's methods.

What has been said of the college in this connection holds true in the main also of the professional and technical schools. In their aims, methods and achievements these schools are, in the nature of the case, foreign to the higher learning. This is, of course, not said in disparagement of their work; rather the contrary. As is the case with the college, so these schools also are often included in the university corporation by ties of an external and factitious kind, frequently by terms of the charter. But this formal inclusion of them under the corporate charter does not set aside the substantial discrepancy between their purpose, work and animus and those of the university proper. It can only serve to trouble the single-mindedness of both. It leaves both the pursuit of learning and the work of preparation for the professions somewhat at loose ends, confused with the bootless illusion that they are, in some recondite way, parallel variants of a single line of work.

In aim and animus the technical and professional schools are "practical," in the most thoroughgoing manner; while the pursuit of knowledge that occupies the scientists and scholars is not "practical" in the slightest degree. The divergent lines of interest to be taken care of by the professional schools and the university, respectively, are as widely out of touch as may well be within the general field of human knowledge. The one is animated wholly by considerations of material expediency, and the range of its interest and efforts is strictly limited by considerations of the useful effect to which the proficiency that it gives is to be turned; the other knows nothing of expediency, and is influenced by no consideration of utility or disutility, in its appreciation of the knowledge to be sought. The animus of the one is worldly wisdom; of the other, idle curiosity. The two are incommensurably at variance so far as regards their purpose, and in great measure also as regards their methods of work, and necessarily so.

But with all this divergence of purpose and animus there is after all a broad and very substantial bond of community between the technical schools, on the one hand, and the proper work of the university, on the other hand, in that the two are, in great measure, occupied with the same general range of materials and employ somewhat the same logical methods in handling these materials. But the relation that results from this community of material is almost wholly external and mechanical. Nor does it set up any presumption that the two should expediently be included in some corporate establishment, or even that they need be near neighbors or need maintain peculiarly close relations of personnel. The technical schools, and in less degree the professional schools not properly classed as technical, depend in large measure on results worked out by the scientists, who properly belong in the universities. But the material so made use of for technical ends is taken over and turned to account without afterthought. The technologist's work is related to that of the scientists very much as the work of the designer is related to that of the inventor. To a considerable extent the scientists similarly depend on the work of the technical men for information, and for correction and verification of their own theoretical work. But there is, on this account, nothing to gain by associating any given technical school with any given university establishment; incorporation in any given university does not in any degree facilitate the utilization of the results of the sciences by the technical men; nor is it found in practice to further the work of the sciences. The schools in question do not in any peculiar degree draw on the work of the scientists attached to their particular university; nor do these scientists, on the other hand, have any special use for the work of their associated technical schools. In either case the source drawn on is the general literature of the subject, the body of materials available at large, not the work of particular men attached to particular schools. The generalizations of science are indispensable to the technical men; but what they draw on is the body of science at large, regardless of what any given university establishment may have had to do with the work out of which the particular items of scientific information have emerged. Nor is the scientific material useful to the technologist for the further pursuit of science; to them the scientific results are data, raw material to be turned to practical use, not means by which to carry scientific inquiry out to further results.

Similarly, the professions and the technical schools, afford valuable data for the use of the professed scholars and scientists, information that serves as material of investigation, or that will at least be useful as a means of extending, correcting, verifying and correlating lines of inquiry on which they are engaged. But the further bearing of these facts upon the affairs of life, their expediency or futility, is of no interest or consequence. The affairs of life, except the affairs of learning, do not touch the interest of the university man as a scholar or scientist. What is of importance to him in all these matters with which the professions and technologists are busy is their bearing on those matters of fact into which his scientific interest leads him to inquire. The tests and experiments carried out at these technical schools, as well as the experience gathered by the members of their staff, will occasionally afford him material for further inquiry or means whereby to check results already arrived at; but for such matter he does not by preference resort to any one of the technical schools as contrasted with any other, and it is quite an idle question whether the source of any such serviceable information is a school attached to his own university. The investigator finds his material where he can; which comes to saying that he draws on the general body of technical knowledge, with no afterthought as to what particular technical school may have stood in some relation or other to the information which he finds useful.

Neither to the man engaged in university work nor to the technical schools that may serve him as occasional sources of material is there any advantage to be derived from their inclusion in the university establishment. Indeed, it is a detriment to both parties, as has already been remarked, but more decidedly to the university men. By including the technical and professional schools in the university corporation the technologists and professional men attached to these schools are necessarily included among the academic staff, and so they come to take their part in the direction of academic affairs at large. In what they so do toward shaping the academic policy they will not only count for all they are worth, but they are likely to count for something more than their due share in this respect; or they are to some extent trained to the conduct of affairs, and so come in for something of that deference that is currently paid to men of affairs, at the same time that this practical training gives them an advantage over their purely academic colleagues, in the greater assurance and adroitness with which they are able to present their contentions. By virtue of this same training, as well as by force of current practical interest, the technologist and the professional man are, like other men of affairs, necessarily and habitually impatient of any scientific or scholarly work that does not obviously lend itself to some practical use. The technologist appreciates what is mechanically serviceable; the professional man, as, for instance, the lawyer, appreciates what promises pecuniary gain; and the two unite with the business-man at large in repudiating whatever does not look directly to such a utilitarian outcome. So that as members of the academics staff these men are likely to count at their full weight toward the diversion of the university's forces from disinterested science and scholarship to such palpably utilitarian ends.

But the active measures so taken by the academic authorities at the instance of the schoolmasters and "practical" men are by no means the only line along which their presence in the academic corporation affects the case. Intimate association with these "utilitarians" unavoidably has its corrupting effect on the scientists and scholars, and induces in them also something of the same bias toward "practical" results in their work; so that they no longer pursue the higher learning with undivided interest, but with more or less of an eye to the utilitarian main chance; whereby the advantages of specialization, which are the reason for these schools, are lost, and the pride of the modern community is wounded in its most sensitive spot — the efficiency of its specialists.

So also, on the other hand, the formal incorporation of these technological and professional men in the academic body, with its professedly single-minded interest in learning, has its effect on their frame of mind. They are, without intending it, placed in a false position, which unavoidably leads them to court a specious appearance of scholarship, and so to invest their technological discipline with a degree of pedantry and sophistication; whereby it is hoped to give these schools and their work some scientific and scholarly prestige, and so lift it to that dignity that is presumed to attach to a non-utilitarian pursuit of learning. Doubtless this pursuit of scholarly prestige is commonly successful, to the extent that it produces the desired conviction of awe in the vulgar, who do not know the difference; but all this make-believe scholarship, however successfully staged, is not what these schools are designed for; or at least it is not what is expected of them, nor is it what they can do best and most efficiently.

To the substantial gain of both parties, though with some lesion of the vanity of both, the separation between the university and the professional and technical schools should be carried through and made absolute. Only on such conditions can either the one or the other do its own work in a workmanlike manner. Within the university precincts any aim or interest other than those of irresponsible science and scholarship — pursuit of matter-of-fact knowledge — are to be rated as interlopers.

To all this there is the ready objection of the school-masters and utilitarians that such a project is fantastic and unpractical, useless and undesirable; that such has not been the mission of the university in the past, nor its accepted place and use in the educational system of today and yesterday; that the universities of Christendom have from their first foundation been occupied with professional training and useful knowledge; that they have been founded for utilitarian purposes and their work has been guided mainly or altogether by utilitarian considerations; — all of which is conceded without argument. The historical argument amounts to saying that the universities were founded before modern civilization took on its modern character, before the disinterested pursuit of knowledge had come to take the first place among the ideals of civilized mankind, and that they were established to take care of those interests which were then accounted of first importance, and that this intellectual enterprise in pursuit of disinterested knowledge consequently was not at that time confided to the care of any special establishment or freely avowed as a legitimate interest in its own right.

It is true that, by historical accident, the university at large has grown out of professional training-schools, — primarily schools for training in theology, secondarily in law and medicine. It is also true, in like wise and in like degree, that modern science and scholarship have grown out of the technology of handicraft and the theological philosophy of the schoolmen.[vii] But just as it would be a bootless enterprise to cut modern science back into handicraft technology, so would it be a gratuitous imbecility to prune back the modern university to that inchoate phase of its life-history and make it again a corporation for the training of theologians, jurists and doctors of medicine. The historical argument does not enjoin a return to the beginning of things, but rather an intelligent appreciation of what things are coming to.

The genesis of the university at large, taken as an institution of civilized life, is an accident of the transition from the barbarian culture of the Middle Ages to modern times, and its later growth and acquirement of character are an incident of the further growth of modern civilization; and the character of this later growth of the university reflects the bent of modern civilization, as contrasted with the barbarian spirit of things in the mediaeval spiritual world.

In a general way, the place of the university in the culture of Christendom is still substantially the same as it has been from the beginning. Ideally, and in the popular apprehension, it is, as it has always been, a corporation for the cultivation and care of the community's highest aspirations and ideals. But these ideals and aspirations have changed somewhat with the changing scheme of the Western civilization; and so the university has also concomitantly so changed in character, aims and ideals as to leave it still the corporate organ of the community's dominant intellectual interest. At the same time, it is true, these changes in the purpose and spirit of the university have always been, and are always being, made only tardily, reluctantly, concessively, against the protests of those who are zealous for the commonplaces of the day before yesterday. Such is the character of institutional growth and change; and in its adaptation to the altered requirements of an altered scheme of culture the university has in this matter been subject to the conditions of institutional growth at large. An institution is, after all, a prevalent habit of thought, and as such it is subject to the conditions and limitations that surround any change in the habitual frame of mind prevalent in the community.

The university of mediaeval and early modern times, that is to say the barbarian university, was necessarily given over to the pragmatic, utilitarian disciplines, since that is the nature of barbarism; and the barbarian university is but another, somewhat sublimated expression of the same barbarian frame of mind. The barbarian culture is pragmatic, utilitarian, worldly wise, and its learning partakes of the same complexion. The barbarian, late or early, is typically an unmitigated pragmatist; that is the spiritual trait that most profoundly marks him off from the savage on the one hand and from the civilized man on the other hand. "He turns a keen, untroubled face home to the instant need of things."

The high era of barbarism in Europe, the Dark and Middle Ages, is marked off from what went before and from what has followed in the cultural sequence, by a hard and fast utilitarian animus. The all-dominating spiritual trait of those times is that men then made the means of life its end.

It is perhaps needless to call to mind that much of this animus still survives in later civilized life, especially in so far as the scheme of civilized life is embodied in the competitive system. In that earlier time, practical sagacity and the serviceability of any knowledge acquired, its bearing on individual advantage, spiritual or temporal, was the ruling consideration, as never before or since. The best of men in that world were not ashamed to avow that a boundless solicitude for their own salvation was their worthiest motive of conduct, and it is plain in all their speculation that they were unable to accept any other motive or sanction as final in any bearing. Saint and sinner alike knew no higher rule than expedience, for this world and the next. And, for that matter, so it still stands with the saint and the sinner, — who make up much of the commonplace human material in the modern community; although both the saint and the sinner in the modern community carry, largely by shamefaced subvention, an ever increasing side-line of other and more genial interests that have no merit in point of expediency whether for this world or the next.

Under the rule of such a cultural ideal the corporation of learning could not well take any avowed stand except as an establishment for utilitarian instruction, the practical expediency of whose work was the sole overt test of its competency. And such it still should continue to be according to the avowed aspirations of the staler commonplace elements in the community today. By subvention, and by a sophisticated subsumption under some ostensibly practical line of interest and inquiry, it is true, the university men of the earlier time spent much of their best endeavor on matters of disinterested scholarship that had no bearing on any human want more to the point than the idle curiosity; and by a similar turn of subvention and sophistication the later spokesmen of the barbarian ideal take much complacent credit for the "triumphs of modern science" that have nothing but an ostensible bearing on any matter of practical expediency, and they look to the universities to continue this work of the idle curiosity under some plausible pretext of practicality.

So the university of that era unavoidably came to be organized as a more or less comprehensive federation of professional schools or faculties devoted to such branches of practical knowledge as the ruling utilitarian interests of the time demanded. Under this overshadowing barbarian tradition the universities of early modern times started out as avowed contrivance for indoctrination in the ways and means of salvation, spiritual and temporal, individual and collective, — in some sort a school of engineering, primarily in divinity, secondarily in law and politics, and presently in medicine and also in the other professions that serve a recognized utilitarian interest. After that fashion a university that answered to this manner of ideals and aspirations had once been installed and gained a secure footing, its pattern acquired a degree of authenticity and prescription, so that later seminaries of learning came unquestioningly to be organized on the same lines; and further changes of academic policy and practice, such as are demanded by the later growth of cultural interests and ideals, have been made only reluctantly and with a suspicious reserve, gradually and by a circuitous sophistication; so that much of the non-utilitarian scientific and scholarly work indispensable to the university's survival under modern conditions is still scheduled under the faculties of law or medicine, or even of divinity.

But the human propensity for inquiry into things, irrespective of use or expediency, insinuated itself among the expositors of worldly wisdom from the outset; and from the first this quest of idle learning has sought shelter in the university as the only establishment in which it could find a domicile, even on sufferance, and so could achieve that footing of consecutive intellectual enterprise running through successive generations of scholars which is above all else indispensable to the advancement of knowledge. Under the régime of unmitigated pragmatic claims that ruled the earlier days of the European universities, this pursuit of knowledge for its own sake was carried on as work of scholarly supererogation by men whose ostensibly sole occupation was the promulgation of some accredited line of salutary information. Frequently it had to be carried on under some colourable masquerade of practicality. And yet so persistent has the spirit of idle curiosity proved to be, and so consonant with the long-term demands even of the laity, that the dissimulation and smuggling-in of disinterested learning has gone on ever more openly and at an ever increasing rate of gain; until in the end, the attention given to scholarship and the non-utilitarian sciences in these establishments has come far to exceed that given to the practical disciplines for which the several faculties were originally installed. As time has passed and as successive cultural mutations have passed over the community, shifting the centre of interest and bringing new ideals of scholarship, and bringing the whole cultural fabric nearer to its modern complexion, those purposes of crass expediency that were of such great moment and were so much a matter of course in earlier academic policy, have insensibly fallen to the rank of incidentals. And what had once been incidental, or even an object of surreptitious tolerance in the university, remains today as the only unequivocal duty of the corporation of learning, and stands out as the one characteristic trait without which no establishment can claim rank as a university.

Philosophy — the avowed body of theoretical science in the late mediaeval time — had grown out of the schoolmen's speculations in theology, being in point of derivation a body of refinements on the divine scheme of salvation; and with a view to quiet title, and to make manifest their devotion to the greater good of eschatological expediency, those ingenious speculators were content to proclaim that their philosophy is the handmaid of theology — *Philosophia thelogia ancillans*. But their philosophy has fallen into the alembic of the idle curiosity and has given rise to a body of modern science, godless and unpractical, that has no intended or even ostensible bearing on the religious fortunes of mankind; and their sanctimonious maxim would today be better accepted as the subject of a limerick than of a homily. Except in degree, the fortunes of the temporal pragmatic disciplines, in Law and Medicine, have been much the same as that of their elder sister, Theology. Professionalism and practical serviceability have been gradually crowded into the background of academic interests and overlaid with the quasi-utilitarian research — such as the history of jurisprudence, comparative physiology, and the like. They have in fact largely been eliminated.[viii]

And changes running to this effect have gone farthest and have taken most consistent effect in those communities that are most fully imbued with the spirit of the modern peaceable civilization. It is in the more backward communities and schools that the barbarian animus of utilitarianism still maintains itself most nearly intact, whether it touches matters of temporal or of spiritual interest. With the later advance of culture, as the intellectual interest has gradually displaced the older ideals in men's esteem, and barring a reactionary episode here and there, the university has progressively come to take its place as a seat of the higher learning, a corporation for the pursuit of knowledge; and barring accidental reversions, it has increasingly asserted itself as an imperative necessity, more and more consistently, that the spirit of disinterested inquiry must have free play in these seminaries of the higher learning, without after-thought as to the practical or utilitarian consequences which this free inquiry may conceivably have for the professional training or for the social, civil or religious temper of the students of the rest of the community. Nothing is felt to be so irremediably vicious in academic policy as coercive bias, religious, political, conventional or professional, in so far as it touches that quest of knowledge that constitutes the main interest of the university.

Professional training and technological work at large have of course not lost ground, either in the volume and the rigour of their requirements or in the application bestowed in their pursuit; but as within the circle of academic interests, these utilitarian disciplines have lost their preferential place and have been pushed to one side; so that the professional and the technical schools are now in fact rated as adjuncts rather than as integral constituents of the university corporation. Such is the unmistakable sense of this matter among academic men. At the same time these vocational schools have, one with another, progressively taken on more of a distinctive, independent and close-knit structure; an individual corporate existence, autonomous and academically self-sufficient, even in those cases where they most tenaciously hold to their formal connection with the university corporation. They have reached a mature phase of organization, developed a type of personnel and control peculiar to themselves and their special needs, and have in effect come out from under the tutelage of the comprehensive academic organization of which they once in their early days were the substantial core. These schools have more in common among themselves as a class than their class have with the academic aims and methods that characterize the university proper. They are in fact ready and competent to go on their own recognizances, — indeed they commonly resent any effective interference or surveillance from the side of the academic corporation of which they know best. Their connection with the university is superficial and formal at the best, so far as regards any substantial control of their affairs and policy by the university authorities at large; it is only in their interference with academic policy, and in injecting their own peculiar bias into university affairs, that they count substantially as corporate members of the academic body. And in these respects, what is said of the professional and technical schools holds true also of the undergraduate departments.

It is quite feasible to have a university without professional schools and without an undergraduate department; but it is not possible to have one without due provision for that non-utilitarian disciplines cluster. And this in spite of the solicitous endeavors of the professional schools to make good their footing as the substantial core of the corporation.

As intimated above, there are two main reasons for the continued and tenacious connection between these schools and the universities: (a) ancient tradition, fortified by the solicitous ambition of the university directorate to make a brave show of magnitude, and (b) the anxiety of these schools to secure some degree of scholarly authentication through such a formal connection with a seat of learning. These two motives have now and again pushed matters fairly to an extreme in the reactionary direction. So, for instance, the chances of intrigue and extra-academic clamor have latterly thrown up certain men of untempered "practicality" as directive heads of certain universities, and some of these have gone so far as to avow a reactionary intention to make the modern university a cluster of professional schools or faculties, after the ancient barbarian fashion.[ix]

So the academic authorities face the choice between scholarly efficiency and vocational training, and hitherto the result has been equivocal. The directorate should presumably be in a position to appreciate the drift of their own action, in so diverting the university's work to ends at variance with its legitimate purpose; and the effect of such a policy should presumably be repugnant to their scholarly tastes, as well as to their sense of right and honest living. But the circumstances of their office and tenure leave them somewhat helpless, for all their presumed insight and their aversion to this malpractice; and these conditions of office require them, as it is commonly apprehended, to take active measures for the defeat of learning, — hitherto with an equivocal outcome. The schools of commerce, even more than the other vocational schools, have been managed somewhat parsimoniously, and the effectual results have habitually fallen far short of the clever promises held out in the prospectus. The professed purpose of these schools is the training of young men to a high proficiency in the larger and more responsible affairs of business, but for the present this purpose must apparently remain a speculative, and very temperately ingenuous, aspiration, rather than a practicable working programme.

As in earlier passages, so here in speaking of profit and loss, the point of view taken is neither that of material advantage, whether of the individuals concerned or of the community at large, nor that of expediency for the common good in respect of prosperity or of morals; nor is the appraisal here ventured upon to be taken as an expression of praise or dispraise at large, touching this incursion of business principles into the affairs of learning.

By and large, the intrusion of businesslike ideals, aims and methods into this field, with all the consequences that follow, may be commendable or the reverse. All that is matter for attention and advisement at the hands of such as aim to alter, improve, amend or conserve the run of institutional phenomena that goes to make up the current situation. The present inquiry bears on the higher learning as it comes into this current situation, and on the effect of this recourse to business principles upon the pursuit of learning.

Not that this learning is therefore to be taken as necessarily of higher and more substantial value than that traffic in competitive gain and competitive spending upon which business principles converge, and in which they find their consummate expression, — even though it is broadly to be recognized and taken account of that such is the deliberate appraisal awarded by the common sense of civilized mankind. The profit and loss here spoken for is not profit and loss, to mankind or to any given community, in respect of that inclusive complex of interests that makes up the balanced total of good and ill; it is profit and loss for the cause of learning, simply; and there is here no aspiration to pass on ulterior questions. As required by the exigencies of such an argument, it is therefore assumed *pro forma* that profit and loss for the pursuit of learning is profit and loss without reservation; very much as a corporation accountant will audit income and outlay within the affairs of the corporation, whereas qua accountant, he will perforce have nothing to say as to the ulterior expediency of the corporation and its affairs in any other bearing.

Business principles take effect in academic affairs most simply, obviously and avowably in the way of a businesslike administration of the scholastic routine; where they lead immediately to a bureaucratic organization and a system of scholastic accountancy. In one form or another, some such administrative machinery is a necessity in any large school that is to be managed on a centralized plan as the American schools commonly are, and as, more particularly, they aim to be. This necessity is all the more urgent in a school that takes over the discipline of a large body of pupils that have not reached years of discretion, as is also commonly the case with those American schools that claim rank as universities; and the necessity is all the more evident to men whose ideal of efficiency is the centralized control exercised through a system of accountancy in the modern large business concerns. The larger American schools are primarily undergraduate establishments, — with negligible exceptions; and under these current American conditions, of excessive numbers, such a centralized and bureaucratic administration appears to be indispensable for the adequate control of immature and reluctant students; at the same time, such an organization conduces to an excessive size. The immediate and visible effect of such a large and centralized administrative machinery is, on the whole, detrimental to scholarship, even in the undergraduate work; though it need not be so in all respects and unequivocally, so far as regards that routine training that is embodied in the undergraduate curriculum. But it is at least a necessary evil in any school that is of so considerable size as to preclude substantially all close or cordial personal relations between the teachers and each of these immature pupils under their charge, as, again, is commonly the case with these American undergraduate establishments. Such a system of authoritative control, standardization, gradation, accountancy, classification, credits and penalties, will necessarily be drawn on stricter lines the more the school takes on the character of a house of correction or a penal settlement; in which the irresponsible inmates are to be held to a round of distasteful tasks and restrained from (conventionally) excessive irregularities of conduct. At the same time this recourse to such coercive control and standardization of tasks has unavoidably given the schools something of the character of a penal settlement.

As intimated above, the ideal of efficiency by force of which a large-scale centralized organization commends itself in these premises is that pattern of shrewd management whereby a large business concern makes money. The underlying business-like presumption accordingly appears to be that learning is a merchantable commodity, to be produced on a piece-rate plan, rated, bought and sold by standard units, measured, counted and reduced to staple equivalence by impersonal, mechanical tests. In all its bearing the work is hereby reduced to a mechanistic, statistical consistency, with numerical standards and units; which conduces to perfunctory and mediocre work throughout, and acts to deter both students and teachers from a free pursuit of knowledge, as contrasted with the pursuit of academic credits. So far as this mechanistic system goes freely into effect it leads to a substitution of salesmanlike proficiency — a balancing of bargains in staple credits — in the place of scientific capacity and addiction to study.

The salesmanlike abilities and the men of affairs that so are drawn into the academic personnel are, presumably, somewhat under grade in their kind; since the pecuniary inducement offered by the schools is rather low as compared with the remuneration for office work of a similar character in the common run of business occupations, and since businesslike employees of this kind may fairly be presumed to go unreservedly to the highest bidder. Yet these more unscholarly members of the staff will necessarily be assigned the more responsible and discretionary positions in the academic organization; since under such a scheme of standardization, accountancy and control, the school becomes primarily a bureaucratic organization, and the first and unremitting duties of the staff are those of official management and accountancy. The further qualifications requisite in the members of the academic staff will be such as make for vendibility, — volubility, tactful effrontery, conspicuous conformity to the popular taste in all matters of opinion, usage and conventions.

The need of such a businesslike organization asserts itself in somewhat the same degree in which the academic policy is guided by considerations of magnitude and statistical renown; and this in turn is somewhat closely correlated with the extent of discretionary power exercised by the captain of erudition placed in control. At the same time, by provocation of the facilities which it offers for making an impressive demonstration, such bureaucratic organization will lead the university management to bend its energies with somewhat more singleness to the parade of magnitude and statistical gains. It also, and in the same connection, provokes to a persistent and detailed surveillance and direction of the work and manner of life of the academic staff, and so it acts to shut off initiative of any kind in the work done.[x]

Intimately bound up with this bureaucratic officialism and accountancy, and working consistently to a similar outcome, is the predilection for "practical efficiency" — that is to say, for pecuniary success — prevalent in the American community.[xi] This predilection is a matter of settled habit, due, no doubt, to the fact that preoccupation with business interests characterizes this community in an exceptional degree, and that pecuniary habits of thought consequently rule popular thinking in a peculiarly uncritical and prescriptive fashion. This pecuniary animus falls in with and reinforces the movement for academic accountancy, and combines with it to further a so-called "practical" bias in all the work of the schools.

It appears, then, that the intrusion of business principles in the universities goes to weaken and retard the pursuit of learning, and therefore to defeat the ends for which a university is maintained. This result follows, primarily, from the substitution of impersonal, mechanical relations, standards and tests, in the place of personal conference, guidance and association between teachers and students; as also from the imposition of a mechanically standardized routine upon the members of the staff, whereby any disinterested preoccupation with scholarly or scientific inquiry is thrown into the background and falls into abeyance. Few if any who are competent to speak in these premises will question that such has been the outcome. To offset against this work of mutilation and retardation there are certain gains in expedition, and in the volume of traffic that can be carried by any given equipment and corps of employees. Particularly will there be a gain in the statistical showing, both as regards the volume of instruction offered, and probably also as regards the enrollment; since accountancy creates statistics and its absence does not.

Such increased enrollment as may be due to businesslike management and methods is an increase of undergraduate enrollment. The net effect as regards the graduate enrollment — apart from any vocational instruction that may euphemistically be scheduled as "graduate" — is in all probability rather a decrease than an increase. Through indoctrination with utilitarian (pecuniary) ideals of earning and spending, as well as by engendering spendthrift and sportsmanlike habits, such a businesslike management diverts the undergraduate students from going in for the disinterested pursuit of knowledge, and so from entering on what is properly university work; as witness the relatively slight proportion of graduate students — outside of the professional schools — who come up from the excessively large undergraduate departments of the more expansive universities, as contrasted with the number of those who come into university work from the smaller and less businesslike colleges.

The ulterior consequences that follow from such businesslike standardization and bureaucratic efficiency are evident in the current state of the public schools; especially as seen in the larger towns, where the principles of business management have had time and scope to work out in a fair degree of consistency. The resulting abomination of desolation is sufficiently notorious. And there appears to be no reason why a similarly stale routine of futility should not overtake the universities, and give similarly foolish results, as fast as the system of standardization, accountancy and piece-work goes consistently into effect, — except only for the continued enforced employment of a modicum of impracticable scholars and scientists on the academic staff, whose unbusinesslike scholarly proclivities and inability to keep the miner's-inch of scholastic credit always in mind, must in some measure always defeat the perfect working of standardization and accountancy.

As might be expected, this régime of graduated sterility has already made fair headway in the undergraduate work, especially in the larger undergraduate schools; and this in spite of any efforts on the part of the administration to hedge against such an outcome by recourse to an intricate system of electives and a wide diversification of the standard units of erudition so offered.

In the graduate work the like effect is only less visible, because the measures leading to it have come into bearing more recently, and hitherto less unreservedly. But the like results should follow here also, just so fast and so far as the same range of business principles come to be worked into the texture of the university organization in the same efficacious manner as they have already taken effect in the public schools. And, pushed on as it is by the progressive substitution of men imbued with the tastes and habits of practical affairs, in the place of unpractical scholarly ideals, the movement toward a perfunctory routine of mediocrity should logically be expected to go forward at a progressively accelerated rate. The visible drift of things in this respect in the academic pursuit of the social sciences, so-called, is an argument as to what may be hoped for in the domain of academic science at large. It is only that the executive is actuated by a sharper solicitude to keep the academic establishment blameless of anything like innovation or iconoclasm at this point; which reinforces the drift toward a mechanistic routine and a curtailment of inquiry in this field; it is not that these sciences that deal with the phenomena of human life lend themselves more readily to mechanical description and enumeration than the material sciences do, nor is their subject matter intrinsically more inert or less provocative of questions.

Throughout the above summary review, as also through the foregoing inquiry, the argument continually returns to or turns about two main interests, — notoriety and the academic executive. These two might be called the two foci about which swings the orbit of the university world. These conjugate foci lie on a reasonably short axis; indeed, they tend to coincide; so that the orbit comes near the perfection of a circle; having virtually but a single centre, which may perhaps indifferently be spoken of as the university's president or as its renown, according as one may incline to conceive these matters in terms of tangible fact or of intangible.

The system of standardization and accountancy has this renown or prestige as its chief ulterior purpose, — the prestige of the university or of its president, which largely comes to the same net result. Particularly will this be true in so far as it its organization is designed to serve competitive ends; which are, in academic affairs, chiefly the ends of notoriety, prestige, advertising in all its branches and bearings.

All of which points unambiguously to the only line of remedial measures that can be worth serious consideration; and at the same time it carries the broad implication that in the present state of popular sentiment, touching these matters of control and administration, any effort that looks to reinstate the universities as effectual seminaries of learning will necessarily be nugatory; inasmuch as the popular sentiment runs plainly to the effect that magnitude, arbitrary control, and businesslike administration are the only sane rule to be followed in any human enterprise. So that, while the measures called for are simple, obvious, and effectual, they are also sure to be impracticable, and for none but extraneous reasons.

While it still remains true that the long-term commonsense judgement of civilized mankind places knowledge above business traffic, as an end to be sought, yet workday habituation under the stress of competitive business has induced a frame of mind that will tolerate no other method of procedure, and no rule of life that does not approve itself as a faithful travesty of competitive enterprise. And since the quest of learning cannot be carried on by the methods or with the apparatus and incidents of competitive business, it follows that the only remedial measures that hold any promise of rehabilitation for the higher learning in the universities cannot be attempted in the present state of public sentiment.

All that is required is the abolition of the academic executive and of the governing board. Anything short of this heroic remedy is bound to fail, because the evils sought to be remedied are inherent in these organs, and intrinsic to their functioning.

Even granting the possibility of making such a move, in the face of popular prejudice, it will doubtless seem suicidal, on first thought, to take so radical a departure; in that it would be held to cripple the whole academic organization and subvert the scheme of things academic, for good and all, — which, by the way, is precisely what would have to be aimed at, since it is the present scheme and organization that unavoidably work the mischief, and since, also (as touches the interest of the higher learning), they work nothing but mischief.

It should be plain, on reflection, to any one familiar with academic matters that neither of these official bodies serves any useful purpose in the university, in so far as bears in any way on the pursuit of knowledge. They may conceivably both be useful for some other purpose, foreign or alien to the quest of learning; but within the lines of the university's legitimate interest both are wholly detrimental, and very wastefully so. They are needless, except to take care of needs and emergencies to which their own presence gratuitously gives rise. In so far as these needs and difficulties that require executive surveillance are not simply and flagrantly factitious, — as, e.g., the onerous duties of publicity — they are altogether such needs as arise out of an excessive size and a gratuitously complex administrative organization; both of which characteristics of the American university are created by the governing boards and their executive officers, for no better purpose than a vainglorious self-complacency, and with no better justification than an uncritical prepossession to the effect that large size, complex organization, and authoritative control necessarily make for efficiency; whereas, in point of fact, in the affairs of learning these things unavoidably make for defeat.

Objection to any such measure of abolition is not to be grounded in their impracticability or their inefficiency, — supposing only that they could be carried out in the face of the prejudices of the ignorant and of the selfishly interested parties; the obstacles to any such move lie simply in the popular prejudice which puts implicit faith in large, complicated, and formidable organizations, and in that appetite for popular prestige that animates the class of persons from which the boards and executives are drawn.

This unreasoning faith in large and difficult combinations has been induced in the modern community by its experience with the large-scale organizations of the mechanical industries, and still more particularly by the convincing pecuniary efficiency of large capital, authoritative control, and devious methods, in modern business enterprise; and of this popular prejudice the boards of control and their executive officers have at least their full share, — indeed they owe their place and power in great part to their being animated with something more than an equitable share of this popular prepossession.

It is undeniable, indeed it is a matter of course, that so long as the university continues to be made up, as is now customary, of an aggregation of divers and sundry schools, colleges, divisions, etc., each and several of which are engaged in a more or less overt rivalry, due to their being so aggregated into a meaningless coalition, — so long will something formidable in the way of a centralized and arbitrary government be indispensable to the conduct of the university's affairs; but it is likewise patent that none of the several constituent schools, colleges, etc., are any the better off, in respect of the work, for being so aggregated in such an arbitrary collective organization. The duties of the executive — aside from the calls of publicity and self-aggrandizement — are in the main administrative duties that have to do with the interstitial adjustments of the composite establishment. These resolve themselves into a co-ordinated standardization of the several constituent schools and divisions, or a mechanically specified routine and scale, which commonly does violence to the efficient working of all these diverse and commensurable elements; with no gain at any point, excepting a gain in the facility of control — control for control's sake, at best. Much of the official apparatus and routine office-work is taken up with this futile control. Beyond this, and requisite to the due working of this control and standardization, there is the control of the personnel, the checking-up of their task work; together with the disciplining of such as do not sufficiently conform to the resulting schedule of uniformity and mediocrity.

These duties are, all and several, created by the imposition of a central control, and in the absence of such control the need of them would not arise. They are essentially extraneous to the work on which each and several of the constituent schools are engaged, and their only substantial effect on that work is to force it into certain extraneous formalities of routine that accountancy, such as to divert and retard the work in hand. So also the control exercised more at large by the governing board; except in so far as it is the mere mischief-making interference of ignorant outsiders, it is likewise directed to the keeping of a balance between units that need no balancing as against one another; except for the need which so is gratuitously induced by drawing these units into an incongruous coalition under the control of such a board; whose duties of office in this way arise wholly out of the creation of their office.

The great and conspicuous effect of abolishing the academic executive and governing board would be, of course, that the university organization as now known would incontinently fall to pieces. The several constitute schools would fall apart, since nothing holds them together except the strong hand of the present central government. This would, of course, seem a monstrous and painful outrage to all those persons who are infatuated with a veneration of big things; to whom a "great" — that is to say voluminous — university is an object of pride and loyal affection. This class of persons is a very large one, and they are commonly given to reflection on the merits of their preconceived ideals of "greatness." So that the dissolution of this "trust"-like university coalition would bitterly hurt their feelings. So intolerable would the shock to this popular sentiment presumably be, indeed, that no project of the kind can have any reasonable chance of hearing.

Apart from such loss of "prestige value" in the eyes of those whose pride centres on magnitude, the move in question would involve no substantial loss. The chief direct and tangible effect would be a considerable saving in "overhead charges," in that the greater part of the present volume of administrative work would fall away. The greater part — say, three-fourths — of the present officers of administration, with their clerical staff, would be lost; under the present system these are chiefly occupied with the correlation and control of matters that need correlation and control only with a view to centralized management.

The aggregate of forces engaged and the aggregate volume of work done in the schools would suffer no sensible diminution. Indeed, the contemplated change would bring a very appreciably heightened efficiency of all the working units that are now tied up in the university coalition. Each of these units would be free to follow its own devices, within the lines imposed by the work in hand, since none of them would then be required to walk in lock-step with several others with which it had no more vital articulation than the lock-step in question.

Articulation and co-ordination are good and requisite where and so far as they are intrinsic to the work in hand; but it all comes to nothing better than systematized lag, leak and friction, so soon as it is articulation and co-ordination in other terms and for other ends than the performance of the work in hand. It is also true, the coalition of these several school units into a pseudo-aggregate under a centralized control gives a deceptive appearance of a massive engine working to some common end; but, again, mass movement comes to nothing better than inhibition and misdirection when it involves a coalition of working units whose work is necessarily to be done in severalty.

Left to themselves the several schools would have to take care each of its own affairs and guide its endeavors by the exigencies of its own powers and purposes, with such regard to inter-collegiate comity and courtesy as would be required by the substantial relations and subsisting between them by virtue of their common employment in academic work.

In what has just been said, it is not forgotten that the burden of their own affairs would be thrown back on the initiative and collective discretion of the several faculties, so soon as the several schools had once escaped from the trust-like coalition in which they are now held. As has abundantly appeared in latter-day practice, these faculties have in such matters proved themselves notable chiefly for futile disputation; which does not give much promise of competent self-direction on their part, in case they were given a free hand. It is to be recalled, however, that this latter-day experience of confirmed incompetence has been gathered under the overshadowing presence of a surreptitiously and irresponsibly autocratic executive, vested with power of use and abuse, and served by a corps of adroit parliamentarians and lobbyists, ever at hand to divert the faculty's action from any measure that might promise to have a substantial effect. By force of circumstances, chief of which is the executive office, the faculties have become deliberative bodies charged with power to talk. Their serious attention has been taken up with schemes for weighing imponderables and correlating incommensurables, with such a degree of verisimilitude as would keep the statistics and accountancy of the collective administration in countenance, and still leave some play in the joints of the system for the personal relation of teacher and disciple. It is a nice problem in self-deception, chiefly notable for an endless proliferation.

At the same time it is well known — too well known to command particular attention — that in current practice, and of necessity, the actual effective organization of each of these constituent school units devolves on the working staff, in so far as regards the effectual work to be done; even to the selection of its working members and the apportionment of the work. It is all done "by authority," of course, and must all be arranged discreetly, with an ulterior view to its sanction by the executive and its due articulation with the scheme of publicity at large; but in all these matters the executive habitually comes into bearing only as a (powerful) extraneous and alien interference, — almost wholly inhibitory, in effect, even though with a show of initiative and creative guidance. And this inhibitory surveillance is exercised chiefly on grounds of conciliatory notoriety towards the outside, rather than on grounds that touch the efficiency of the staff for the work in hand. Such efficiency is commonly not barred, it is believed, so long as it does not hinder the executive's quest of the greater glory. There is, in effect, an inhibitory veto power touching the work and its ways and means.

But even when taken at its best, and when relieved of the inhibition and deflection worked by the executive, such an academic body can doubtless be counted on to manage its collective affairs somewhat clumsily and incompetently. There can be no hope of trenchant policy and efficient control at their hands; and, it should be added, there need be no great fear of such an outcome. The result should, in so far, be nearly clear gain, as against the current highly efficient management by an executive. Relatively little administration or control would be needed in the resulting small-scale units; except in so far as they might carry over into the new régime an appreciable burden of extra-scholastic traffic in the way of athletics, fraternities, student activities, and the like; and except so far as regards those schools that might still continue to be "gentlemen's colleges," devoted to the cultivation of the irregularities of adolescence and to their transfusion with a conventional elegance; these latter, being of the nature of penal settlements, would necessarily require government by a firm hand. That work of intimately personal contact and guidance, in a community of intellectual enterprise, that makes up the substance of efficient teaching, would, it might fairly be hoped, not be seriously hindered by the ill co-ordinated efforts of such an academic assembly, even if its members had carried over a good share of the mechanistic frame of mind induced by their experience under the régime of standardization and accountancy.

Indeed, there might even be grounds to hope that, on the dissolution of the trust, the underlying academic units would return to that ancient footing of small-scale parcelment and personal communion between teacher and student that once made the American college, with all its handicap of poverty, chauvinism and denominational bias, one of the most effective agencies of scholarship in Christendom.

The hope — or illusion — would be that the staff in each of the resulting disconnected units might be left to conduct its own affairs, and that they would prove incapable of much concerted action or detailed control. It should be plain that no other and extraneous power, such as the executive or the governing boards, is as competent — or, indeed, competent in any degree — to take care of these matters, as are the staff who have the work to do. All this is evident to any one who is at all conversant with the run of academic affairs as currently conducted on the grand scale; inasmuch as it is altogether a matter of course and of common notoriety within the precincts, that this is precisely what these constituent schools and units now have to do, each and several; with the sole qualification that they now have to take care of these matters under the inhibitory surveillance of the executive and his extraneous interests, and under the exactions of a super-imposed scheme of mechanical standardization and accountancy that accounts for nothing with its superimposition. At the same time the working force of the staff is hampered with a load of dead timber imported into its body to administer a routine of control and accountancy exacted by the executive's need of a credible publicity.[xii]

This highly conjectural tracing of consequences to follow from this hypothetical dissolution of the trust, may as well be pursued into a point or two of detail, as touches those units of the university coalition that have an immediate interest in point of scholarship, — the Collegiate ("Arts") division and the Graduate School. The former being left to its own devices and, it might be hoped, being purified of executive megalomania, it should seem probable that something of a reversion would take effect, in the direction of that simpler scheme of scholarship that prevailed in the days before the coming of electives. It was in the introduction of electives, and presently of alternatives and highly flexible curricula, that the move first set in which carried the American college off its footing as a school of probation and introduction to the scholarly life, and has left it a job-lot of ostensibly conclusive short-cuts into the trades and professions. It need not follow that the ancient curriculum would be re-established, but it should seem reasonable that a move would take effect in the direction of something like a modern equivalent. The Graduate School, on the other hand, having lost the drag of the collegiate division and the vocational schools, should come into action as a shelter where the surviving remnant of scholars and scientists might pursue their several lines of adventure, in teaching and in inquiry, without disturbance to or from the worldly-wise who clamor for the greater glory.

Now, all this speculation as to what might happen has, of course, little else than a speculative value. It is not intended, seriously and as a practical measure, to propose the abolition of the president's office, or of the governing board; nor is it intended to intimate that the captain of erudition can be dispensed with in fact. He is too dear to the commercialized popular imagination, and he fits too convincingly into the businessmen's preconceived scheme of things, to permit any such sanguine hope of surcease from skilled malpractice and malversation. All that is here intended to be said is nothing more than the obiter dictum that, as seen from the point of view of the higher learning, the academic executive and all his works are anathema, and should be discontinued by the simple expedient of wiping him off the slate; and that the governing board, in so far as it presumes to exercise any other than vacantly perfunctory duties, has the same value and should with advantage be lost in the same shuffle.

Notes

i An inquiry of this kind has been attempted elsewhere: Cf. *The Instinct of Workmanship*, chapter vii, pp. 321—340; "The Place of Science in Modern Civilisation," *American Journal of Sociology*, Vol. XI (March, 1996), pp. 585—609; "The Evolution of the Scientific Point of View," *University of California Chronicle* (1908), Vol. X, No. 4, pp. 395—416.

ii Cf. *The Instinct of Workmanship and the State of the Industrial Arts*, ch. i and pp. 39—45, 52—62, 84—89.

iii In the crude surmises of the pioneers in pragmatism this proposition was implicitly denied; in their later and more advisedly formulated positions the expositors of pragmatism have made their peace with it.

iv The essential function of the university is to bring together by the transmission of experience and impulse, the sages of the passing and the picked youths of the coming generation. By the extent and fullness with which they establish these social contacts, and thus transmit the wave of cumulative experience and idealist impulse — the real sources of moral and intellectual progress — the universities are to be judged. — Victor Branford *Interpretations and Forecasts*, ch. VI. "The Present as a Transition," p. 288.

v Cf. Geo. T. Ladd, *University Control*, p. 349.

vi i. Cf., e.g., J. McKeen Cattell, University Control, Part III, Ch. V., "concerning the American University." "The university is those who teach and those who learn and the work they do." "The university is its men and their work. But certain externals are necessary or at least usual — buildings and equipment, a president and trustees."

The papers by other writers associated with Mr. Cattell in this volume run the same effect whenever they touch the same topic; and, indeed, it would be difficult to find a deliberate expression to the contrary among men entitled to speak in these premises.

It may be in place to add here that the volume referred to, on University Control, has been had in mind throughout the following analysis and has served as ground and material for much of the argument.

vii Cf. *The Instinct of Workmanship*, ch. vi, vii.

viii With the current reactionary trend of things political and civil toward mediaeval-barbarian policies and habits of thought in the Fatherland, something of a correlative change has also latterly come in evidence in the German universities; so that what is substantially "cameralisitic science" — training and information for prospective civil servants and police magistrates — is in some appreciable measure displacing and police magistrates — is in some appreciable measure displacing disinterested inquiry in the field of economics and political theory. This is peculiarly true of those corporations of learning that come closely in touch with the *Cultus Ministerium*.

ix Cf. "Some Considerations on the Function of the State University." (Inaugural Address of Edmund Janes James, Ph.D., LL.D.), *Science*, November 17, 1905.

x "He has stifled all manly independence and individuality wherever it has exhibited itself at college. All noble idealism, and all the graces of poetry and art have been shriveled by his brutal and triumphant power. He has made mechanical efficiency and administrative routine the goal of the university's endeavor. The nobler ends of academic life will never be served so long as this spokesman of materialism remains in power."

History will relate that one of the eminent captains, through an incumbency of more than a quarter of a century, in a university of eminent wealth and volume, has followed a settled policy of defeating any overt move looking to scientific or scholarly inquiry on the part of any member of his faculty. Should a man of scholarly proclivities by any chance sift through the censorship exercised in virtue of the executive's appointing power, as might happen, since the captain was himself not qualified to pass a grounded opinion on any man's qualifications in that respect; and should he then give evidence of continuing to spend time and thought on matters of that nature, his burden of administrative and class-room tasks would presently be increased sufficiently to subdue his wayward bent; or, in any incorrigible case, the offender against the rule of academic sterility would eventually be retired by severance of his connection with this seat of learning.

In some sinister sense the case reflects credit on the American academic community at large, in that, by the close of this quarter-century of preventive regimen, the resulting academic staff had become a byword of nugatory intrigue and vacant pedantry.

xi So far has this predilection made its way in the counsels of the "educators" that much of the current discussion of *desideranda* academic policy reads like controversial argument on "efficiency engineering," — an "efficiency engineer" is an accountant competent to advise business concerns how best to increase their saleable output per unit of cost. And there has, indeed, been at least one tour of inspection of American universities by such an "efficiency engineer," undertaken in the service of an establishment founded with a view to academic welfare and governed by a board of university presidents. The report submitted by the inquiry in question duly conforms to the customary lines of "scientific management."

xii It will be objected, and with much reason, that these underlying "school units" that go to make up the composite American university habitually see no great evil in so being absorbed into the trust. They lend themselves readily, if not eagerly, to schemes of coalition; they are in fact prone to draw in under the aegis of the university corporation by "annexation," "affiliation," "absorption," etc. Anyone who cares to take stock of that matter and is in a position to know what is going on can easily assure himself that the reasons which decide in such a case are to advisedly accepted reasons intrinsic to the needs of efficiency for the work in hand, but rather reasons of competitive expediency, of competitive advantage and of prestige; except in so far as it may all be — as perhaps it commonly is — mere unreflecting conformity to the current fashion. In this connection it is to be remarked, however, that even if the current usage has no intrinsic advantage, as against another way of doing, failure to conform with the current way of doing will always entail a disadvantage.

6

Sabotage

"Sabotage" is a derivative of "sabot," which is French for a wooden shoe. It means going slow, with a dragging, clumsy movement, such as that manner of footgear may be expected to bring on. So it has come to describe any manoeuver of slowing-down, inefficiency, bungling, obstruction. In American usage the word is very often taken to mean a forcible obstruction, destructive tactics, industrial frightfulness, incendiarism and high explosives, although that is plainly not its first meaning nor its common meaning. Nor is that its ordinary meaning as the word is used among those who have advocated a recourse to sabotage as a means of enforcing an argument about wages or the conditions of work. The ordinary meaning of the word is better defined by an expression which has latterly come into use among the I.W.W., "conscientious withdrawal of efficiency" — although that phrase does not cover all that is rightly to be included under this technical term.

The sinister meaning which is often attached to the word in American usage, as denoting violence and disorder, appears to be due to the fact that the American usage has been shaped chiefly by persons and newspapers who have aimed to discredit the use of sabotage by organized workmen, and who have therefore laid stress on its less amiable manifestations. This is unfortunate. It lessens the usefulness of the word by making it a means of denunciation rather than of understanding. No doubt violent obstruction has had its share in the strategy of sabotage as carried on by disaffected workmen, as well as in the similar tactics of rival business concerns. It comes into the case as one method of sabotage, though by no means the most usual or the most effective; but it is also a spectacular and shocking method that it has drawn undue attention to itself. Yet such deliberate violence is, no doubt, a relatively minor fact in the case, as compared with that deliberate malingering, confusion, and misdirection of work that make up the bulk of what the expert practitioners would recognize as legitimate sabotage.

The word first came into use among the organized French workmen, the members of certain *syndicats*, to describe their tactics of passive resistance, and it has continued to be associated with the strategy of these French workmen, who are known as syndicalists, and with their like-minded running-mates in other countries. But the tactics of these syndicalists, and their use of sabotage, do not differ, except in detail, from the tactics of other workmen elsewhere, or from the similar tactics of friction, obstruction, and delay habitually employed, from time to time, by both employees and employers to enforce an argument about wages and prices. Therefore, in the course of a quarter-century past, the word has quite unavoidably taken on general meaning in common speech, and has been extended to cover all such peaceable or surreptitious manoeuvres of delay, obstruction, friction, and defeat, whether employed by the workmen to enforce their claims, or by the employers to defeat their employees, or by competitive business concerns to get the better of their business rivals or to secure their own advantage.

Such manoeuvres of restriction, delay, and hindrance have a large share in the ordinary conduct of business; but it is only lately that this ordinary line of business strategy has come to be recognized as being substantially of the same nature as the ordinary tactics of the syndicalists. So that it has not been usual until the last few years to speak of manoeuvres of this kind as sabotage when they are employed by employers and their business concerns. But all this strategy of delay, restriction, hindrance, and defeat is manifestly of the same character, and should conveniently be called by the same name, whether it is carried on by business men or by workmen; so that is no longer unusual now to find workmen speaking of "capitalistic sabotage" as freely as the employers and the newspapers speak of syndicalist sabotage. As the word is now used, and as it is properly used, it describes a certain system of industrial strategy or management, whether it is employed by one or another. What is describes is a resort to peaceable or surreptitious restriction, delay, withdrawal, or obstruction.

Sabotage commonly works within the law, although it may often be within the letter rather than the spirit of the law. It is used to secure some special advantage or preference, usually of a businesslike sort. It commonly has to do with something in the nature of a vested right, which one or another of the parties in the case aims to secure or defend, or to defeat or diminish; some preferential right or special advantage in respect of income or privilege, something in the way of a vested interest. Workmen have resorted to such measures to secure improved conditions of work, or increased wages, or shorter hours, or to maintain their habitual standards, to all of which they have claimed to have some sort of a vested right. Any strike is of the nature of sabotage, of course. Indeed, a strike is a typical species of sabotage. That strikes have not been spoken of as sabotage is due to the accidental fact that strikes were in use before this word came into use. So also, of course, a lockout is another typical species of sabotage. That the lockout is employed by the employers against the employees does not change the fact that it is a means of defending a vested right by delay, withdrawal, defeat, and obstruction of the work to be done. Lockouts have not usually been spoken of as sabotage, for the same reason that holds true in the case of strikes. All the while it has been recognized that strikes and lockouts are of identically the same character.

All this does not imply that there is anything discreditable or immoral about this habitual use of strikes and lockouts. They are part of the ordinary conduct of industry under the existing system, and necessarily so. So long as the system remains unchanged these measures are a necessary and legitimate part of it. By virtue of this industrial plant and workmen, it is altogether unlikely that prices could be maintained at a reasonably profitable figure for any appreciable time. A businesslike control of the rate and volume of output is indispensable for keeping up a profitable market, and a profitable market is the first and unremitting condition of prosperity in any community whose industry is owned and managed by business men. And the ways and means of this necessary control of the output of industry are always and necessarily something in the nature of sabotage — something in the way of retardation, restriction, withdrawal, unemployment of plant and workmen — whereby production is kept short of productive capacity.

The mechanical industry of the new order is inordinately productive. So the rate and volume of output have to be regulated with a view to what the traffic will bear — that is to say, what will yield the largest net return in terms of price to the business men who manage the country's industrial system. Otherwise there will be "over-production," business depression, and consequent hard times all around. Over-production means production in excess of what the market will carry off at a sufficiently profitable price. So it appears that the continued prosperity of the country from day to day hangs on a "conscientious withdrawal of efficiency" by the business men who control the country's industrial output. They control it all for their own use, of course, and their own use means always a profitable price.

In any community that is organized on the price system, with investment and business enterprise, habitual unemployment of the available industrial plant and workmen, in whole or in part, appears to be the indispensable condition without which tolerable conditions of life cannot be maintained. That is to say, in no such community can the industrial system be allowed to work at full capacity for any appreciable interval of time, on pain of business stagnation and consequent privation for all classes and conditions of men. The requirements of profitable business will not tolerate it. So the rate and volume of output must be adjusted to the needs of the market, not to the working capacity of the available resources, equipment and man power, nor to the community's need of consumable goods. Therefore there must always be a certain variable margin of unemployment of plant and man power. Rate and volume of output can, of course, not be adjusted by exceeding the productive capacity of the industrial system. So it has to be regulated by keeping short of maximum production by more or less as the condition of the market may require. It is always a question of more or less unemployment of plant and man power, and a shrewd moderation in the unemployment of these available resources, a "conscientious withdrawal of efficiency," therefore, is the beginning of wisdom in all sound workday business enterprise that has to do with industry.

All this is matter of course, and notorious. But it is not a topic on which one prefers to dwell. Writers and speakers who dilate on the meritorious exploits of the nation's business men will not commonly allude to this voluminous running administration of sabotage, this conscientious withdrawal of efficiency, that goes into their ordinary day's work. One prefers to dwell on those exceptional, sporadic, and spectacular episodes in business where business men have now and again successfully gone out of the safe and sane highway of conservative business enterprise that is hedged about with a conscientious withdrawal of efficiency, and have endeavored to regulate the output by increasing the productive capacity of the industrial system at one point or another.

But after all, such habitual recourse to peaceable or surreptitious measures of restraint, delay, and obstruction in the ordinary businesslike management of industry is too widely known and too well approved to call for much exposition or illustration. Yet, as one capital illustration of the scope and force of such businesslike withdrawal of efficiency, it may be in place to recall that all the civilized nations are just now undergoing an experiment of businesslike sabotage on an unexampled scale and carried out with unexampled effrontery. All these nations that have come through the war, whether as belligerents or as neutrals, have come into a state of more or less pronounced distress, due to a scarcity of the common necessaries of life; and this distress falls, of course, chiefly on the common sort, who have at the same time borne the chief burden of the war which has brought them to this state of the distress.

The common man has won the war and lost his livelihood. This need not be said by way of praise or blame. As it stands it is, broadly, an objective statement of fact, which may need some slight qualification, such as broad statements of fact will commonly need. All these nations that have come through the war, and more particularly the common run of their populations, are very much in need of all sorts of supplies for daily use, both for immediate consumption and for productive use. So much so that the prevailing state of distress rises in many places to an altogether unwholesome pitch of privation, for want of the necessary food, clothing, shelter, and fuel. Yet in all these countries the staple industries are slowing down. There is an ever increasing withdrawal of efficiency. The industrial plant is increasingly running idle or half idle, running increasingly short of its productive capacity. Workmen are being laid off; an increasing number of these workmen who have been serving in the armies are going idle for want of work, at the same time that troops which are no longer needed in the service are being demobilized as slowly as popular sentiment will tolerate, apparently for fear that the number of unemployed workmen in the country may presently increase to such proportions as to bring on a catastrophe. And all the while all these peoples are in great need of all sorts of goods and services which these idle plants and idle workmen are fit to produce. But for reasons of business expediency it is impossible to let these idle plants and idle workmen go to work — that is to say for reasons of insufficient profit to the business men interested, or in other words, of the reasons of insufficient income to the vested interests which control the staple industries and so regulate the output of product. The traffic will not bear so large a production of goods as the community needs for current consumption, because it is considered doubtful whether so large a supply could be sold at prices that would yield a reasonable profit on the investment — or rather on the capitalization; that is to say, it is considered doubtful whether an increased production, such as to employ more workmen and supply the goods needed by the community, would result in an increased net aggregate income for the vested interests which control these industries. A reasonable profit always means, in effect, the largest obtainable profit.

All this is simple and obvious, and it should scarcely need explicit statement. It is for these business men to manage the country's industry, of course, and therefore to regulate the rate and volume of output; and also of course any regulation of the output by them will be made with a view to the needs of business; that is to say, with a view to the largest obtainable net profit, not with a view to the physical needs of these peoples who have come through the war and have made the world safe for the business of the vested interests. Should the business men in charge, by any chance aberration, stray from this straight and narrow path of business integrity, and allow the community's needs unduly to influence their management of the community's industry, they would presently find themselves discredited and would probably face insolvency. Their only salvation is a conscientious withdrawal of efficiency. All this lies in the nature of the case. It is the working of the price system, whose creatures and agents these business men are. Their case is rather pathetic, as indeed they admit quite volubly. They are not in a position to manage with a free hand, the reason being that they have in the past, under the routine requirements of the price system as it takes effect in corporation finance, taken on so large an overhead burden of fixed charges that any appreciable decrease in the net earnings of the business will bring any well-managed concern of this class face to face with bankruptcy.

At the present conjuncture, brought on by the war and its termination, the case stands somewhat in this typical shape. In the recent past earnings have been large; these large earnings (free income) have been capitalized; their capitalized value has been added to the corporate capital and covered with securities bearing a fixed income-charge; this income-charge, representing free income, has thereby become a liability on the earnings of the corporation; this liability cannot be met in case the concern's net aggregate earnings fall off in any degree; therefore prices must be kept up to such a figure as will bring the largest net aggregate return, and the only means of keeping up prices is a conscientious withdrawal of the efficiency in these staple industries on which the community depends for a supply of the necessaries of life.

The business community has hopes of tiding things over by this means, but it is still a point in doubt whether the present unexampled large use of sabotage in the businesslike management of the staple industries will now suffice to bring the business community through this grave crisis without a disastrous shrinkage of its capitalization, and a consequent liquidation; but the point is not in doubt that the physical salvation of these peoples who have come through the war must in any case wait on the pecuniary salvation of these owners of corporate securities which represent free income. It is a sufficiently difficult passage. It appears that production must be curtailed in the staple industries, on pain of unprofitable prices. The case is not so desperate in those industries which have immediately to do with the production of superfluities; but even these, which depend chiefly on the custom of those kept classes to whom the free income goes, are not feeling altogether secure. For the good of business it is necessary to curtail production of the means of life, on pain of unprofitable prices, at the same time that the increasing need of all sorts of the necessaries of life must be met in some passable fashion, on pain of such popular disturbances as will always come of popular distress when it passes the limit of tolerance.

Those wise business men who are charged with administering the salutary modicum of sabotage at this grave juncture may conceivably be faced with a dubious choice between a distasteful curtailment of the free income that goes to the vested interests, on the one hand, and an unmanageable onset of popular discontent on the other hand. And in either alternative lies disaster. Present indications would seem to say that their choice will fall out according to ancient habit, that they will be likely to hold fast by an undiminished free income for the vested interests at the possible cost of any popular discontent that may be in prospect — and then, with the help of the courts and the military arm, presently make reasonable terms with any popular discontent that may arise. In which event it should all occasion no surprise or resentment, inasmuch as it would be nothing unusual or irregular and would presumably be the most expeditious way of reaching a *modus vivendi*. During the past few weeks, too, quite an unusually large number of machine guns have been sold to industrial business concerns of the larger sort, here and there, at least so they say. Business enterprise being the palladium of the Republic, it is right to take any necessary measures for its safeguarding. Price is of the essence of the case, whereas livelihood is not.

The grave emergency that has arisen out of the war and its provisional conclusion is, after all, nothing exceptional except in magnitude and severity. In substance it is the same sort of thing that goes on continually but unobtrusively and as a matter of course in ordinary times of business as usual. It is only that the extremity of the case is calling attention to itself. At the same time it serves impressively to enforce the broad proposition that a conscientious withdrawal of efficiency is the beginning of wisdom in all established business enterprise that has to do with industrial production. But it has been found that this grave interest which the vested interests always have in a salutary retardation of industry at one point or another cannot well be left altogether to the haphazard and ill-coordinated efforts of individual business concerns, each taking care of its own particular line of sabotage within its own premises. The needed sabotage can best be administered on a comprehensive plan and by a central authority, since the country's industry is of the nature of a comprehensive interlocking system, whereas the business concerns which are called on to control the motions of this industrial system will necessarily work piecemeal, in severalty and at cross-purposes. In effect, their working at cross-purposes results in a sufficiently large aggregate retardation that is necessarily somewhat blindly apportioned and does not converge to a neat and perspicuous outcome. Even a reasonable amount of collusion among the interested business concerns will not by itself suffice to carry on that comprehensive moving equilibrium of sabotage that is required to preserve the business community from recurrent collapse or stagnation, or to bring the nation's traffic into line with the general needs of the vested interests.

Where the national government is charged with the general care of the country's business interests, as is invariably the case among the civilized nations, it follows from the nature of the case that the nation's lawgivers and administration will have some share in administering that necessary modicum of sabotage that must always go into the day's work of carrying on industry by business methods and for business purposes. The government is in a position to penalize excessive or unwholesome traffic. So, it is always considered necessary, or at least expedient, by all sound mercantilists, as by a tariff or by subsidies, to impose and maintain a certain balance or proportion among the several branches of industry and trade that go to make up the nation's industrial system. The purpose commonly urged for measures of this class is the fuller utilization of the nation's industrial resources in material, equipment, and man power; the invariable effect is a lowered efficiency and a wasteful use of these resources, together with an increase of international jealousy. But measures of that kind are thought to be expedient by the mercantilists for these purposes — that is to say, by the statesmen of these civilized nations, for the purposes of the vested interests. The chief and nearly the sole means of maintaining such a fabricated balance and proportion among the nation's industries is to obstruct the traffic at some critical point by prohibiting or penalizing any exuberant undesirables among these branches of industry. Disallowance, in whole or in part, is the usual and standard method.

The great standing illustration of sabotage administered by the government is the protective tariff, of course. It protects certain special interests by obstructing competition from beyond the frontier. This is the main use of a national boundary. The effect of the tariff is to keep the supply of goods down and thereby keep the price up, and so to bring reasonably satisfactory dividends to those special interests which deal in the protected articles of trade, at the cost of the underlying community. A protective tariff is a typical conspiracy in restraint of trade. It brings a relatively small, though absolutely large, run of free income to the special interests which benefit by it, at a relatively, and absolutely, large cost to the underlying community, and so it gives rise to a body of vested rights and intangible assets belonging to these special interests.

Of a similar character, in so far that in effect they are in the nature of sabotage — conscientious withdrawal of efficiency — are all manner of excise and revenue-stamp regulations; although they are not always designed for that purpose. Such would be, for instance, the partial or complete prohibition of alcoholic beverages, the regulation of the trade in tobacco, opium, and other deleterious narcotics, drugs, poisons, and high explosives. Of the same nature, in effect if not in intention, are such regulations as the oleomargarine law; as also the unnecessarily costly and vexatious routine of inspection imposed on the production of industrial (denatured) alcohol, which has inured to the benefit of certain business concerns that are interested in other fuels for use in internal-combustion engines; so also the singularly vexatious and elaborately imbecile specifications that limit and discourage the use of the parcel post, for the benefit of the express companies and other carriers which have a vested interest in traffic of that kind.

It is worth noting in the same connection, although it comes in from the other side of the case, that ever since the express companies have been taken over by the federal administration there has visibly gone into effect a comprehensive system of vexation and delay in the detail conduct of their traffic, so contrived as to discredit federal control of this traffic and thereby provoke a popular sentiment in favor of its early return to private control. Much the same state of things has been in evidence in the railway traffic under similar conditions. Sabotage is serviceable as a deterrent, whether in furtherance of the administration's work or in contravention of it.

In what has just been said there is, of course, no intention to find fault with any of these uses of sabotage. It is not a question of morals and good intentions. It is always to be presumed as a matter of course that the guiding spirit in all such governmental moves to regularize the nation's affairs, whether by restraint or by incitement, is a wise solicitude for the nation's enduring gain and security. All that can be said here is that many of these wise measures of restraint and incitement are in the nature of sabotage, and that in effect they habitually, though not invariably, inure to the benefit of certain vested interests — ordinarily vested interests which bulk large in the ownership and control of the nation's resources. That these measures are quite legitimate and presumably salutary, therefore, goes without saying. In effect they are measures for hindering traffic and industry at one point or another, which may often be a wise business precaution.

During the period of the war administrative measures in the nature of sabotage have been greatly extended in scope of kind. Peculiar and imperative exigencies have had to be met, and the staple means of meeting many of these new and exceptional exigencies has quite reasonably been something in the way of avoidance, disallowance, penalization, hindrance, a conscientious withdrawal of efficiency from work that does not fall in with the purposes of the Administration. Very much as is true in private business when a situation of doubt and hazard presents itself, so also in the business of government at the present juncture of exacting demand and inconvenient limitations, the Administration has been driven to expedients of disallowance and obstruction with regard to some of the ordinary processes of life, as, for instance, in the nonessential industries. It has also appeared that the ordinary equipment and agencies for gathering and distributing news and other information have in the past developed a capacity far in excess of what can safely be permitted in time of war or of returning peace. The like is true for the ordinary facilities for public discussion of all sorts of public questions. The ordinary facilities, which may have seemed scant enough in time of peace with the slack interest, had after all developed a capacity far beyond what the governmental traffic will bear in these uneasy times of war and negotiations, when men are very much on the alert to know what is going on. By a modern use of the later improvements in the technology of transport and communication, the ordinary means of disseminating information and opinions have grown so efficient that the traffic can no longer be allowed to run at full capacity during a period of stress in the business of government. Even the mail service has proved insufferably efficient, and a selective withdrawal of efficiency has gone into effect. To speak after the analogy of private business, it has been found best to disallow such use of the mail facilities as does not inure to the benefit of the Administration in the way of good will and vested rights of usufruct.

These peremptory measures of disallowance have attracted a wide and dubious attention; but they have doubtless been of a salutary nature and intention, in some way which is not to be understood by outsiders — that is to say, by citizens of the Republic. An unguarded dissemination of information and opinions or an unduly frank canvassing of the relevant facts by these outsiders, will be a handicap on the Administration's work, and may even defeat the Administration's aims. At least so they say.

Something of much the same color has been observed elsewhere and in other times, so that all this nervously alert resort to sabotage on undesirable information and opinions is nothing novel, nor is it peculiarly democratic. The elder statesmen of other great monarchies, east and west, have long seen and approved the like. But these elder statesmen of the dynastic régime have gone to their work of sabotage on information because of a palpable division of sentiment between their government and the underlying population, such as does not exist in the advanced democratic commonwealths. The case of Imperial Germany during the period of the war is believed to show such a division of sentiment between the government and the underlying population, and also to show how such a divided sentiment on the part of a distrustful and distrusted population had best be dealt with. The method approved by German dynastic experience is sabotage, of a somewhat free-swung character, censorship, embargo on the communication, and also, it is confidently alleged, elaborate misinformation.

Such procedure on the part of the dynastic statesmen of the Empire is comprehensible even to a layman. But how it all stands with those advanced democratic nations, like America, where the government is the dispassionately faithful agent and spokesman of the body of citizens, and where there can consequently be no division of aims and sentiment between the body of officials and any underlying population — all that is a more obscure and hazardous subject of speculation. Yet there has been censorship, somewhat rigorous, and there has been selective refusal of mail facilities, somewhat arbitrary, in these democratic commonwealths also, and not least in America, freely acknowledged to be the most naïvely democratic of them all. And all the while one would like to believe that it all has somehow served some useful end. It is all sufficiently perplexing.

7

Patriotism

Patriotism may be defined as a sense of partisan solidarity in respect of prestige. What the expert psychologists, and perhaps the experts in Political Science, might find it necessary to say in the course of an exhaustive analysis and definition of this human faculty would presumably be something more precise and more extensive. There is no inclination here to forestall definition, but only to identify and describe the concept that loosely underlies the colloquial use of this term, so far as seems necessary to an inquiry into the part played by the patriotic animus in the life of modern peoples, particularly as it bears on questions of war and peace.

On any attempt to divest this concept of all extraneous or adventitious elements it will be found that such a sense of undivided joint interest in a collective body of prestige will always remain at an irreducible minimum. This is the substantial core about which many and divers subsidiary interests cluster, but without which these other clustering interests and aspirations will not, jointly or severally, make up a working palladium of the patriotic spirit.

It is true, seen in some other light or rated in some other bearing or connection, one and another of these other interests, ideals, aspirations, beatitudes, may well be adjudged nobler, wiser, possibly more urgent than the national prestige; but in the forum of patriotism all these other necessaries of human life — the glory of God and the good of man — rise by comparison only to the rank of subsidiaries, auxiliaries, and amenities. He is an indifferent patriot who lets "life, liberty and the pursuit of happiness" cloud the issue and get in the way of the main business in hand.

There once were, we are told, many hardy and enterprising spirits banded together along the Spanish Main for such like ends, just as there are in our day an even greater number of no less single-minded spirits bent on their own "life, liberty and the pursuit of happiness," according to their light, in the money-markets of the modern world; but for all their admirable qualities and splendid achievements, their passionate quest of these amenities has not entitled them these Gentlemen Adventurers to claim rank as patriots. The poet says:

> "Strike for your altars and your fires!
> Strike for the green graves of your sires!
> God and your native land!"

But, again, a temperate scrutiny of the list of desiderata so enumerated in the poet's flight, will quickly bring out the fact that any or all of them might drop out of the situation without prejudice to the plain call of patriotic duty. In the last resort, when the patriotic spirit falls back on its naked self alone, it is not reflection on the merits of these good and beautiful things in Nature that gives him his cue and enforces the ultimate sacrifice. Indeed it is something infinitely more futile and infinitely more urgent, — provided only that the man is imbued with the due modicum of patriotic devotion, as, indeed, men commonly are. It is not faith, hope or charity that abide as the irreducible minimum of virtue in the patriot's scheme of things; particularly not that charity that has once been highly spoken of as being the greatest of these. It may be that, viewed in the light of reason, as Doctor Katzenberger would say, patriotic devotion is the most futile thing in the world; but, for good or ill, the light of reason has nothing to do with the case, — no more than "The flowers that bloom in the spring."

The patriotic spirit is a spirit of emulation, evidently, at the same time that it is emulation shot through with a sense of solidarity. It belongs under the general caption of sportsmanship, rather than of workmanship. Now, any enterprise in sportsmanship is bent on an invidious success, which most involve as its major purpose the defeat and humiliation of some competitor, whatever else may be comprised in its aim. Its aim is a differential gain, as against a rival; and the emulative spirit that comes under the head of patriotism commonly, if not invariably, seeks this differential advantage by injury of the rival rather than by an increase of home-bred well-being.

Indeed, well-being is altogether out of perspective, except as underpinning for an edifice of national prestige. It is, at least, a safe generalization that the patriotic sentiment never has been known to rise to the consummate pitch of enthusiastic abandon except when bent on some work of concerted malevolence. Patriotism is of a contentious complexion, and finds its full expression in no other outlet than warlike enterprise; its highest and final appeal is for its death, damage, discomfort and destruction of the party of the second part.

It is not that the spirit of patriotism will tolerate no other sentiments bearing on matters of public interest, but only that it will tolerate none that traverse the call of the national prestige. Like other men, the patriot may be moved by many and divers other considerations, besides that of the national prestige; and these other considerations may be of the most genial and reasonable kind, or they may also be as foolish and mischievous as any comprised in the range of human infirmities. He may be a humanitarian given over to the kindliest solicitude for the common good, or a religious devotee hedged about in all his motions by the ever present fear of God, or taken up with artistic, scholarly or scientific pursuits; or, again, he may be a spendthrift devotee of profane dissipation, whether in the slums or on the higher levels of gentility, or he may be engaged on a rapacious quest of gain, as a businessman within the law or as a criminal without its benefit, or he may spend the rest of his best endeavors in advancing the interests of his class at the cost of the nation at large. All that is understood as a matter of course and is beside the point. In so far as he is a complete patriot, these other interests will fall away from him when the one clear call of patriotic duty comes to enlist him in the cause of national prestige. There is, indeed, nothing to hinder a bad citizen being a good patriot; nor does it follow that a good citizen — in other respects — may not be a very indifferent patriot.

Many and various other preferences and considerations may coincide with the promptings of the patriotic spirit, and so may come in to coalesce with and fortify its driving force; and it is usual for patriotic men to seek support for their patriotic impulses in some reasoned purpose of their extraneous kind that is believed to be served by following the call of the national prestige; — it may be a presumptive increase and diffusion of culture at large, or the spread and enhancement of a presumptively estimable religious faith, or a prospective liberation of mankind from servitude to obnoxious masters and outworn institutions; or, again, it may be the increase of peace and material well-being among men, within the national frontiers or impartially throughout the civilized world.

There are, substantially, none of the desirable things in this world that are not so counted on by some considerable body of patriotic aspirations. What they will not come to an understanding about is the particular national ascendancy with which the attainment of these admirable ends is conceived to be bound up.

The ideals, needs and aims that so are brought into the patriotic argument to lend a color of rationality to the patriotic aspiration in any given case will of course be such ideals, needs and aims as are currently accepted and felt to be authentic and self-legitimating among the people in whose eyes the given patriotic enterprise is to find favor. So one finds that, e. g., among the followers of Islam, devout and resolute, the patriotic statesman (that is to say the politician who designs to make use of the popular patriotic fervor) will in the last resort appeal to the claims and injunctions of the faith. In a similar way the Prussian statesman bent on dynastic enterprise will conjure in the name of dynasty and of culture and efficiency; or, if worse comes to worst, an outbreak will be decently covered with a plea of mortal peril and self-defense. Among English-speaking peoples much is to be gained by showing that the path of patriotic glory is at the same time the way of equal-handed justice under the rule of free institutions; at the same time, in a fully commercialized community, such as the English-speaking commonly are, material benefits in the way of trade will go far to sketch in a background of decency for any enterprise that looks to the enhancement of the national prestige.

But any promise of gain, whether in the nation's material or immaterial assets, will not of itself carry full conviction to the commonplace modern citizen; or even to such modern cities as are best endowed with a national spirit. By and large, and overlooking that appreciable contingent of morally defective citizens that is be counted on any hybrid population, it will hold true that no contemplated enterprise or line of policy will fully commend itself to the popular sense of merit and expediency until it is given a moral turn, so as to bring it to square with the dictates of right and honest dealing. On no terms short of this will it effectually coalesce with the patriotic fervor that animates any modern nation, and so turn it to use in the most effective way, it is necessary to show that the demands of equity are involved in the case. Any cursory survey of modern historical events bearing on this point, among the civilized peoples, will bring out the fact that no concerted and sustained movement of the national spirit can be had without enlisting the community's moral convictions. The common man must be persuaded that right is on his side. "Thrice is he armed who knows his quarrel just." The grounds of his convictions may often be tawdry enough, but the conviction is a necessary factor in the case.

The requisite moral sanction may be had on various grounds, and, on the whole, it is not an extremely difficult matter to arrange. In the simplest and not infrequent case it may turn in a question of equity in respect of trade or investment as between the citizens or subjects of the several rival nations; the Chinese "Open Door" affords as sordid an example as may be desired. Or it may be only an envious demand for a share in the world's material resources "A Place in the Sun," as picturesque phrase describes it; or "The Freedom of the Seas," as another equally vague and equally invidious demand for international equity phrases it. These demands are put forward with a color of demanding something in the way of equitable opportunity for the commonplace peaceable citizen; but quite plainly they have none but a fanciful bearing on the fortunes of the common man in the time of peace, and they have a meaning to the nation only as a fighting unit; apart from their prestige value, these things are worth fighting for only as prospective means of fighting. The like appeal to the moral sensibilities may, again, be made in the way of a call to self-defense, under the rule of live and let live; or it may also rest on the more tenuous obligation to safeguard the national integrity of a weaker neighbor, under a broader interpretation of the same equitable rule of live and let live. But in one way or another it is necessary to set up the conviction that the promptings of patriotic ambition have the sanction of moral necessity.

It is not that the line of national policy or patriotic enterprise so entered upon with the support of popular sentiment needs to be right and equitable as seen in dispassionate perspective from the outside, but only that it should be capable of being made to seem right and equitable to the biased populace whose moral convictions are requisite to its prosecution; which is quite another matter. Nor is it that any such patriotic enterprise is, in fact, entered on simply or mainly on these moral grounds that are so alleged in its justification, but only that some colorable ground of justification of extenuation is necessary to be alleged, and to be credited by popular belief.

It is not that the common man is not sufficiently patriotic, but only that he is a patriot hampered with a plodding and uneasy sense of right and honest dealing, and that one must make up one's account with this moral bias in looking to any sustained and concerted action that draws on the sentiment of the common man for its carrying on. But the moral sense in the case may be somewhat easily satisfied with a modicum of equity, in case the patriotic bias of the people is well pronounced, or in case it is re-inforced with a sufficient appeal to self-interest. In those cases where the national fervor rises to an excited pitch, even very; attenuated considerations of right and justice, such as would under ordinary conditions doubtfully bear scrutiny as extenuating circumstances, may come to serve as moral authentication for any extravagant course of action to which the craving for national prestige may incite. The higher the pitch of patriotic fervor, the more tenuous and more threadbare may be the requisite moral sanction. By cumulative excitation some very remarkable results have latterly been attained along this line.

Patriotism is evidently a spirit of particularism, of saliency and animosity between contrasted groups of persons; it lives on invidious comparison, and works out in mutual hindrance and jealousy between nations. It commonly goes the length of hindering intercourse and obstructing traffic that would patently serve the material and cultural well-being of both nationalities; and not infrequently, indeed normally, it eventuates in competitive damage to both.

All this holds true in the world of modern civilization, at the same time that the modern civilized scheme of life is, notoriously, of a cosmopolitan character, both in its cultural requirements and in its economic structure. Modern culture is drawn on too a large scale, is of too complex and multiform a character, requires the cooperation of too many and various lines of inquiry, experience and insight, to admit of its being confined within national frontiers, except at the cost of insufferable crippling and retardation. The science and scholarship that is the peculiar pride of civilized Christendom are not only international, but rather they are homogeneously cosmopolitan; so that in this bearing there are, in effect, no national frontiers; with the exception, of course, that in a season of patriotic intoxication, such as the current war has induced, even the scholars and scientists will be temporarily overset by their patriotic fervor. Indeed, with the best efforts of obscurantism and national jealousy to the contrary, it remains patently true that modern culture is the culture of Christendom at large, not the culture of one and another nation in severalty within the confines of Christendom. It is only as and in so far as they partake in and contribute to the general run of Western civilization at large that the people of any one of these nations of Christendom can claim standing as a cultured nation; and even any distinctive variation from this general run of civilized life, such as may give a "local color" of ideals, tastes and conventions, will, in point of cultural value, have to be rated as an idle detail, a species of lost motion, that serves no better purpose than a transient estrangement.

So also, the modern state of the industrial arts is of a like cosmopolitan character, in point of scale, specialization, and the necessary use of diversified resources, of climate and raw materials. None of the countries of Europe, e. g., is competent to carry on its industry by modern technological methods without constantly drawing on resources outside of its national boundaries. Isolation in this industrial respect, exclusion from the world market, would mean intolerable loss of efficiency, more pronounced the more fully the given country has taken over this modern state of the industrial arts. Exclusion from the general body of outlying resources would seriously cripple any one or all of them, and effectually deprive them of the usufruct of this technology; and partial exclusion, by prohibitive or protective tariffs and the like, unavoidably results in a partial lowering of the efficiency of each, and therefore a reduction of the current well-being among them all together.

Into this cultural and technological system of the modern world the patriotic spirit fits like dust in the eyes and sand in bearings. Its net contribution to the outcome is obscuration, distrust, and retardation at every point where it touches the fortunes of modern mankind. Yet it is forever present in the counsels of the statesmen and in the affections of the common man, and it never ceases to command the regard of all men as the prime attribute of manhood and the final test of the desirable citizen. It is scarcely an exaggeration to say that no other consideration is allowed in abatement of the claims of patriotic loyalty, and that such loyalty will be allowed to cover any multitude of sins. When the ancient philosopher described Man as a "political animal," this, in effect, was what he affirmed; and today the ancient maxim is as good as new. The patriotic spirit is at cross-purposes with modern life, but in any test case it is found that the claims of life yield before those of patriotism; and any voice that dissents from this order of things is as a voice crying in the wilderness.

To anyone who is inclined to moralize on the singular discrepancies of human life this state of the case will be fruitful of much profound speculation. The patriotic animus appears to be an enduring trait of human nature, an ancient heritage that has stood over unshorn from time immemorial, under the Mendelian rule of the stability of racial types. It is archaic, not amenable to elimination or enduring suppression, and apparently not appreciably to be mitigated by reflection, education, experience or selective breeding.

Throughout the historical period, and presumably through an incalculable period of the unrecorded past, patriotic manslaughter has consistently been seeding out of each successive generation of men the most patriotic among them; with the net result that the level of patriotic ardor today appears to be no lower than it ever was. At the same time, with the advance of population, of culture and of the industrial arts, patriotism has grown increasingly disserviceable; and it is to all appearance as ubiquitous and as powerful as ever, and is held in as high esteem.

The continued prevalence of this archaic animus among the modern peoples, as well as the fact that it is universally placed high among the virtues, must be taken to argue that it is, in its elements, and hereditary trait, of the nature of an inborn impulsive propensity, rather than a product of habituation. It is, in substance, not something that can be learned and unlearned. From one generation to another, the allegiance may shift from one nationality to another, but fact of unreflecting allegiance at large remains. And it all argues also that no sensible change has taken effect in the hereditary endowment of the race, at least in this respect, during the period known by record or by secure inference, — say, since the early Neolithic in Europe; and this in spite of the fact that there has all this while been opportunity for radical changes in the European population by cross-breeding, infiltration and displacement of the several racial stocks that go to make up this population. Hence, on slight reflection the inference has suggested itself and has gained acceptance that this trait of human nature must presumably have been serviceable to the peoples of the earlier time, on those levels of savagery or of the lower barbarism on which the ancestral stocks of the European population first made good their survival and proved their fitness to people that quarter of the earth. Such, indeed, is the common view; so common as to pass for matter-of-course, and therefore habitually to escape scrutiny.

Still it need not follow, as more patient reflection will show. All the European peoples show much the same animus in this respect; whatever their past history may have been, and whatever the difference in past experience that might be conceived to have shaped their temperament. Any difference in the pitch of patriotic conceit and animosity, between the several nationalities or the several localities, is by no means wide, even in cases where the racial composition of the population is held to be very different, as, e. g., between the people on the Baltic seaboard and those on the Mediterranean. In point of fact, in this matter of patriotic animus there appears to be a wider divergence, temperamentally, between individuals within any one of these communities than between the common run in any one community and the corresponding common run in any other. But even such divergence of individual temper in respect of patriotism as is to be met with, first and last, is after all surprisingly small in view of the scope for individual variation which this European population would seem to offer.

These peoples of Europe, all and several, are hybrids compounded out of the same run of racial element, but mixed in varying proportions. On any parallel of latitude — taken in the climatic rather than in the geometric sense — the racial composition of the west-European population will be much the same, virtually identical in effect, although always of a hybrid complexion; whereas on any parallel of longitude — also in the climatic sense — the racial composition will vary progressively, but always within the limits of the same general scheme of hybridisation, — the variation being a variation in the proportion in which the several racial elements are present in any given case. But in no case does a notable difference in racial composition coincide with a linguistic or national frontier. But in point of patriotic animus these European people are one as good as another, whether the comparison be traced on parallels of latitude or of longitude. And the inhabitants of each national territory, or of each detailed locality, appear also to run surprisingly uniform in respect of their patriotic spirit.

Heredity in any such community of hybrids will, superficially, appear to run somewhat haphazard. There will, of course, be no traceable difference between social or economic classes, in point of heredity, — as is visibly the case in Christendom. But variation — of an apparently haphazard description — will be large and ubiquitous among the individuals of such a populace. Indeed, it is a matter of course and of easy verification that individual variation within such a hybrid stock will greatly exceed the extreme differences that may subsist between the several racial types that have gone to produce the hybrid stock. Such is the case of the European peoples. The inhabitants vary greatly among themselves, both in physical and in mental traits, as would be expected; then the variation between individuals in point of patriotic animus should accordingly also be expected to be extremely wide, — should, in effect, greatly exceed the difference, if any, in this respect between the several racial elements engaged in the European population. Some appreciable difference in this respect there appears to be, between individuals; but individual divergence from the normal or average appears always to be of a sporadic sort, — it does not run on class lines, whether of occupation, status or property, nor does it run at all consistently from parent to child. When all is told the argument returns to the safe ground that these variations in point of patriotic animus are sporadic and inconsequential, and do not touch the general proposition that, one with another, the inhabitants of Europe and the European Colonies are sufficiently patriotic, and that the average endowment in this respect runs with consistent uniformity across all differences of time, place and circumstance. It would, in fact, be extremely hazardous to affirm that there is a sensible difference in the ordinary pitch of patriotic sentiment as between any two widely diverse samples of these hybrid populations, in spite of that fact that the diversity in visible physical traits may be quite pronounced.

In short, the conclusion seems safe, on the whole, that in this respect the several racial stocks that have gone to produce the existing populations of Christendom have all been endowed about as richly one as another. Patriotism appears to be a ubiquitous trait, at least among the races and peoples of Christendom. From which it should follow, that since there is, and has from the beginning been, no differential advantage favoring one racial stock or one fashion of hybrid as against another, in this matter of patriotic animus, there should also be no ground of selective survival or selective elimination of this account as between these several races and peoples. So that the undisturbed and undiminished prevalence of this trait among the European population, early or late, argues nothing as to its net serviceability or disserviceability under any of the varying conditions of culture and technology to which these Europeans have been subjected, first and last; except that it has, in any case, not proved so disserviceable under the conditions prevailing hitherto as to result in the extinction of these Europeans, one with another.[i]

The patriotic frame of mind has been spoken of above as if it were an hereditary trait, something after the fashion of Mendelian unit character. Doubtless this is not a competent account of the matter; but the present argument scarcely needs a closer analysis. Still, in a measure to quiet title and avoid annoyance, it may be noted that this patriotic animus is of the nature of a "frame of mind" rather than a Mendelian unit of character; that it so involves a concatenation of several impulsive propensities (presumably hereditary); and that both the concatenation and the special mode and amplitude of the response are a product of habituation, very largely of the nature of conventionalised use and wont. What is said above, therefore, goes little farther than saying that the underlying aptitudes requisite to this patriotic frame of mind are heritable, and that use and wont as bearing on this point run with sufficient uniformity to bring a passably uniform result. It may be added that in this concatenation spoken of there seems to be comprised, ordinarily, that sentimental attachment to habitat and custom that is called love of home, or in its accentuated expression, home-sickness; so also an invidious self-complacency, coupled with a gregarious bent which gives the invidious comparison a group content; and further, commonly if not invariably, a bent of abnegation, self-abasement, subservience, or whatever it may best be called, that inclines the bearer unreasoningly and unquestioningly to accept and serve a prescriptive ideal given by custom or by customary authority.

The conclusion would therefore provisionally run to the effect that under modern conditions the patriotic animus is wholly a disserviceable trait in the spiritual endowment of these peoples, — in so far as it bears on the material conditions of life unequivocally, and as regards the cultural interests more at large presumptively; whereas there is no assured ground for a discriminating opinion as touches its possible utility or disutility at any remote period in the past. There is, or course, always room for the conservative estimate that, as the possession of this spiritual trait has not hitherto resulted in the extinction of the race, so it may also in the calculable future continue to bring no more grievous results than a degree of mischief, without even stopping or greatly retarding the increase of population.

All this, of course, is intended to apply only so far as it goes. It must not be taken as intending to say any least word in derogation of those high qualities that inspire the patriotic citizen. In its economic, biological and cultural incidence patriotism appears to be an untoward trait of human nature; which has, of course, nothing to say as to its moral excellence, its aesthetic value, or its indispensability to a worthy life. No doubt, it is in all these respects deserving of all the esteem and encomiums that fall to its share. Indeed, its well-known moral and aesthetic value, as well as the reprobation that is visited on any shortcomings in this respect, signify, for the purposes of the present argument, nothing more than that the patriotic animus meets the unqualified approval of men because they are, all and several, infected with it. It is evidence of the ubiquitous, intimate and ineradicable presence of this quality in human nature; all the more since it continues untiringly to be held in the highest esteem in spite of the fact that a modicum of reflection should make its disserviceability plain to the meanest understanding. No higher praise of moral excellence, and no profounder test of loyalty, can be asked than this current unreserved commendation of a virtue that makes invariably for damage and discomfort. The virtuous impulse must be deep-seated and indefeasible that drives men incontinently to do good that evil may come to it. "Though He slay me, yet will I trust in Him."

In the light — and it is a dim and wavering light — of the archaeological evidence, helped out by circumstantial evidence from such parallel or analogous instances as are afforded by existing communities on a comparable level of culture, one may venture more or less confidently on a reconstruction of the manner of life among the early Europeans, of early neolithic times and later.[ii] And so one may form some conception of the part played by this patriotic animus among those beginnings, when, if not the race, at least its institutions were young; and when the native temperament of these peoples was tried out and found fit to survive through the age-long and slow-moving eras of stone and bronze. In this connection, it appears safe to assume that since early neolithic times no sensible change has taken effect in the racial complexion of the European peoples; and therefore no sensible change in their spiritual and mental make-up. So that in respect of the spiritual elements that go to make up this patriotic animus the Europeans of today will be substantially identical with the Europeans of that early time. The like is true as regards those other traits of temperament that come in question there, as being included among the stable characteristics that still condition the life of these peoples under the altered circumstances of the modern age.

The difference between prehistoric Europe and the present state of these peoples resolves itself on analysis into a difference in the state of the industrial arts, together with such institutional changes as have come on in the course of working out this advance in the industrial arts. The habits and the exigencies of life among these peoples have greatly changed; whereas in temperament and capacities the peoples that now live by and under the rule of this altered state of the industrial arts are the same as they were. It is to be noted, therefore, that the fact of their having successfully come through the long ages of prehistory by the use of this mental and spiritual endowment cannot be taken to argue that these peoples are thereby fit to meet the exigencies of this later and gravely altered age; nor will it do to assume that because these peoples have themselves worked out this modern culture and its technology, therefore it must all be suitable for their use and conductive to their biological success. The single object lesson of the modern urban community, with its endless requirements in the way of sanitation, police, compulsory education, charities, — all this and many other discrepancies in modern life should enjoin caution on anyone who is inclined offhand to hold that because modern men have created these conditions, therefore these must be the most suitable conditions of life for modern mankind.

In the beginning, that is to say in the European beginning, men lived in small and close groups. Control was close within the group, and the necessity of subordinating individual gains and preferences to the common good was enjoined on the group by the exigencies of the case, on pain of common extinction. The situation and usages of existing Eskimo villages may serve to illustrate and enforce the argument on this head. The solidarity of sentiment necessary to support the requisite solidarity of action in the case would be a prime condition of survival in any racial stock exposed to the conditions which surrounded these early Europeans. This needful sense of solidarity would touch not simply or most imperatively the joint prestige of the group, but rather the joint material interests; and would enforce a spirit of mutual support and dependence. Which would be rather helped than hindered by a jealous attitude of joint prestige; so long as no divergent interests of members within the group were in a position to turn this state of the common sentiment to their own particular advantage.

This state of the case will have lasted for a relatively long time; long enough to have tested the fitness of these peoples for that manner of life, — longer, no doubt, than the interval that has elapsed since history began. Special interests - e.g., personal and family interests — will have been present and active in these days of the beginning; but so long as the group at large was small enough to admit of a loose neighborly contact throughout its extent and throughout the workday routine of life, at the same time that it was too small and feeble to allow any appreciable dissipation of its joint energies in such pursuit of selfish gains as would run counter to the paramount business of the common livelihood, so long the sense of a common livelihood and a joint fortune would continue to hold any particular ambitions effectually in check. Had it fallen out otherwise, the story of the group in question would have been ended, and another and more suitably endowed type of men would have taken the place vacated by its extinction.

With a sensible advance in the industrial arts the scale of operations would grow larger, and the group more numerous and extensive. The margin between production and subsistence would also widen and admit additional scope for individual ambitions and personal gains. And as this process of growth and increasing productive efficiency went on, the control exercised by neighborly surveillance, through the sentiment of the common good as against the self-seeking pursuits of individuals and sub-groups, would gradually slacken; until by progressive disuse it would fall into a degree of abeyance; to be called into exercise and incite to concerned action only in the face of unusual exigencies touching the common fortunes of the group at large, or on persuasion that the collective interest of the group at large was placed in jeopardy in the molestation of one and another of its members from without. The group's prestige at least would be felt to suffer in the defeat or discourtesy suffered by any of its members at the hands of any alien; and, under compulsion of the ancient sense of group solidarity, whatever material hardship or material gain might so fall to individual members in their dealings with the alien would pass easy scrutiny as material detriment or gain inuring to the group at large, — in the apprehension of men whose sense of community interest is inflamed with a jealous disposition to safeguard their joint prestige.

With continued advance in the industrial arts the circumstances conditioning life will undergo a progressive change of such a character that the joint interest of the group at large, in the material respect, will progressively be less closely bound up with the material fortunes of any particular member of members; until in the course of time and change there will, in effect, in ordinary times be no general and inclusive community or material interest binding the members together in a common fortune and working for common livelihood. As the rights of ownership begin to take effect, so that the ownership of property and the pursuit of a livelihood under the rules of ownership come to govern men's economic relations, these material concerns will cease to be a matter of undivided joint interest, and will fall into the shape of interest in severalty. So soon and so far as this institution of ownership or property takes effect, men's material interests cease to run on lines of group solidarity. Solely, or almost solely, in the exceptional case of defense against a predatory incursion from outside, do the members of the group have a common interest of a material kind. Progressively as the state of the arts advances, the industrial organisation advances to a larger scale and a more extensive specialisation, with increasing divergence among individual interests and individual fortunes; and intercourse over larger distances grows easier and makes a larger grouping practicable; which enables a larger, prompter and more effective mobilisation of forces with which to defend or assert any joint claims. But by the same move it also follows, or at least appears uniformly to have followed in the European case, that the accumulation of property and the rights of ownership have progressively come into the first place among the material interests of these peoples; while anything like a community or usufruct has imperceptibly fallen into the background, and has presently gone virtually into abeyance, except as an eventual recourse in extremis for the common defense. Property rights have displaced community or usufruct; and invidious distinctions as between persons, sub-groups, and classes have displaced community of prestige in the workday routine of these peoples; and the distinctions between contrasted persons or classes have come to rest, in an ever increasing degree, directly or indirectly, on invidious comparisons in respect of pecuniary standing rather than on personal affiliation with the group at large.

So, with the advance of the industrial arts a differentiation of a new character sets in and presently grows progressively more pronounced and more effectual, giving rise to regrouping on lines that run regardless of those frontiers that divide one community from another for purposes of patriotic emulation. So far as it comes chiefly and typically in question here, this regrouping takes place on two distinct but somewhat related principles of contrast: that of wealth and poverty, and that of master and servant, or authority and obedience. The material interests of the population in this way come to be divided between the group of those who own and those who command, on the one hand, and of those who work and who obey, on the other hand.

Neither of these two contrasted categories of persons have any direct material interest in the maintenance of the patriotic community; or at any rate no such interest as should reasonably induce them to spend their own time and substance in support of the political (patriotic) organisation within which they live. It is only in so far as one or another of these interests looks for a more than proportionate share in any prospective gain from the joint enterprise, that the group or class in question can reasonably be counted on to bear its share in the joint venture. And it is only when and in so far as their particular material or self-regarding interest is re-inforced by patriotic conceit, that they can be counted on to spend themselves in furtherance of the patriotic enterprise, without the assurance of a more than proportionate share in any gains that may be held in prospect from any such joint enterprise; and it is only in its patriotic bearing that the political community continues to be a joint venture. That is to say, in more generalised terms, through the development of the rights of property, and of such like prescriptive claims of privilege and prerogative, it has come about that other community interests have fallen away, until the collective prestige remains as virtually the sole community interest which can hold the sentiment of the group in a bond of solidarity.

To one or another of these several interested groups or classes within the community the political organisation may work a benefit; but only to one or another, not to each and several, jointly or collectively. Since by no chance will the benefit derived from such joint enterprise on the part of the community at large equal the joint cost; in as much as all joint enterprise of the kind that looks to material advantage works by one or another method of inhibition and takes effect, if at all, by lowering the aggregate efficiency of the several countries concerned, with a view to the differential gain of one at the cost of another. So, e.g., a protective tariff is plainly a conspiracy in restraint of trade, with a view to benefit the conspirators by hindering their competitors. The aggregate cost to the community at large of such an enterprise in retardation is always more than the gains it brings to those who may benefit by it.

In so speaking of the uses to which the common man's patriotic devotion may be turned, there is no intention to underrate its intrinsic value as genial and generous trait of human nature. Doubtless it is best and chiefly to be appreciated as a spiritual quality that beautifies and ennobles its bearer, and that endows him with the full stature of manhood, quite irrespective of ulterior considerations. So it is to be conceded without argument that this patriotic animus is a highly meritorious frame of mind, and that it has an aesthetic value scarcely to be overstated in the farthest stretch of poetic license. But the question of its serviceability to the modern community, in any other than this decorative respect, and particularly its serviceability to the current needs of the common man in such a modern community, is not touched by such an admission; nor does this recognition of its generous spiritual nature afford any help toward answering a further question as to how and with what effect this animus may be turned to account by anyone who is in position to make use of the forces which it sets free.

Among Christian nations there still is, on the whole, a decided predilection for that ancient and authentic line of national repute that springs from warlike prowess. This repute for warlike prowess is what first comes to mind among civilised peoples when speaking of national greatness. And among those who have best preserved this warlike ideal of worth, the patriotic ambition is likely to converge on the prestige of their sovereign; so that it takes the concrete form of personal loyalty to a master, and so combines or coalesces with a servile habit of mind.

But peace hath its victories no less renowned than war, it is said; and peaceable folk of a patriotic temper have learned to make the best of their meager case and have found self-complacency in these victories of the peaceable order. So it may broadly be affirmed that all nations look with complacency on their own peculiar culture — the organised complex of habits of thought and of conduct by which their own routine of life is regulated — as being in some way worthier than the corresponding habits of their neighbors. The case of the German culture has latterly come under a strong light in this way. But while it may be that no other nation has been so naïve as to make a concerted profession of faith to the effect that their own particular way of life is altogether commendable and is the only fashion of civilization that is fit to survive; yet it will scarcely be an extravagance to assert that in their own secret mind these others, too, are blest with much the same consciousness of unique worth. Conscious virtue of this kind is a good and sufficient ground for patriotic inflation, so far as it goes. It commonly does not go beyond a defensive attitude, however. Now and again, as in the latter-day German animation on this head, these phenomena of national use and wont may come to command such a degree of popular admiration as will incite to an aggressive or proselytizing campaign.

In all this there is nothing of a self-seeking or covetous kind. The common man who so lends himself to the aggressive enhancement of the national culture and its prestige has nothing of a material kind to gain from the increase of renown that so comes to his sovereign, his language, his countrymen's art of science, his diet, or his God. There are no sordid motives in all this. These spiritual assets of self-complacency are, indeed, to be rated as grounds of high-minded patriotism without afterthought. These aspirations and enthusiasms would perhaps be rated as Quixotic by men whose horizon is bounded by the main chance; but they make up that substance of things hoped for that inflates those headlong patriotic animosities that stir universal admiration.

So also, men find a invidious distinction in such matters of physical magnitude as their country's area, the number of its population, the size of its cities, the extent of its natural resources, its aggregate wealth and its wealth per capita, its merchant marine and its foreign trade. As a ground of invidious complacency these phenomena of physical magnitude and pecuniary traffic are no better and no worse than such immaterial assets as the majesty of the sovereign or the perfections of the language. They are matters in which the common man is concerned only by the accident of domicile, and his only connection with these things is an imaginary joint interest in their impressiveness. To these things he has contributed substantially nothing, and from them he derives no other merit of advantage than a patriotic inflation. He takes pride in these things in an invidious way, and there is no good reason why he should not; just as there is also no good reason why he should, apart from the fact that the common man is so constituted that he, mysteriously, takes pride in these things that concern him not.

Of the several groups of classes of persons within the political frontiers, whose particular interests run systematically at cross-purposes with those of the community at large under modern conditions, the class of masters, rulers, authorities, — or whatever term may seem most suitable to designate that category of persons whose characteristic occupation is to give orders and command deference, — of the several orders than conditions of men these are, in point of substantial motive and interest, most patently at variance with all the rest, or with the fortunes of the common man. The class will include civil and military authorities and whatever nobility there is of a prescriptive and privileged kind. The substantial interest of these classes in the common welfare is of the same kind as the interest which the parasite has in the well-being of his host; a sufficiently substantial interest, no doubt, but there is in this relation nothing like a community of interest. Any gain on the part of the community at large will materially serve the needs of this group of personages, only in so far as it may afford them a larger volume or a wider scope for what has in latter-day colloquial phrase been called "graft." These personages are, of course, not to be spoken of with disrespect or with the slightest inflection of discourtesy. They are all honorable men. Indeed they afford the conventional pattern of human dignity and meritorious achievement, and the "Fountain of Honor" is found among them. The point of the argument is only that their material or other self-regarding interests are of such a nature as to be furthered by the material wealth of the community, and more particularly by the increasing volume of the body politic; but only with the proviso that this material wealth and this increment of power must accrue without anything like a corresponding cost to this class. At the same time, since this class of the superiors is in some degree a specialised organ of prestige, so that their value, and therefore their tenure, both in the eyes of the community and in their own eyes, is in the main a "prestige value" and a tenure by prestige and since the prestige that invests their persons is a shadow cast by the putative worth of the community at large, it follows that their particular interest in the joint prestige is peculiarly alert and insistent. But it follows also that these personages cannot of their own substance or of their own motion contribute this collective prestige in the same proportion in which it is necessary for them to draw on it in support of their own prestige value. It would, in other words, be a patent absurdity to call on any of the current ruling classes, dynasties, nobility, military and diplomatic corps, in any of the nations of Europe, e.g., to preserve their current dignity and command the deference that is currently accorded them by recourse to their own powers and expenditure of their own substance, without the usufruct of the commonalty whose organ of dignity they are. The current prestige value which they enjoy is beyond their unaided powers to create or maintain, without the usufruct of the community. Such an enterprise does not lie within the premises of the case.

In this bearing, therefore, the first concern with which these personages are necessarily occupied is the procurement and retention of a suitable usufruct in the material resources and good-will of a sufficiently large and industrious population. The requisite good-will in these premises is called loyalty, and its retention by the line of personages that so trade on prestige rests on a superinduced association of ideas, whereby the national honor comes to be confounded in popular apprehension with the prestige of these personages who have the keeping of it. But the potentates and the establishments, civil and military, on whom this prestige value rests will unavoidably come into invidious comparison with others of their kind; and, as invariably happens in matters of invidious comparison, the emulative needs of all the competitors for prestige are "indefinitely extensible," as the phrase of the economists has it. Each and several of them incontinently needs a further increment of prestige, and therefore also a further increment of the material assets in men and resources that are needful as ways and means to assert and augment the national honor.

It is true, the notion that their prestige value is in any degree conditioned by the material circumstances and the popular imagination of the underlying nation is distasteful to many of these vicars of the national honor. They will incline rather to the persuasion that this prestige value is a distinctive attribute, of a unique order, intrinsic to their own persons. But, plainly, any such detached line of magnates, notables, kings and mandarins resting their notability on nothing more substantial than a slightly sub-normal intelligence and a moderately scrofulous habit of body could not long continue to command that eager deference that is accounted their due. Such a picture of majesty would be sadly out of drawing. There is little conviction and no great dignity to be drawn from the unaided pronouncement:

> "We're here because,
> "We're here because,
> "We're here because
> "We're here,"

Even when the doggerel is duly given the rhetorical benefit of a "Tenure by the Grace of God." The personages that carry this dignity require the backing of a determined and patriotic populace in support of their prestige value, and they commonly have no great difficulty in procuring it. And their prestige value is, in effect, proportioned to the volume of material resources and patriotic credulity that can be drawn on for its assertion. It is true, their draught on the requisite sentimental and pecuniary support is fortified with large claims of serviceability to the common good, and these claims are somewhat easily, indeed eagerly, conceded and acted upon; although the alleged benefit to the common good will scarcely be visible except in the light of glory shed by the blazing torch of patriotism.

In so far as it is of a material nature the benefit which the constituted authorities so engage to contribute to the common good, or in other words to confer on the common man, falls under two heads: defense against aggression from without; and promotion of the community's material gain. It is to be presumed that the constituted authorities commonly believe more or less implicitly in their own professions in so professing to serve the needs of the common man in these respects. The common defense is a sufficiently grave matter, and doubtless it claims the best affections and endeavor of the citizen; but it is not a matter that should claim much attention at this point in the argument, as bearing on the service rendered the common man by the constituted authorities, taken one with another. Any given governmental establishment at home is useful in this respect only as against another governmental establishment elsewhere. So that on the slightest examination it resolves itself into a matter of competitive patriotic enterprise, as between the patriotic aspirations of different nationalities led by different governmental establishments; and the service so rendered by the constituted authorities in the aggregate takes on the character of remedy for evils of their own creation. It is invariably a defense against the concerted aggressions of other patriots. Taken in the large, the common defense of any given nation becomes a detail of the competitive struggle between rival nationalities animated with a common spirit of patriotic enterprise and led by authorities constituted for this competitive purpose.

Notes

i For a more extended discussion of this matter, cf. *Imperial Germany and the Industrial Revolution*, ch. i. and Supplementary Notes i. and ii.

ii Cf. *Imperial Germany and the Industrial Revolution*, as above.

8

The Barbarian Status of Women

It seems altogether probable that in the primitive groups of mankind, when the race first took to a systematic use of tools, and so emerged upon the properly human plane of life, there was but the very, slightest beginning of status, with little of invidious distinction between classes and little of a corresponding division of employments. In an earlier paper, [...], it has been argued that the early division of labor between classes comes in as the result of an increasing efficiency of labor, due to a growing effectiveness in the use of tools. When, in the early cultural development, the use of tools and the technical command of material forces had reached a certain degree of effectiveness, the employments which occupy the primitive community would fall into two distinct groups — (a) the honorific employments, which involve a large element of prowess, and (b) the humiliating employments, which call for diligence and into which the sturdier virtues do not enter. An appreciable advance in the use of tools must precede the differentiation of employments, because (1) without effective tools (including weapons) men are not sufficiently formidable in conflict with the ferocious beasts to devote themselves so exclusively to the hunting of large game as to develop that occupation into a conventional mode of life reserved for a distinct class; (2) without tools of some efficiency, industry is not productive enough to support a dense population, and therefore the groups into which the population gathers will not come into such a habitual hostile contact with one another as would give rise to a life of warlike prowess; (3) until industrial methods and knowledge have made some advance, the work of getting a livelihood is too exacting to admit of the consistent exemption of any portion of the community from vulgar labor; (4) the inefficient primitive industry yields no such disposable surplus of accumulated goods as would be worth fighting for, or would tempt an intruder, and therefore there is little provocation to warlike prowess.

With the growth of industry comes the possibility of a predatory life; and if the groups of savages crowd one another in the struggle for subsistence, there is a provocation to hostilities, and a predatory habit of life ensues. There is a consequent growth of a predatory culture, which may for the present purpose be treated as the beginning of the barbarian culture. This predatory culture shows itself in a growth of suitable institutions. The group divides itself conventionally into a fighting and a peace-keeping class, with a corresponding division of labor. Fighting, together with other work that involves a serious element of exploit, becomes the employment of the able-bodied men; the uneventful everyday work of the group falls to the women and the infirm.

In such a community the standards of merit and propriety rest on an invidious distinction between those who are capable fighters and those who are not. Infirmity, that is to say incapacity for exploit, is looked down upon. One of the early consequences of this depreciation of infirmity is a tabu on women and women's employments. In the apprehension of the archaic, animistic barbarian, infirmity is infectious. The infection may work its mischievous effect both by sympathetic influence and transfusion. Therefore it is well for the able-bodied man who is mindful of his virility to shun all undue contact and conversation with the weaker sex to avoid all contamination with the employments that are characteristic of the sex. Even the habitual food of women should not be eaten by men, lest their force be thereby impaired. The injunction against womanly employments and foods and against intercourse with women applies with especial rigor during the season of preparation for any work of manly exploit, such as a great hunt or a warlike raid, or induction into some manly dignity or society of mystery. Illustrations of this special tabu abound in the early history of all peoples that have had a warlike or barbarian past. The women, their occupations, their food and clothing, their habitual place in the house or village and in extreme cases even their speech, become ceremonially unclean to the men. This imputation of ceremonial uncleanness on the ground of their infirmity has lasted on in the later culture as a sense of the unworthiness of Levitical inadequacy of women; so that even now we feel the impropriety of women taking rank with men, or representing the community in any relation that calls for dignity and ritual competency; as for instance, in priestly or diplomatic offices, or even in representative civil offices, and likewise, and for a like reason, in such offices of domestic and body servants as are of a seriously ceremonial character — footmen, butlers, etc.

The changes that take place in the everyday experiences of a group or horde when it passes from a peaceable to a predatory habit of life have their effect on the habits of thought prevalent in the group. As the hostile contact of one group with another becomes closer and more habitual, the predatory activity and the bellicose animus become more habitual to the members of the group. Fighting comes more and more to occupy men's everyday thoughts, and the other activities of the group fall into the background and become subsidiary to the fighting activity. In the popular apprehension the substantial core of such a group — that on which men's thoughts run when the community and the community's life is thought of — is the body of fighting men. The collective fighting capacity becomes the most serious question that occupies men's minds, and gives the point of view from which persons and conduct are rated. The scheme of life of such a group is substantially a scheme of exploit. There is much of this point of view to be found even in the common-sense views held by modern populations. The inclination to identify the community with its fighting men comes into evidence today whenever warlike interests occupy the popular attention in an appreciable degree.

The work of the predatory barbarian group is gradually specialized and differentiated under the dominance of this idea of prowess, so as to give rise to a system of status in which the non-fighters fall into a position of subservience to the fighters. The accepted scheme of life or consensus of opinions which guides the conduct of men in such a predatory group and decides what may properly be done of course comprises a great variety of details; but it is, after all, a single scheme — a more or less organic whole — so that the life carried on under its guidance in any case makes up a somewhat consistent and characteristic body of culture. This is necessarily the case, because of the simple fact that the individuals between whom the consensus holds are individuals. The thinking of each one is the thinking of the same individual, on whatever head and in whatever direction his thinking may run. Whatever may be the immediate point or object of his thinking, the frame of mind which governs his aim and manner of reasoning in passing on any given point of conduct is, on the whole, the habitual frame of mind which experience and tradition have enforced upon him. Individuals whose sense of what is right and good departs widely from the accepted views suffer some repression, and in case of an extreme divergence they are eliminated from the effective life of the group through ostracism. Where the fighting class is in the position of dominance and prescriptive legitimacy, the canons of conduct are shaped chiefly by the common-sense of the body of fighting men. Whenever conduct and whatever code of proprieties have the authentication of this common-sense are definitely right and good, for the time being, and the deliverance of this common-sense are, in their turn, shaped by the habits of life of the able-bodied men. Habitual conflict acts, by selection and the habituation, to make these male members tolerant of any infliction of damage and suffering. Habituation to the sight and infliction of suffering, and to the emotions that go with fights and brawls, may even end in making the spectacle of misery a pleasing diversion to them. The result is in any case a more or less consistent attitude of plundering and coercion on the part of the fighting body, and this animus is incorporated into the scheme of life of the community. The discipline of predatory life makes for an attitude of mastery on the part of the able-bodied men in all their relations with the weaker members of the group, and especially in their relations with the women. Men who are trained in predatory ways of life and modes of thinking come by habituation to apprehend this form of the relation between the sexes as good and beautiful.

All the women in the group will share in the class repression and depreciation that belongs to them as women, but the status of women taken from hostile groups has an additional feature. Such a woman not only belongs to a subservient and low class, but she also stands in a special relation to her captor. She is the trophy of the raid, and therefore an evidence of exploit, and on this ground it is to her captors' interest to maintain a peculiarly obvious relation of mastery toward her. And since, in the early culture, it does not detract from her subservience to the life of the group, this peculiar relation of the captive to her captor will meet but slight, if any, objection from other members of the group. At the same time, since his peculiar coercive relation to the woman serves to mark her as a trophy of his exploit, he will somewhat jealously resent any similar freedom taken by other men, or any attempt on their part to parade a similar coercive authority over her and so usurp the laurels of his prowess, very much as a warrior would under like circumstances resent a usurpation or an abuse of the scalps or skulls which he had taken from the enemy.

After the habit of appropriating captured women has hardened into custom, and so given rise on the one hand to the form of marriage resting on coercion, and on the other hand to the concept of ownership, a development of certain secondary features of the institution so inaugurated is to be looked for. In time this coercive ownership-marriage receives the sanction of the popular taste and morality. It comes to rest in men's habits of thought as the right form of marriage relation, and it comes at the same time to be gratifying to men's sense of beauty and of honor. The growing predilection for mastery and coercion, as a manly trait, together with the growing moral and aesthetic and approbation of marriage on the basis of coercion and ownership, will affect the tastes of the men most immediately and most strongly; but since the men are the superior class whose views determine the current views of the community, their common-sense in the matter will shape the current canons of taste in its own image. The tastes of the women also, in point of morality and of propriety alike, will presently be affected in the same way. Through the precept and example of those who make the vogue, and through selective repression of those who are unable to accept it, the institution of ownership-marriage makes its way into definitive acceptance as the only beautiful and virtuous form of the relation. As the conviction of its legitimacy grows stronger in each succeeding generation, it comes to be appreciated unreflectingly as a deliverance of common-sense and enlightened reason that the good and beautiful attitude of the man toward the woman is an attitude of coercion. "None but the brave deserve the fair."

As the predatory habit of life gains a more unquestioned and undivided sway, other forms of the marriage relation fall under a polite odium. The masterless, unattached woman consequently loses caste. It becomes imperative for all men who would stand well in the eyes of their fellows to attach some woman or women to themselves by the honorable bonds of seizure. In order to attain a decent standing in the community a man is required to enter into this virtuous and honorific relation of ownership-marriage, and a publicly acknowledged marriage relation which has not the sanction of capture becomes unworthy of able-bodied men. But as the group increases in size, the difficulty of providing wives by capture becomes very great, and it becomes necessary to find a remedy that shall save the requirements of decency and at the same time permit the marriage of women from within the group. To this end the status of women married from within the group is sought to be mended by a mimic or ceremonial capture. The ceremonial capture effects an assimilation for the free woman into the more acceptable class of women who are attached by bonds of coercion to some master, and so gives a ceremonial legitimacy and decency to the resulting marriage relation. The probable motive for adopting the free women into the honorable class of bondwomen in this way is not primarily a wish to improve their standing or their lot, but rather a wish to keep those good men in countenance, who, for dearth of captives, are constrained to seek a substitute from among the home-bred women of the group. The inclinations of men in high standing who are possessed of marriageable daughters would run in the same direction. It would not seem right that a woman of high birth should irretrievably be outclassed by any chance-comer from outside.

According to this view, marriage by feigned capture within the tribe is a case of mimicry — "protective mimicry," to borrow a phrase from the naturalists. It is substantially a case of adoption. As is the case in all human relations where adoption is practiced, this adoption of the free women into the class of the unfree proceeds by as close an imitation as may be of the original fact for which it is a substitute. And as in other cases of adoption, the ceremonial performance is by no means looked upon as a fatuous make-believe. The barbarian has implicit faith in the efficiency of imitation and ceremonial execution as a means of compassing a desired end. The entire range of magic and religious rites is testimony to that effect. He looks upon external objects and sequences naïvely, as organic and individual things, and as expressions of a propensity working toward an end. The unsophisticated common-sense of the primitive barbarian apprehends sequences and events in terms of will-power or inclination. As seen in the light of this animistic preconception, any process is substantially teleological, and the propensity imputed to it will not be thwarted of its legitimate end after the course of events in which it expresses itself has once fallen into shape or got under way. It follows logically, as a matter of course, that, if once the motions leading to desired consummation have been rehearsed in the accredited form and sequence, the same substantial result will be attained as that produced by the process imitated. This is the ground of whatever efficiency is imputed to ceremonial observances on all planes of culture, and it is especially the chief element in formal adaptation and initiation. Hence, probably, the practice of mock-seizure or mock-capture, and hence the formal profession of fealty and submission on the part of the woman in the marriage rites of peoples among whom the household with a male head prevails. This form of the household is almost always associated with some survival or reminiscence of wife-capture. In all such cases, marriage is, by derivation, a ritual of initiation into servitude. In the words of the formula, even after it has been appreciably softened under the latter-day decay of the sense of status, it is the woman's place to love, honor, and obey.

According to this view, the patriarchal household or, in other words, the household with a male head is an outgrowth of emulation between the members of a warlike community. It is, therefore, in point of derivation, a predatory institution. The ownership and control of women is a gratifying evidence of prowess and high standing. In logical consistency, therefore, the greater the number of women so held, the greater the distinction which their possession confers upon their master. Hence the prevalence of polygamy, which occurs almost universally at one stage of culture among peoples which have the male household. There may, of course, be other reasons for polygamy, but the ideal development of polygamy which is met with in the harems of very powerful patriarchal despots and chieftains can scarcely be explained on other grounds. But whether it works out in a system of polygamy or not, the male household is in any case a detail of a system of status under which the women are included in the class of unfree subjects. The dominant feature in the institutional structure of these communities is that of status, and the groundwork of their economic life is a rigorous system of ownership.

The institution is found at its best, or in its most effectual development, in the communities in which status and ownership prevail with the least mitigation; and with the decline of the sense of status and of the extreme pretensions of ownership, which as has been going on for some time past in the communities of the western culture, the institution of the patriarchal household has also suffered something of a disintegration. There has been some weakening and slackening of the bonds, and this deterioration is most visible in the communities which have departed farthest from the ancient system of status, and have gone farthest in reorganizing their economic life on the lines of industrial freedom. And the deference for an indissoluble tie of ownership-marriage, as well as the sense of its definitive virtuousness, has suffered the greatest decline among the classes immediately engaged in the modern industries. So that there seems to be fair ground for saying that the habits of thought fostered by modern industrial life are, on the whole, not favorable to the maintenance of this institution or to that status of women which the institution in its best development implies. The days of its best development are in the past, and the discipline of modern life — if not supplemented by a prudent inculcation of conservative ideals — will scarcely afford the psychological basis for its rehabilitation.

This form of marriage, or of ownership, by which the man becomes the head of the household, the owner of the woman, and the owner and discretionary consumer of the household's output of consumable goods, does not of necessity imply a patriarchal system of consanguinity. The presence or absence of maternal relationship should, therefore, not be given definite weight in this connection. The male household, in some degree of elaboration, may well coexist with a counting of relationship in the female line, as, for instance, among many North American tribes. But where this is the case it seems probable that the ownership of women, together with the invidious distinctions of status from which the practice of such an ownership sprints, has come into vogue at so late a stage of the cultural development that the maternal system of relationship had already been thoroughly incorporated into the tribe's scheme of life. The male household in such cases is ordinarily not developed in good form or entirely free from traces of a maternal household. The traces of a maternal household which are found in these cases commonly point to a form of marriage which disregards the man rather than places him under the surveillance of the woman. It may well be named the household of the unattached woman. This condition of things argues that the tribe or race in question has entered upon a predatory life only after a considerable period of peaceable industrial life, and after having achieved a considerable development of social structure under the régime of peace and industry, whereas the unqualified prevalence of the patriarchate, together with the male household, may be taken to indicate that the predatory phase was entered early, culturally speaking.

Where the patriarchal system is in force in fully developed form, including the paternal household, and hampered with no indubitable survivals of a maternal household or a maternal system of relationship, the presumption would be that the people in question have entered upon the predatory culture early, and have adopted the institutions of private property and class prerogative at an early stage of their economic development. On the other hand, where there are well-preserved traces of a maternal household, the presumption is that the predatory phase has been entered by the community in question at a relatively late point in its life history, even if the patriarchal system is, and long has been the prevalent system of relationship. In the latter case the community or the group of tribes, may, perhaps for geographical reasons, not have independently attained the predatory culture in accentuated form but may at a relatively late date have contracted the agnatic system and paternal household through contact with another, higher, or characteristically different, culture, which has included these institutions among its cultural furniture. The required contact would take place most effectually by way of invasion and conquest by an alien race occupying the higher plane or divergent line of culture. Something of this kind is the probable explanation, for instance, of the equivocal character of the household and relationship system in the early Germanic culture, especially as it is seen in such outlying regions as Scandinavia. The evidence, in this latter case, as in some other communities lying farther south, is somewhat obscure, but it points to a long-continued coexistence of the two forms of the household; of which the maternal seems to have held its place most tenaciously among the subject or lower classes of the population, while the paternal was the honorable form of marriage in vogue among the superior class. In the earliest traceable situation of these tribes there appears to have been a relatively feeble, but growing, preponderance of the male household throughout the community. This mixture of marriage institutions, as well as the correlative mixture of ambiguity of property institutions associated with it in the Germanic culture, seems most easily explicable as being due to the mingling of two distinct racial stocks, whose institutions differed in these respects. The race or tribe which had the maternal household and common property would probably have been the more numerous and the more peaceable at the time the mixing process began, and would fall into some degree of subjection to its more warlike consort race.

No attempt is hereby made to account for the various forms of human marriage or to show how the institution varies in detail from place to place and from time to time, but only to indicate what seems to have been the range of motives and of exigencies that have given rise to the paternal household, as it has been handed down from the barbarian past of the peoples of the western culture. To this end, nothing but the most general features of the life history of the institution have been touched upon, and even the evidence on which this much of generalization is based is, perforce, omitted. The purpose of the argument is to point out that there is a close connection, particularly in point of psychological derivation, between individual ownership, the system of status, and paternal household, as they appear in this culture.

This view of the derivation of private property and of the male household, as already suggested, does not imply the prior existence of a maternal household of the kind in which the woman is the head and master of a household group and exercises a discretionary control over her husband or husbands and over the household effects. Still less does it imply a prior state of promiscuity. What is implied by the hypothesis and by the scant evidence at hand is rather the form of the marriage relation above characterized as the household of the unattached woman. The characteristic feature of this marriage seems to have been an absence of coercion or control in the relation between the sexes. The union (probably monogamic and more or less enduring) seems to have been terminable at will by either party, under the constraint of some slight conventional limitations. The substantial difference introduced into the marriage relation on the adoption of ownership-marriage is the exercise of coercion by the man and the loss on the part of the woman of the power to terminate the relation at will. Evidence running in this direction, and in part hitherto unpublished, is to be found both in the modern and in the earlier culture of Germanic communities.

It is only in cases where circumstances have, in an exceptional degree, favored the development of ownership-marriage that we should expect to find the institution worked out to its logical consequences. Wherever the predatory phase of social life has not come in early and has not prevailed in unqualified form for a long time, or wherever a social group or race with this form of the household has received a strong admixture of another race not possessed of the institution, there the prevalent form of marriage should show something of a departure from this paternal type. And even where neither of these two conditions is present, this type of the marriage relation might be expected in the course of time to break down with the change of circumstances, since it is an institution that has grown up as a detail of a system of status, and, therefore, presumably fits into such a social system, but does not fit into a system of a different kind. It is at present visibly breaking down in modern civilised communities, apparently because it is at variance with the most ancient habits of thought of the race, as well as with the exigencies of a peaceful, industrial mode of life. There may seem some ground for holding that the same reassertion of ancient habits of thought which is now apparently at work to disintegrate the institution of ownership-marriage may be expected also to work a disintegration of the correlative institution of private property; but that is perhaps a question of speculative curiosity rather than of urgent theoretical interest.

9

The Economic Theory of Women's Dress

In human apparel the element of dress is readily distinguishable from that of clothing. The two functions — of dress and of clothing the person — are to a great extent subserved by the same material goods, although the extent to which the same material serves both purposes will appear very much slighter on second thought than it does at first glance. A differentiation of materials has long been going on, by virtue of which many things that are worn for the one purpose no longer serve, and are no longer expected to serve, the other. The differentiation is by no means complete. Much of human apparel is worn both for physical comfort and for dress; still more of it is worn ostensibly for both purposes. But the differentiation is already very considerable and is visibly progressing.

But, however united in the same object, however the two purposes may be served by the same material goods, the purpose of physical comport and that of a reputable appearance are not to be confounded by the meanest understanding. The elements of clothing and of dress are distinct; not only that, but they even verge on incompatibility; the purpose of either is frequently best subserved by special means which are adapted to perform only a single line of duty. It is often true, here as elsewhere, that the most efficient tool is the most highly specialised tool.

Of these two elements of apparel dress came first in order of development, and it continues to hold the primacy to this day. The element of clothing, the quality of affording comfort, was from the beginning, and to a great extent it continues to be, in some sort an afterthought.

The origin of dress is sought in the principle of adornment. This is a well-accepted fact of social evolution. But that principle furnished the point of departure for the evolution of dress rather than the norm of its development. It is true of dress, as of so much else of the apparatus of life, that its initial purpose has not remained its sole or dominant purpose throughout the course of its later growth. It may be stated broadly that adornment, in the *naïve* aesthetic sense, is a factor of relatively slight importance in modern dress.

The line of progress during the initial stage of the evolution of apparel was from the simple concept of adornment of the person by supplementary accessions from without, to the complex concept of an adornment that should render the person pleasing, or of an enviable presence, and at the same time serve to indicate the possession of other virtues than that of a well-favored person only. In this latter direction lies what was to evolve into dress. By the time dress emerged from the primitive efforts of the savage to beautify himself with gaudy additions to his person, it was already an economic factor of some importance. The change from a purely aesthetic character (ornament) to a mixture of the aesthetic and economic took place before the progress had been achieved from pigments and trinkets to what is commonly understood by apparel. Ornament is not properly an economic category, although the trinkets which serve the purpose of ornament may also do duty as an economic factor, and in so far be assimilated to dress. What constitutes dress an economic fact, properly falling within the scope of economic theory, is its function as in index of the wealth of its wearer — or, to be more precise, of its owner, for the wearer and owner are not necessarily the same person. It will hold with respect to more than one half the values currently recognised as "dress," especially that portion with which this paper is immediately concerned — women's dress — that the wearer and the owner are different persons. But while they need not be united in the same person, they must be organic members of the same economic unit; and the dress is the index of the wealth of the economic unit which the wearer represents.

Under the patriarchal organisation of society, where the social unit was the man (with his dependents), the dress of the women was an exponent of the wealth of the man whose chattels they were. In modern society, where the unit is the household, the woman's dress sets forth the wealth of the household to which she belongs. Still, even today, in spite of the nominal and somewhat celebrated demise of the patriarchal idea, there is that about the dress of women which suggests that the wearer is something in the nature of a chattel; indeed, the theory of women's dress quite plainly involves the implication that the woman is a chattel. In this respect the dress of women differs from that of men. With this exception, which is not of first-rate importance, the essential principles of woman's dress are not different from those which govern the dress of men; but even apart from this added characteristic the element of dress is to be seen in a more unhampered development in the apparel of women. A discussion of the theory of dress in general will gain in brevity and conciseness by keeping in view the concrete facts of the highest manifestation of the principles with which it has to deal, and its highest manifestation of dress is unquestionably seen in the apparel of the women of the most advanced modern communities.

The basis of the award of social rank and popular respect is the success, or more precisely the efficiency, of the social unit, as evidenced by its visible success. When efficiency eventuates in possessions, in pecuniary strength, as it eminently does in the social system of our time, the basis of the award of social consideration becomes the visible pecuniary strength of the social unit. The immediate and obvious index of pecuniary strength is the visible ability to spend, to consume unproductively; and men early learned to put in evidence their ability to spend by displaying costly goods that afford no return to their owner, either in comfort or in gain. Almost as early did a differentiation set in, whereby it became the function of woman, in a peculiar degree, to exhibit the pecuniary strength of her social unit by means of a conspicuously unproductive consumption of valuable goods.

Reputability is in the last analysis, and especially in the long run, pretty unfairly coincident with the pecuniary strength of the social unit in question. Woman, primarily, originally because she was herself a pecuniary possession, has become in a peculiar way the exponent of the pecuniary strength of her social group; and with the progress of specialisation of functions in the social organism this duty tends to devolve the more entirely upon the woman. The best, most advanced, most highly developed societies of our time have reached the point in their evolution where it has (ideally) become the great, peculiar, and almost the sole function of woman in the social system to put in evidence her economic unit's ability to pay. That is to say, woman's place (according to the ideal scheme of our social system) has come to be that of a means of conspicuously unproductive expenditure.

The admissible evidence of the woman's expensiveness has considerable range in respect of form and method, but in substance it is always the same. It may take the form of manners, breeding, and accomplishments that are, *prima facie*, impossible to acquire or maintain without such leisure as bespeaks a considerable and relatively long-continued possession of wealth. It may also express itself in a peculiar manner of life, on the same grounds and with much the same purpose. But the method in vogue always and everywhere, alone or in conjunction with other methods, is that of dress. "Dress," therefore, from the economic point of view, comes pretty near being synonymous with "display of wasteful expenditure."

The extra portion of butter, or other unguent, with which the wives of the magnates of the African interior anoint their persons, beyond what comfort requires, is a form of this kind of expenditure lying on the border between primitive personal embellishment and incipient dress. So also the brass-wire bracelets, anklets, etc., at times aggregating some thirty pounds in weight, worn by the same class of persons, as well as, to a less extent, by the male population of the same countries. So also the pelt of the arctic fur seal, which the women of civilised countries prefer to fabrics that are preferable to it in all respects but that of expense. So also the ostrich plumes and the many curious effigies of plants and animals that are dealt in by the milliners. The list is inexhaustible, for there is scarcely an article of apparel of male or female, civilised or uncivilised, that does not partake largely of this element, and very many may be said, in point of economic principle, to consist of virtually nothing else.

It is not that the wearers or the buyers of these wasteful goods desire the waste. They desire to make manifest their ability to pay. What is sought is not the *de facto* waste, but the appearance of waste. Hence there is a constant effort on the part of the consumers of these goods to obtain them at as good a bargain as may be; and hence also a constant effort on the part of the producers of these goods to lower the cost of their production, and consequently to lower the price. But as fast as the price of the goods declines to such a figure that their consumption is no longer *prima facie* evidence of a considerable ability to pay, the particular goods in question fall out of favor, and consumption is diverted to something which more adequately manifests the wearer's ability to afford wasteful consumption.

This fact, that the object sought is not the waste but the display of waste, develops into a principle of pseudo-economy in the use of material; so that it has come to be recognised as a canon of good form that apparel should not show lavish expenditure simply. The material used must be chosen so as to give evidence of the wearer's (owner's) capacity for making it go as far in the way of display as may be; otherwise it would suggest incapacity on the part of the owner, and so partially defeat the main purpose of the display. But what is more to the point is that such a mere display of crude waste would also suggest that the means of display had been acquired so recently as not to have permitted that long-continued waste of time for the effect required for mastering the most effective methods of display. It would argue recent acquisition of means; and we are still near enough to the tradition of pedigree and aristocracy of birth to make long-continued possession of means second in point of desirability only to the possession of large means. The greatness of the means possessed is manifested by the volume of display; the length of possession is, in some degree, evidenced by the manifestation of a thorough habituation to the methods of display. Evidence of a knowledge and habit of good form in dress (as in manners) is chiefly to be valued because it argues that much time has been spent in the acquisition of this accomplishment; and as the accomplishment is in no wise of direct economic value, it argues pecuniary ability to waste time and labor. Such accomplishment, therefore, when possessed in a high degree, is evidence of a life (or of more than one life) spent to no useful purpose; which, for purposes of respectability, goes as far as a very considerable unproductive consumption of goods. The offensiveness of crude taste and vulgar display in matters of dress is, in the last analysis, due to the fact that they argue the absence of ability to afford a reputable amount of waste of time and effort.

Effective use of the means at hand may, further, be taken to argue efficiency in the person making the display; and the display of efficiency, so long as it does not manifestly result in pecuniary gain or increased personal comfort, is a great social desideratum. Hence it happens that, surprising as it may seem at first glance, a principle of pseudo-economy in the use of materials has come to hold a well-secured though pretty narrowly circumscribed place in the theory of dress, as that theory expresses itself in the facts of life. This principle, acting in concert with certain other requirements of dress, produces some curious and otherwise inexplicable results, which will be spoken of in their place.

The first principle of dress, therefore, is conspicuous expensiveness. As a corollary under this principle, but of such magnificent scope and consequence as to claim rank as a second fundamental principle, there is the evidence of expenditure afforded by a constant supersession of one wasteful garment or trinket by a new one. This principle inculcates the desirability, amounting to a necessity wherever circumstances allow, of wearing nothing that is out of date. In the most advanced communities of our time, and so far as concerns the highest manifestations of dress — e.g., in ball dress and apparel worn on similar ceremonial occasions, when the canons of dress rule unhampered by extraneous considerations — this principle expresses itself in the maxim that no outer garment may be worn more than once.

This requirement of novelty is the underlying principle of the whole of the difficult and interesting domain of fashion. Fashion does not demand continual flux and change simply because that way of doing is foolish; flux and change and novelty are demanded by the central principle of all dress — conspicuous waste.

This principle of novelty, acting in concert with the motive of pseudo-economy already spoken of, is answerable for that system of shams that figures so largely, openly and aboveboard, in the accepted code of dress. The motive of economy, or effective use of material, furnishes the point of departure, and, this being given, the requirement of novelty acts to develop a complex and extensive system of pretenses, ever varying and transient in point of detail, but each imperative during its allotted time — facings, edgings, and the many (pseudo) deceptive contrivances that will occur to any one that is at all familiar with the technique of dress. This pretense of deception is often developed into a pathetic, childlike make-believe. The realities which it simulates, or rather symbolises, could not be tolerated. They would be in some cases too crudely expensive, in others inexpensive and more nearly adapted to minister to personal comport than to visible expense; and either alternative is obnoxious to the canons of good form.

But apart from the exhibition of pecuniary strength afforded by an aggressive wasteful expenditure, the same purpose may also be served by conspicuous abstention from useful effort. The woman is, by virtue of the specialisation of social functions, the exponent of the economic unit's pecuniary strength, and it consequently also devolves on her to exhibit the unit's capacity to endure this passive form of pecuniary damage. She can do this by putting in evidence the fact (often a fiction) that she leads a useless life. Dress is her chief means of doing so. The ideal of dress, on this head, is to demonstrate to all observers, and to compel observation of the fact, that the wearer is manifestly incapable of doing anything that is of any use. The modern civilised woman's dress attempts this demonstration of habitual idleness, and succeeds measurably.

Herein lies the secret of the persistence, in modern dress, of the skirt and of all the cumbrous and otherwise meaningless drapery which the skirt typifies. The skirt persists because it is cumbrous. It hampers the movement of the wearer and disables her, in great measure, for any useful occupation. So it serves as an advertisement (often disingenuous) that the wearer is backed by sufficient means to be able to afford the idleness, or impaired efficiency, which the skirt implies. The like is true of the high heel, and in less degree of several other features of modern dress.

Herein is also to be sought the ground of the persistence (probably not the origin) of the one great mutilation practiced by civilised occidental womankind — the constricted waist, as well as of the analogous practice of the abortive foot among their Chinese sisters. This modern mutilation of woman is perhaps not to be classed strictly under the category of dress; but it is scarcely possible to draw the line so as to exclude it from the theory, and it is so closely coincident with that category in point of principle that an outline of the theory would be incomplete without reference to it.

A corollary of some significance follows from this general principle. The fact that voluntarily accepted physical incapacity argues the possession of wealth practically establishes the futility of any attempted reform of woman's dress in the direction of convenience, comfort, or health. It is of the essence of dress that it should (appear to) hamper, incommode, and injure the wearer, for in so doing it proclaims their wearer's pecuniary ability to endure idleness and physical incapacity.

It may be noted, by the way, that this requirement, that women must appear to be idle in order to be respectable, is an unfortunate circumstance for women who are compelled to provide their own livelihood. They have to supply not only the means of living, but also the means of advertising the fiction that they live without any gainful occupation; and they have to do all this while encumbered with garments specially designed to hamper their movements and decrease their industrial efficiency.

The cardinal principles of the theory of woman's dress, then, are these three:

1 Expensiveness: Considered with respect to its effectiveness as clothing, apparel must be uneconomical. It must afford evidence of the ability of the wearer's economic group to pay for things that are in themselves of no use to any one concerned — to pay without getting an equivalent in comfort or in gain. From this principle there is no exception.
2 Novelty: Woman's apparel must afford *prima facie* evidence of having been worn but for a relatively short time, as well as, with respect to many articles, evidence of inability to withstand any appreciable amount of wear. Exceptions from this rule are such things as are of sufficient permanence to become heirlooms, and of such surpassing expensiveness as normally to be possessed only by persons of superior (pecuniary) rank. The possession of an heirloom is to be commended because it argues the practice of waste through more than one generation.
3 Ineptitude: it must afford *prima facie* evidence of incapacitating the wearer for any gainful occupation; and it should also make it apparent that she is permanently unfit for any useful effort, even after the restraint of the apparel is removed. From this rule there is no exception.

Besides these three, the principle of adornment, in the aesthetic sense, plays some part in dress. It has a certain degree of economic importance, and applies with a good deal of generality; but it is by no means imperatively present, and when it is present its application is closely circumscribed by the three principles already laid down. Indeed, the office of the principle of adornment in dress is that of handmaid to the principle of novelty, rather than that of an independent or co-ordinate factor. There are, further, minor principles that may or may not be present, some of which are derivatives of the great central requisite of conspicuous waste; others are of alien origin, but all are none the less subject to the controlling presence of the three cardinal principles enumerated above. These three are essential and constitute the substantial norm of woman's dress, and no exigency can permanently set them aside so long as the chance of rivalry between persons in respect of wealth remains. Given the possibility of a difference in wealth, and the sway of this norm of dress is inevitable. Some spasm of sense, or sentiment, or what not, may from time to time create a temporary and local diversion in woman's apparel; but the great norm of "conspicuous waste" cannot be set aside or appreciably qualified so long as this its economic ground remains.

To single out an example of the temporary effect of a given drift of sentiment, there has, within the past few years, come, and very nearly gone, a recrudescence of the element of physical comfort of the wearer, as one of the usual requirements of good form in dress. The meaning of this proposition, of course, is not what appears on its face; that seldom happens in matters of dress. It was the show of personal comfort that was lately imperative, and the show was often attained only at the sacrifice of the substance. This development, by the way, seems to have been due to a ramification of the sentimental athleticism (flesh-worship) that has been dominant of late; and now that the crest of this wave of sentiment has passed, this alien motive in dress is also receding.

The theory of which an outline has now been given is claimed to apply in full force only to modern woman's dress. It is obvious that, if the principles arrived at are to be applied as all-deciding criteria, "woman's dress" will include the apparel of a large class of persons who, in the crude biological sense, are men. This feature does not act to invalidate the theory. A classification for the purpose of economic theory must be made on economic grounds alone, and cannot permit considerations whose validity does not extend beyond the narrower domain of the natural sciences to mar its symmetry so far as to exclude this genial volunteer contingent from the ranks of womankind.

There is also a second, very analogous class of persons, whose apparel likewise, though to a less degree, conforms to the canons of woman's dress. This class is made up of the children of civilised society. The children, with some slight reservation of course, are, for the purpose of the theory, to be regarded as ancillary material serving to round out the great function of civilised womankind as the conspicuous consumers of goods. The child in the hands of civilised woman is an accessory organ of conspicuous consumption, much as any tool in the hands of a laborer is an accessory organ of productive efficiency.

Note

i Reprinted From *Popular Science Monthly*, Vol. XLVI, November, 1894.

10

Dementia Praecox

It is evident now, beyond cavil, that no part of Europe is better off for America's having taken part in the great war. So also it is evident that the Americans are all the worse off for it. Europe is balancing along the margin of bankruptcy, famine, and pestilence, while America has gone into moral and industrial eclipse. This state of things, in both cases, is traceable directly to America's having taken part in the war, whatever may have been the ulterior determining circumstances that brought European politics to a boil in 1914.

As regards the state of Europe, the immediate effect of American intervention was to bring the war to an inconclusive settlement; to conclude hostilities before they were finished and thereby reinstate the status quo ante out of which the war has arisen; to save the Junkers from conclusive defeat. There is every reason to believe that in the absence of American intervention the hostilities would have been continued until the German nation had been exhausted and the German forces had been broken and pushed back across their frontiers and across their own territory; which would have demoralised and discredited the rule of privilege and property in the Fatherland to such effect that the control of affairs would have passed out of the hands of the kept classes. The outcome should then have been an effectual liquidation of the old order and the installation of something like an industrial democracy resting on other ground than privilege and property, instead of the camouflage of a pro forma liquidation in 1918—19 and the resulting pseudo-republic of the Ebert Government. Noske could not have functioned and the Junkers would not have been war-heroes. It was the apprehension of some such eventuality that brought out the Lansdowne letters, which served warning on the kept classes of the Entente and prepared the way for an inconclusive peace — a compact to preserve the elements of dissension, the vested interests and national ambitions out of which the war arose.

There can be no grounded surmise as to what might have been the ulterior fortunes of any conceivable revolutionary establishments that so might have been set up in the German lands on some other basis than vested interests and national ambition; but it may at least be confidently believed that no such foot-loose establishment or group of establishments could have constituted a warlike menace to the rest of Europe, or even a practicable war-bogy. The outcome would presumably have been a serious peaceful menace to absentee ownership and imperial politics, throughout Christendom, but assuredly not a menace of war — Germany would have ceased to be a Power, in the usual minatory sense of the term. And when Germany, with Austria, had fallen out of line as a Power, the rest of the line of Powers would be in a precarious case for want of something formidable to lean against. A practicable Power has to rest its case on a nerve-shattering popular fear of aggression from without.

The American intervention saved the life of the German Empire as a disturber of the peace, by saving the German forces from conclusive defeat, and so saving the rule of the kept classes in Germany. It will be said, of course, by vainglorious Americans and by obsequious politicians of the Entente, that America's entrance into the war decided the case against the Central Powers; which is a sufficiently idle piece of stage-bravery. So also the German war-lords cover their shame with the claim that America turned their assured victory to defeat; but the reason for that claim is the need of it. When the whole adventure is seen in perspective it is evident that the defeat of the Germans was decided at the battle of the Marne in 1914, and the rest of the conflict was a desperate fight for negotiable terms on which the German war-lords hoped to save their face at home; and America's intervention has helped them save the remnants of their face.

If Imperial Germany had dropped out of the running, as a practicable war-Power, at the same time that Imperial Russia had gone into collapse, the French Government would have had no practicable war-scare at hand with which to frighten the French people into a policy of increased armament. On the same grounds coercion and submission would have ceased to characterise the administration of their internal affairs; the existing Government of French profiteers would have lost control; and expenditures would have been covered in part by taxes on income and capital, instead of the present deficit-financiering and constantly increasing debt. France would have returned to a peace-footing. At the same time the prosecution of hostilities through the winter of 1918—19 would have carried the exhaustion of French resources and the inflation of French indebtedness to such a point as to ensure a drastic and speedy liquidation of their fiscal and commercial affairs.

It will be said, of course, that the American intervention hastened the return of peace and thereby saved much property and very many lives of men, women, and children that would otherwise have been wasted in hostilities carried on to no effect for another four or five months; all of which is not reasonably to be questioned. But it is also not reasonably to be questioned that the past three or four years of dissension, disorder, privation, and disease that have been brought on by the precipitate conclusion of hostilities, have taken twice as heavy a toll in wasted time and substance and in wasted lives — not counting the debauch of waste and confusion which their unselfish participation in the war has brought upon the Americans.

Assuredly, none of these untoward consequences was aimed at or contemplated by the Administration when it shifted from a footing of quasi-neutrality to formal hostilities in 1917. Still less was anything of the kind contemplated in that run of popular sentiment that came to the support of the Administration in its declaration of war. So far as the case can be covered with any general formula, America entered the war "to make the world safe for democracy." If it is only that, instead of what was aimed at, the untoward state of things described above has followed in the chain of consequence. The motives of the Americans in the case are not to be impugned. They were as nearly blameless as might reasonably be expected under the circumstances. It is only that the unintended and unforeseen ulterior outcome of the adventure has now, after the event, shown that America's participation in the war was a highly deplorable mistake. In so far, this unhappy turn of events has gone to vindicate the protests of the pacifists and the conscientious objectors. Their arguments may have been unsound, and the conscientious objectors have at least found themselves on the wrong side of the law, and their motives may have been unworthy as often as not. There is no call to argue the legalities or the moralities of the case in this connection. It is only that now, after the event, it has unhappily become evident that the course of public policy against which they contended — perhaps unworthily — was not the wiser course to pursue. Their morals may have been bad and their manners worse, and the courts have decided, with great spontaneity, that their aim was criminal in high degree, and popular sentiment has borne out the sentiment of the courts in this matter, on the whole and for the time being. Yet the turn of events has, unhappily, gone to show that, barring the statutory infirmities of their case, these statutory criminals were in effect contending for the wiser course. And for so having, in some wrongheaded ways, spoken for a wiser course of action than that adopted by the constituted authorities, these statutory criminals have been and continue to be subjected to cruel and unusual punishment. All of which invites reflection on the vagaries of dementia praecox.

The current situation in America is by way of being something of a psychiatrical clinic. In order to come to an understanding of this situation there is doubtless much else to be taken into account, but the case of America is after all not fairly to be understood without making due allowance for a certain prevalent unbalance and derangement of mentality, presumably transient but sufficiently grave for the time being. Perhaps the commonest and plainest evidence of this unbalanced mentality is to be seen in a certain fearsome and feverish credulity with which a large proportion of the Americans are effected. As contrasted with their state of mind before the war, they are predisposed to believe in footless outrages and odious plots and machinations — "treasons, stratagems, and spoils." They are readily provoked to a headlong intolerance, and resort to unadvised atrocities as a defense against imaginary evils. There is advisable lack of composure and logical coherence, both in what they will believe and in what they are ready to do about it.

Throughout recent times the advance of exact knowledge in the material sciences has been progressively supplanting the received barbarian beliefs in magical and supernatural agencies. This progressive substitution of matter-of-fact in the place of superstition has gone forward unremittingly and at a constantly accelerated rate, being the most characteristic and most constructive factor engaged in modern civilisation. But during the past six or eight years, since the outbreak of the war, and even more plainly since its conclusion, the churches, high and low, have been gaining both in numbers and in revenues, as well as in pontifical unction. The logical faculty appears to have suffered a notable degree of prostration throughout the American community; and all the while it is the more puerile crudities of superstitious fear that have been making particular and inordinate gains. So, for example, it is since the outbreak of the war that the Rev. Billy Sunday has effectively come into his own, and it is since the peace that he has become such a power of obscurity as to command a price as an agency of intimidation and misrule. So also it is during these last few years of the same period of nervous prostration that the Fundamentalists are effectually making headway in their campaign of obscuration designed to reinstate the Fear of God in place of common-sense. Driven by a nerve-shattering fear that some climax of ghostly atrocities is about to be visited on all persons who are found lacking in bigotry, this grosser sort of devout innocents now impugn certain findings of material science on the ground that these findings are presumed to be distasteful to a certain well-known anthropomorphic divinity, to whom His publicity-agents impute a sadistic temper and an unlimited power of abuse. These evidences of a dilapidated mentality are growing more and more obvious. Meantime even a man of such signal good sense and humanity as Mr. Bryan is joining forces with the Rev. Billy Sunday in the propaganda of intolerance, while the gifts of so engaging a raconteur as Sir Conan Doyle are brought in to cover the flanks of this drive into intellectual twilight.

It may be said, of course, that such-like maggoty conceits are native to the religious fancy and are due to come into the foreground in all times of trouble; but just now the same fearsome credulity is running free and large through secular affairs as well, and its working-out is no more edifying in that department of human conduct. At the date when America formally entered the war, American popular sentiment had already been exposed to a protracted stress of apprehension and perplexity and was ready for alarms and excursions into intolerance. All manner of extravagant rumors met with ready belief, and, indeed, few were able to credit anything that was not extravagant. It was a period dominated by illusions of frightfulness and persecution. It was the peculiar misfortune of the American people that they were called into action only after their mental poise had been shattered by a long run of enervating perplexity and agitation. The measures taken under these circumstances were drawn on such lines of suspicion and intolerance as might be looked for under these circumstances. Differences of opinion were erected into statutory crimes, to which extravagant penalties were attached. Persons charged with these new-found statutory crimes were then convicted on a margin of legal interpretation. In effect, suspected persons were held guilty until proved innocent, with the doubt weighing against them. In one of these episodes of statutory frightfulness, that of the far-famed "Lusk Committee," some ten thousand persons were arrested on ungrounded suspicions, with extensive destruction of papers and property. The foreign-language press was laid under disabilities and the use of the mails was interrupted on general grounds of hysterical consternation. On the same grounds circulation and credence were given to extravagantly impossible fictions of Bolshevik propaganda, and the I.W.W. were by interpretation erected into a menace to the Republic, while the Secret Service kept faithfully on the job of making two suspicions grow where one grew before. Under cover of it all the American profiteers have diligently gone about their business of getting something for nothing at the cost of all concerned, while popular attention has been taken up with the maudlin duties of civil and religious intolerance.

The Republic has come through this era of spiritual dilapidation with an unbalanced budget and an increased armament by use of which to "safeguard American Interests" — that is to say, negotiate profitable concessions for American oil companies — a system of passports, deportations, and restricted immigration, and a Legion of veterans organised for a draft on the public funds and the cultivation of warlike distemper. Unreflecting patriotic flurry has become a civic virtue. Drill in patriotic — that is to say military — ritual has been incorporated in the ordinary routine of the public schools, and it has come to be obligatory to stand uncovered through any rendition of the "National Anthem" — a musical composition of which one could scarcely say that it might have been worse. The State constabularies have been augmented; the right of popular assembly freely interfered with; establishment of mercenary "gunmen," under the formal name of detective-agencies, have increased their output; the Ku-Klux-Klan has been reanimated and reorganised for extra-legal intimidation of citizens; and the American Legion now and again enforces "law and order" on the unfortunate by extra-legal measures. Meantime the profiteers do business as usual and the Federal authorities are busied with a schedule of increased protective duties designed to enhance the profits of their business.

Those traits in this current situation wherein it is different from the relatively sober state of things before the war, have been injected by America's participation in the war; and it is, in effect, for their failure to join hands and help in working up this state of things that the conscientious objectors, draft-evaders, I.W.W.'s, Communists, have been penalised in a manner unexampled in American history. This is not saying that the pacifists, conscientious objectors, etc., are not statutory criminals or that they foresaw such an outcome of the traffic against which they protested, or that they were moved by peculiarly high-minded or unselfish considerations in making their protest; but only that the subsequent course of events has unhappily brought out the fact that these distasteful persons took a stand for the sounder side of a debatable question. Except for the continued prevalence of a distempered mentality that still runs on illusions of persecution, it might reasonably have been expected that this sort of *de facto* vindication of the stand taken by these statutory criminals would be allowed to count in extenuation of their *de jure* fault. But the distemper still runs its course. Indeed, it is doubtless the largest, profoundest, and most enduring effect brought upon the Americans by America's intervention in the great war.

Typically and commonly, dementia praecox is a distemper of adolescence or of early manhood, at least such appears to be the presumption held among psychiatrists. Yet its occurrence is not confined within any assignable age-limits. Typically, if not altogether commonly, it takes the shape of a dementia praecox, an illusion of persecution and a derangement of the logical faculty such as to predispose the patient to the belief that he and his folks are victims of plots and systematic atrocities. A fearsome credulity is perhaps the most outstanding symptom, and this credulity may work out in a fear of atrocities to be suffered in the next world or in the present; that is to say a fear of God or of evil men. Prolonged or excessive worry appears to be the most usual predisposing cause. Expert opinions differ as to how far the malady is to be reckoned as a curable disease; the standard treatment being rest, security, and nutrition. The physiological ground of such a failure of mentality appears to be exhaustion and consequent deterioration of nerve-tissue, due to shock or prolonged strain; and recuperation is notoriously slow in the case of nerve-tissue.

No age, sex, or condition is immune, but dementia praecox will affect adolescents more frequently than mature persons, and men more frequently than women; at least so it is said. Adolescent males are peculiarly subject to this malady, apparently because they are — under modern circumstances — in a peculiar degree exposed to worry, dissipation, and consequent nervous exhaustion. The cares and unfamiliar responsibilities of manhood fall upon them at that period, and under modern circumstances these cares and responsibilities are notably exacting, complex, and uncertain. Given a situation of widespread apprehension, uncertainty, and agitation, such as the war-experience brought on the Americans, and the consequent derangement of mentality should be of a similarly widespread character — such as has come in evidence.

The peculiar liability of the adolescent male carries the open suggestion that a similar degree of liability should also extend to those males of more advanced years in whom a puerile mentality persists, men in whom a boyish temper continues into later life. These boyish traits may be seen in admirably systematised fashion in such organisations as the Boy Scouts. Much the same range of characteristics marks the doings and aspirations, individual and collective, of high-school boys, undergraduate students, and organisations of the type of the Y.M.C.A. In this connection it would perhaps be ungraceful to direct attention to the clergy of all denominations, where self-selection has resulted in a concentration on the lower range of the intellectual spectrum. One is also not unprepared to find a sensible infusion of the same puerile traits among military men. A certain truculent temper is conspicuous among the stigmata. Persons in whom the traits and limitations of the puerile mentality persist in a particularly notable degree are called "morons," but there are also many persons who approximate more or less closely to the moronic grade of mentality without being fully entitled to the technical designation.

11

Manufacture and Salesmanship

Loosely, the organisation-table of industry falls into three main branches or divisions: the Key Industries; manufacturers; and Farming; [...]. These lines of division are not sharp and clear; the running contact and interdependence between these divisions being close and critical, [...]. But such a three-fold division is after all, effectual, and it is readily to be seen in the large. So also, the network of business organisation and management runs into three similar divisions, although in the organisation of business the lines of cleavage are even less clear and less fixed.

Of these three divisions, the Key Industries stand at the apex of the industrial system and control the issues of industrial life for the rest. The control which is exercised in this way at the apex is exercised not for the benefit of industry at large but for the profit of the owners (and management) of the key industries, as has also appeared already. The manufacturers — continuation industries — and their management stand in a relation to the rest of the community which is analogous to that in which the key industries stand to the rest of the industrial system; but with the difference that the management of these continuation industries have only a vicarious or delegated power, in that their initiative and discretion are bounded by the measures which may be taken independently by the management of the key industries.

Whenever and in so far as the use of mechanical ways and means is the ruling factor in the work to be done, the processes of industry are inordinately productive, as has already been explained. Therefore it is necessary for the businesslike management of these industries to observe a degree of moderation, if the market is not to be overstocked to an unprofitable extent. It is necessary to regulate the rate and volume of output with a view to profitable prices, and this will involve more or less unemployment of the available equipment and man-power, a variable margin of unemployment, a strategic withholding of productive efficiency for business ends. The Conscientious Withdrawal of Efficiency is what is had in mind here in speaking of Sabotage. The urgency of such a salutary margin of sabotage on output, as well as the ordinary width of the margin, has increased unremittingly during the past half-century, and this increasing urgency of it has been more particularly notable during the past two or three decades.

It is by this reasonable restriction of output that the management of the key industries controls the issues of life for the rest of the industrial system. So it is also by measures of the same character that the management of the manufacturing industries governs the conditions of the life for the rest of the community, in a businesslike endeavor to meet the needs of the market in a profitable way. For one reason and another the Farmers, on the other hand, are not in a position to apply such a salutary modicum of sabotage to their work and output or to regulate prices to their own liking in the same way. They are too many, too scattered, too widely varied in their work and their interests, besides being inveterately rooted in self-help and sharp practice. So that the Farmers are by way of being the residuary losers, at whose cost much of this business is carried on.

Ever since this country began to make the turn from an agricultural to an "industrial" footing, the American manufacturing industry has been producing for a closed market. The American tariff polity also took on an aggravated form about that time, and this has contributed greatly to restrict the available market to the purchasing power of the home population, at the same time that it has enabled American special interests to maintain a high level of prices for their output. The volume of this closed market has continually grown greater, with the growth of population and the use of larger resources; but the productive capacity of the manufacturing industries has also continually increased at a more rapid rate, due to the same circumstances and to the additional factor of a continually increasing efficiency in the industrial arts. Industry has continued to be "inordinately" productive, increasingly so. Therefore the urgency of a strategic limitation of the output has also continually increased. The various concerns that have been doing business in manufactures have been competitive sellers in a limited market whose purchasing capacity has habitually fallen short of the productive capacity of the industries which supply the marketable output. On pain of bankruptcy, therefore, it has been incumbent on these business concerns to use moderation and limit their saleable output to the needs of the market,[i] and at the same time to compete among themselves for profitable sales. Any business concern's need of sales is indefinitely extensible, while the total volume of sales at any given time is fixed within a narrow margin. Salesmanship is the art of taking over a disproportionate share of this run of sales, at a profitable price.

These business concerns are competitive sellers, but they are so circumstanced by their closed market that they can, on the whole, not underbid one another at all effectually in the price of their wares. Underbidding involves an enlarged aggregate output, which implies an enlarged market. In effect, their competitive strategy is confined to two main lines of endeavor: — to reduce the production-cost of a restricted output; and to increase their sales without lowering prices.

On the cost side of this account, again, their constant recourse has been, habitually and increasingly, to endeavor to keep production-costs down by keeping down wages.[ii] On the side of sales and salesmanship the outcome has been a continued increase of selling-costs and a continually more diligent application to salesmanship. Under both of these heads the passing years of the new century have shown a rising curve, and under both heads the ruse has been steeper since the War.

By degrees, as absentee ownership has progressively taken over the ways and means of industrial life, the relation of the workman to the work in hand has lost the personal note and has come to be the relation of a hired man to his job. By degrees also, as the workmen have progressively learned that they are transients and bystanders in whatever concerns the organisation and aims of any given industrial enterprise, they have also learned to draw together on a more or less lucidly collusive plan to make the most of their position in the impersonal employment market. The resulting organisations of workmen have been "trade unions" — that is to say they have been drawn on lines of workmanship — but they have been formed for a businesslike purpose. The avowed spirit of the thing has been the spirit of salesmanship. The unions have been organized with a view to drive a bargain, and from the outset it has been their constant aim to sell dear, and from near the outset they have also aimed to deliver a minimum. Through it all there has run the ancient bent of workmanship, to the effect that a workman has work to do as well as a job to hold. But with time and continued experience in businesslike negotiations it has by degrees been borne in upon them that as a business proposition it is the first duty of a workman to hold a job; that he has work to do is a secondary consideration.

In all bargaining, in all transactions of merchandising and price-making, the limitation of the merchantable supply is of the essence of the case. And the more single-minded and salesmanlike the parties to the transaction may be, the more diligently will they consider ways and means of limiting the supply to such a point as will most profitably enforce a scarcity value of their vendible output. In the course of time and continued attention to salesmanship, therefore, the unions and their members have been learning that, as regards the work to be done in holding their jobs, it is to be their constant concern to devise plausible ways of withholding it. In the nature of things, — that is to say in the nature of salesmanship, — the unions are organizations for the restraint of trade. It is a delicate question, hitherto not finally decided, how far they are to be accounted "conspiracies" in restraint of trade. Necessarily they are of that general complexion, being business organizations; and they have been continually taking on more of that businesslike complexion, since there can be no effectual salesmanship without some limitation on the supply of the vendible goods. The American Federation of Labor may be taken as a type. The outcome is that both parties to the negotiations in the employment market have now reached a passably unequivocal recognition of this state of things. Employers and worker, both, have come to realise that the sole decisive argument on either side is a refusal to go on. The rest of the voluminous disputation which habitually surrounds their negotiations is known to both parties to be so much verbiage designed to cloud the issue.

Hitherto this outcome has not been worked out to a finished clarity. There still remains, especially on the side of the workmen, a lingering sense of unworthiness in so putting salesmanship in the place of workmanship. The habitual position taken by the employer-owners in these disputes is fairly clear and unembarrassed, but hitherto the workmen have been unable to go all the way along these lines of salesmanlike strategy, such as to draw them together into an inclusive and massive formation driving to a common onset against a common adversary; such, e.g., as has sometimes been sketched out under the dread catchword of "One Big Union." They are still tangled in personalities, nor realising that their common adversary is a state of affairs rather than a conspiracy of sinners. And there is also still extant among them a tenacious residue of that ancient way of thinking according to which a workman should work for a living and should, in some moral sense, be able to claim a livelihood for which he is ready to work. In one way and another they are unable to see their own case in the untroubled perspective of salesmanship, in which it is to be seen that the chief end of man is to get a margin of something for nothing, at the cost of any whom it may concern. Their spiritual complexion is not yet fully commercialised, even though the great body of them may already have begun to realise that sabotage is the beginning of wisdom in industrial business. They may already believe it with their head, but they do not yet know it with their heart.

Something is also to be said in abatement on the other side, on the side of the business men who manage the industries and who hire and fire. They too are not quite clear, have not yet come into a fully objective appreciation of the facts in the case; although the remnant of handicraft tradition that sticks in their habitual thinking is not precisely to the same effect, and can scarcely be rated as a handicap. Stripped of its adventitious verbiage the position habitually taken by these substantial citizens comes to this, that in common honesty the workmen should work for a living and the owner-employers should invest for a profit; leaving the substantial citizens to decide what may be a suitable livelihood for the workmen. In substance the constituted authorities of the nation also fall into line with the substantial citizens on this head; as how should they not? Again it is a position taken on bounds of inveterate prepossession rather than objective reasoning. Neither side has yet contemplated the converse of this proposition, that the owner-employers should invest for a living and the workmen should work for a profit; leaving the workmen to fix on a suitable livelihood for the employer-owners.

The outcome of it all is simple enough. These various business concerns are competitors for a closed volume of traffic. Or more specifically, they are competitive sellers each of which necessarily endeavors to increase his net share in the available purchasing fund; the total volume of purchasing funds available at any given time being fixed within a relatively narrow margin of fluctuation. So that each of these competitive sellers can gain only at a corresponding loss to the rest. At the same time there is, by and large, no outlook for competition in this market by the method of increased output at substantially reduced prices. That expedient was tried and found wanting. The large and progressively larger net returns do not come on that footing, on the whole.[iii] That type of competition presumes an open market and a declining price level, all of which is obsolete.

The manufacturers and merchants, therefore, are engaged on a business of competitive selling in a closed market in which prices may fluctuate but cannot substantially decline; a market in which one seller's gain is another's loss.[iv] The business reduces itself to a traffic in salesmanship, running wholly on the comparative merit of the rival commodities, or rather of the rival salesmen. One result has been a very substantial and progressive increase of sales-cost; very appreciably larger than an inspection of the books would show. The producers have been giving continually more attention to the saleability of their product, so that much of what appears on the books as production-cost should properly be charged to the production of saleable appearances. The distinction between workmanship and salesmanship has progressively been blurred in this way, until it will doubtless hold true now that the shop-cost of many articles produced for the market is mainly chargeable to the production of saleable appearances, ordinarily meretricious. So, e.g., whatever its other (and undeniable) merits may be, the vogue of "package goods" is to be credited wholly to salesmanship, and its cost is chargeable in the main to that account.

The designing and promulgation of saleable containers, — that is to say such containers as will sell the contents on the merits of the visual effect of their container, — has become a large and, it is said, a lucrative branch of the business publicity. It employs a formidable number of artist and "copy writers" as well as of itinerant spokesmen, demonstrators, interpreters; and more than one psychologist of eminence has been retained by the publicity agencies for consultation and critical advice on the competitive saleability of rival containers and of the labels and doctrinal memoranda which embellish them. The cost of all this is very appreciable, but it is a necessary cost. Taking them one with another, it is presumably safe to say that the containers account for one-half the shop-cost of what are properly called "package goods," and for something approaching one-half of the price paid by the consumer. In certain lines doubtless, as, e.g., in cosmetics and household remedies, this proportion is exceeded by a very substantial margin; in these lines, indeed, the choice of suitable — that is to say saleable — containers surrounded with suitable — that is to say saleable specific natures of the contents being, on the whole, of subsidiary consequence, if any.[v] It is also the confident testimony of persons who are in a position to know, that except for line and color, shape and surface, of the containers, and apart from verbal differences in the doctrinal matter which surrounds them, any distinctive character in these various articles of intimate personal use is something very difficult to get at.[vi]

Saleable containers are only the beginning of wisdom in latter-day manufacture and merchandising. But they merit attention as being typical and illustrative of the latter-day growth of salesmanship and of the latter-day spirit of business at its homeliest and best. They are typical of the ways and means of salesmanship also in the respect that they serve a useful purpose for the consumer in the way of convenience and cleanliness at the same time that they enable the contents to be sold at an enhanced price. There is always something of such a variable fringe of substantial service attaching to the ordinary ways and means of salesmanlike publicity, whether in the way of containers or in that standard run of doctrinal pronouncements that will come to mind as the type-form of such publicity;[vii] and it is the ordinary duty of the salesman to make it appear that this outlying fringe of usefulness is the whole end and purpose of it all. One will be a competent salesman in much the same measure as one effectually "puts over" this line of make believe.

The concerns which do business in this field are competitors in a closed market. This is to say, they are competitors for a share in the available purchasing-power that comes into the market, so that the one concern gains at the other's cost. From which it follows that any device or expedient which approves itself as a practicable means of cutting into the market, on the part of any one of the competitive concerns, presently becomes a necessity to all the rest, on pain of extinction. The means of "getting ahead" is also the means of "keeping up." Any concern which neglects its opportunities and falls behind is in a way to fall out of the game.[viii] The net aggregate result is a competitive multiplication of the ways and means of salesmanship at a competitively increasing net aggregate cost. The selling-cost per unit of the goods sold rises accordingly, and the price to the consumer rises to meet the enhanced selling-cost. The rising cost of salesmanship becomes a rising overhead charge on the business, regulated by the pressure of competitive selling, but hitherto trending upwards, apparently with a gradually accelerated rise.

As is the case with other business charges and expenditures, the effectual limit on sales-costs, including whatever is to be counted in as ways and means of selling, is what the traffic will bear. But sales-costs present some slight peculiarities in this respect, being subject to certain peculiar circumstances. But use of the proper expedients — which may be taken to mean the same as saying, by judicious expenditure of sufficiently large sums — the sales of any given line of merchantable goods, or of any given concern dealing in such goods, may be increased indefinitely. This is a well-assured proposition in folk-psychology. Beyond a certain point (to be determined by experience) an increase of sales will be had only at an increasing sales-cost per unit of goods sold; and beyond a certain further point (similarly to be determined by experience) any further increase of sales will cost more than it will bring, — that is to say the selling-cost per unit will then exceed the seller's net price-margin over production-cost, which is more than the traffic will bear. A judicious expenditure on sales-cost should evidently approach this point, without passing it.

But the other sellers in the same market, whether they sell the same line of goods or other lines, are competitors for the same custom and will push their sales-enterprise on the same plan. Which puts the sellers, all and several, on the defensive against one another's salesmanship; which comes to a competitively defensive expenditure on sales-costs, of such a character that none of the competing sellers can afford to fall short in his expenditures on salesmanship, — on penalty of failure. That is to say, as a business proposition, the traffic in manufacturing the merchandising will no longer bear a scant overhead charge in the way of sales-costs; or such a charge as would once have been called a reasonable overhead on that score. The conditions imposed by a closed competitive market have taken such a turn that parsimony in the matter of sales-costs will be fatal, in the ordinary case. He who hesitates is lost. Taking one such sales-enterprise with another, what the traffic will bear appears, in effect, to run between the two points indicated above, but to rise consistently toward the higher. Judicious expenditure on salesmanship, therefore, will play between these limits, touching the higher limit more frequently than the lower; with certain consequences to be noted presently.

The experience of the last few years, since salesmanship has come unequivocally to take the first place in the business of manufacturing and merchandising, has also brought out a further peculiar circumstance which attaches to this enterprise of selling goods and services in a closed market. A large, and increasing, number of the competing lines lend themselves effectually to large-scale production in the matter of salesmanship. Judicious and continued expenditure on publicity and the like expedients of salesmanship will result in what may fairly be called a quantity-production of customers for the purchase of the goods or services in question.[ix] Experience has shown what might be expected, that the cost of production per unit of customers by the use of the later perfected methods and appliances of sales-publicity is subject to the well-known economic law of increasing returns, very much as it applies to quantity production generally, wherever machine processes are employed on an appreciably large scale.

It may be called to mind, though the fact should be familiar enough, that with the continued growth and standardisation of the business and its procedure in recent years, very much of sales-publicity has with good effect been reduced to mechanical units of space, speed, number, frequency, and the like. Much the same is true for very much of the other apparatus of salesmanship, including a reasonable proportion of the personnel. It has accordingly become practicable now to check and tally this work and its major effects in units of tangible performance. So that the fabrication of customers can now be carried on as a routine operation, quite in the spirit of the mechanical industries and with much the same degree of assurance as regards the quality, rate and volume of the output; the mechanical equipment as well as its complement of man-power employed in such production of customers being held to its work under the surveillance of technically trained persons who might fairly be called publicity engineers. Such technicians are now diligently bred and trained for this use by all the reputable seminaries of learning.[x]

It is familiarly known to economists that up to a certain, fluctuating but effectual, limit an increasing volume of output may be turned out by methods of quantity production at a decreasing cost per unit. This law of increasing returns, or decreasing cost, will apply in the production to customers by large-scale publicity very much as in the large-scale mechanical industry generally. In the business of sales-publicity this upper limit of increasing returns is relatively high. So that up to a fairly high limit the aggregate sales-costs on a larger volume of sales will be progressively more reasonable, relatively to the net aggregate returns from the sales. The rule does not apply throughout or uniformly, but it applies rather widely and in an increasing number of lines, particularly among the staple lines of merchandise. It follows that within the application of the rule the larger selling-concerns, with larger funds and expenditures, will have something of an advantage over concerns of a smaller and middling size.

It should and appears to follow that so far as this rule of quantity-production applies, the larger advertisers among these competing concerns will tend to displace those of a smaller and middling size. The latter will drop out of the running, inconspicuously. This traffic in publicity and customers runs within a closed market, as has already been remarked, and it feeds on a loosely fixed aggregate volume of purchasing-power; so that at any given time, whatever increase of custom is gained by any given selling-concern will be lost by others, and whatever custom is shifted by publicity to any given commodity (e.g., yeast-cakes) is thereby shifted away from another or others (e.g., soap-powders).[xi] Hitherto the rule appears to hold good, on the whole, that the large selling concerns and the large adventures in publicity are gaining at the expense of the smaller ones and are displacing the latter, particularly those of a middling size. The rule is by no means hard and fast, no more so here than in the industrial use of quantity-production. And it is also noticeable that the growth of these lager absentee selling concerns is not greatly reducing the number of those small-scale concerns that continue to do business on a footing of intimate personal attention to their customers, and that carry their point by word and gesture. What may be called "hand tooling" still holds its place in the field of salesmanship. Very much as is the case in productive industry, where many minor and intimate trades and crafts still find a living in the crevices of the industrial system, so here also.

In this market virtually all sellers (manufacturers and merchants) are competitors of virtually all other sellers, irrespective, on the whole, of the diversity of goods offered for sale. The total offering of goods for sale takes up the total volume of available purchasing-power.[xii] But not all kinds and classes of merchantable goods lend themselves equally to propaganda by methods of the large-scale absentee salesmanship. The quantity-production of customers if visibly more applicable in some lines than in others. The experience of the past few years teaches, on the whole, that articles of intimate personal use and articles of conspicuous personal use lend themselves in some peculiar degree to this manner of propaganda. The volume of publicity devoted to the sale of such articles, as well as the resulting increased volume of sales, argues quite unequivocally to that effect. These articles and their consumption bear, or are plausibly alleged to bear, in a felicitous way on the personal well-being or the personal prestige of the consumer; and customers appear to be peculiarly open to argument and persuasion on these heads.[xiii]

As has already been remarked, the quantity-production of customers by appliances of publicity is a craft which runs on applied psychology. The raw material in which the work is to be done is human credulity, and the output aimed at is profitable fixed ideas. Current experience in publicity appears to show that among the human sensibilities upon which a sagacious salesmanship will spend its endeavors the most fruitful are Fear and Shame. Human credulity appears to be peculiarly tractable under the pressure of a well conceived appeal to fear and shame, and to set into obstinate and extraordinary shapes (action patterns) on relatively slight habituation along these lines. The fear and shame on which the sales-publicity[xiv] proceeds in its work of turning credulous persons into profitable customers are the fear of mortal disease and the fear of losing prestige. It is not easy, nor perhaps is it worth while, to attempt any hard and fast distinction between the sense of shame and the fear of losing prestige; at least in this connection and for the present argument. These are ubiquitous traits of the race. The former rises, apparently, to a gradually advancing pitch of sensibility (and credulity) with advancing age; while the latter, the solicitude for instant personal prestige, counts for more in the period of adolescence and early maturity.[xv] So the publicity agents of the sovereign remedies "throw a scare into" the old generation, while the salesmen of the proprietary beautifiers are in the nature of "pacifiers." Between them they account for a very large and lucrative volume of absentee salesmanship, as well as a large aggregate of sales-costs, and a large diversion of custom from other lines of expenditures. The intrinsic merits of this traffic in fear and credulity will call for no reflections.

Salesmanship which has to do with merchandising follows two main lines: publicity (advertising), and personal bargaining.[xvi] Of the two, quantity-production of publicity has been gaining over the personal bargain ever since the business of selling began its advance to the larger scale. Publicity is absentee salesmanship, and fits into the run of things along with absentee ownership. It is as an expedient of merchandising in absentia that publicity has fully come into its own.[xvii] But while sales-publicity has been gaining ground, it is doubtful if personal bargaining has lost ground, even relatively to the increased volume of sales. What is not doubtful is that between them the two account for a larger employment of manpower and a larger consumption of materials than ever before, whether counted in absolute figures or relatively to the aggregate volume of goods sold. In other words more time, effort, and equipment — per unit of merchandise — goes into salesmanship, now than in the past; the sales-cost per unit is larger now, whether the unit be counted in terms of price or by weight and tale.

The cause of this advancing sales-cost is quite simple: — production-cost by modern industrial methods being less, the margin which can be taken up in sales-cost is more. In the nature of things sales-cost will rise to the maximum which the traffic will bear. If the net returns to any or all of the sellers who are already in the market should rise to any figure that can be called inordinate, one or another of two alternatives will follow. The sellers already in the market will competitively push their sales-cost, their expenditures on publicity and bargainers, to such a figure as to leave no inordinate returns; or new sellers will see their chance to come in for a profit and so will cut into the volume of sales and the margin of returns.

Both methods are in constant operation. Just now their action is masked and in some degree held in abeyance, in that the situation is undergoing a somewhat sweeping change. The large-scale publicity has made good as a profitable enterprise, and the large-scale competitors have not yet begun that closer-shorn and truceless competition among themselves for dominant control of the market, which is presumably coming to a head in due time. It is all contained in the workday premises of absentee ownership and absentee salesmanship. For the time being, the pioneers in this large sales-publicity are enjoying the fruits of their businesslike initiative, in the way of generous net returns; particularly the very large ones among them, who are having things very much their own way; which means low shop-costs, ample sales-costs, high selling-prices, and lucrative margins, with large aggregate net returns. But very much as is true in the mechanical industry, so also in this large-scale mechanical publicity, what one concern with ample funds can do another concern with funds of the same amplitude in the same or another line of merchandising can do as well, just so soon as the pioneers have sufficiently proved the case. The pioneers — the current sellers of soap-powders, yeast-cakes, rubber heels, motor cars, "cost-plus" clothing for young men, and the like — are due presently to be overtaken, and their easy market cut into by others who are ready to do just as well, with the result that sales-costs by this method will rise to the maximum which the traffic will bear, leaving no more than ordinary returns on the investment. The net result in the end should be a further increase of the prices paid by consumers and a further growth of advertising agencies and their business.

The number of concerns and the aggregate capital and personnel engaged in the business of sales-publicity is already very considerable, and the growth in all these respects, as well as in the volume of the business hitherto, goes on unchecked, with a very promising outlook for continued growth at an accelerated rate in the near future.[xviii] The growth of this business, and the growing necessity of it as a means of competitive selling, have been particularly notable during the past dozen years; and at the same time it has undergone an extensive standardisation and specialisation, by which the work has come to be effectually subdivided and apportioned among the personnel within each concern at the same time that the field of publicity has been divided among the several concerns, according to locality and according to the nature of the work, particularly according to the ways and means employed, as, e.g., between news-print and "outdoor advertising."[xix]

News-print publicity, as the use of printed matter in circulation may conveniently be called, is doubtless the largest "medium" employed for the making of sales; as it is also the most familiar and habitual, as well as the most costly in the aggregate, whether cost be counted in terms of the work and material consumed, in the price paid for it by the advertisers, or in what it adds to the prices paid for goods by the consumers. It will include primarily advertising matter in newspapers and periodicals, but it includes also circulars, circular letters, and leaflets distributed by mail or by hand, and there is also to be counted in virtually all of the very considerable and constantly increasing number of trade periodicals devoted to special lines of the manufacturing and merchandising business, as well as the pages of trade-news and business information carried by the common run of papers, dailies, weeklies and others. On a deliberate estimate based on such data as are readily available it appears that advertising matter of the standard forms will account for something like one-half of the space occupied by printed matter in newspapers, including weeklies, rather under than over, and something appreciably less than one-half of the printed space in magazines, taking them one with another. If to this total of what would be listed as advertising space proper be added the trade-news, fashion, and financial columns, of the newspapers and the papers and magazines that are wholly or chiefly occupied with the interests of salesmanship, the total will rise appreciably over one-half the printed matter that goes into circulation the way of newspapers and magazines. In point of expense the aggregate which is so devoted to sales-publicity doubtless runs very appreciably over one-half of the total of printed matter; advertising matter, financial news, and business comment and review being on the whole the most costly reading matter that goes to the make-up of a newspaper, both in the production of its "copy" and in the typographical composition and press work.[xx]

The two major division of sales-advertising are "News-Print," and "Outdoor" Advertising.[xxi] But there are also many and various minor devices employed in the service of absentee salesmanship, which between them make up a sufficiently formidable total. They comprise, e.g., such things as show-windows,[xxii] indoor display of wares, decorative interiors, posters and personnel, trade marks, "slogans," demonstrators, decorative and doctrinal containers.

None of these ways and means are new, in principle, though some of them, as, e.g., the "spectacular" outdoor signs, are as new in detail as the mechanical devices which they turn to account. Nor is their use confined to what would be precisely called sales-publicity. Yet in all the use of these things there is this much in common, that they are employed competitively in an endeavour to draw on the sympathies and the substance of the underlying population; they are useful as a means by which those who make use of them come in for a competitive share in the usufruct of the underlying population, its services, workmanship, and material output. They have all been turned to account, early and late, in such enterprises as public loans, recruiting campaigns for army and navy, electioneering recruiting campaigns, campaigns for contributions to charities, relief, and such demi-military enterprises as the Red Cross; and most notably of all for the Propaganda of the Faith.

Writers who discuss these matters have not directed attention to the Propaganda of the Faith as an object-lesson in sales-publicity, its theory and practice, its ways and means, its benefits and its possibilities of gain.

Yet it is altogether the most notable enterprise of the kind. The Propaganda of the Faith is quite the largest, oldest, most magnificent, most unabashed, and most lucrative enterprise in sales-publicity in all Christendom. Much is to be learned from it as regards media and suitable methods of approach, as well as true perseverance, tact, and effrontery. By contrast, the many secular adventures in salesmanship are no better than upstarts, raw recruits, late and slender capitalisations out of the ample fund of human credulity. It is only quite recently, and even yet only with a dawning realisation of what may be achieved by consummate effrontery in the long run, that these others are beginning to take on anything like the same air of stately benevolence and menacing solemnity. No pronouncement on rubber-heels, soap-powders, lipsticks, or yeast-cakes, not even Sapphira Buncombe's Vegetative Compound, are yet able to ignore material facts with the same magisterial detachment, and none has yet commanded the same unreasoning assent or acclamation. No others have achieved that pitch of unabated assurance which has enabled the publicity-agents of the Faith to debar human reason from scrutinizing their pronouncements. These others are doing well enough, no doubt; perhaps as well as might reasonably be expected under the circumstances, but they are a feeble thing in comparison. Saul has slain his thousands, perhaps, but David has slain his tens of thousands.

There is, of course, no occasion of levity in so calling to mind these highly significant works of human infatuation, past and current. Nor should it cast any shadow of profanation on any of the sacred verities when it is so called to mind that, when all is said, they, too, rest after all on the same ubiquitously human ground of unreasoning fear, aspiration, and credulity, as do the familiar soap-powders, yeast-cakes, lip-sticks, rubber tires, chewing-gum, and restoratives of lost manhood, whose profitable efficacy is likewise created and kept in repair by a well-advised sales-publicity. Indeed, it should rather seem the other way about. That the same principles of sales-publicity are found good and profitable for the traffic in spiritual amenities and in these material comforts should serve to show how deep and pervasively the scheme of deliverance and rehabilitation is rooted in the merciful gift of credulous infatuation. It should redound to the credit of the secular arm of sales-publicity rather than cast an aspersion on those who traffic in man's spiritual needs; and should go to show how truly business-as-usual articulates with the business of the Kingdom of Heaven. As it is with the traffic in these divinely beneficial intangibles, so it is with the like salesmanship on the material plane; the marvels of commercial make-believe, too, seek and find a lodgment in the popular knowledge and belief by way of a tireless publicity, such as blessed experience has long and profitably proved and found good in the Propaganda of the Faith. Ways and means which so have proved gainful to His publicity-agents and conductive to the glory of God — indeed indispensable to the continued upkeep of that Glory — are being drawn into the service of the secular Good of man; so attesting the excellence of the devoutly familiar form of words which describes the *summum bonum* as a balanced ration of divine glory and human use. It is worth noting in this connection that those Godfearing business men who administer the nation's affairs appear to realise this congruity between sacred and secular salesmanship; so much so that they have on due consideration found that investment in commercial advertising is rightfully exempt from the income tax, very much as the assets and revenues of the churches are tax-exempt. The one line of publicity, it appears is intrinsic to the good of man, as the other is essential to the continued Glory of God.

There is more than one reason for speaking of these matters here, and for speaking of them in a detached and objective way as mere workday factors of human conduct, — leaving all due sanctimony on one side for the time being, without thereby questioning the need and merit of such sanctimony as an ordinary means of grace, or the expediency of it as a standard vehicle of sales-publicity in putting over the transcendent verities of the Faith. It all implies no call and no inclination to lay profane hands on these verities. Taken objectively as a human achievement, the high example of the Propaganda of the Faith should serve as a moral stimulus and a pacemaker. The whole duty of sales-publicity is to "put it over," as the colloquial phrasing has it; and in the matter of putting it over, it is plain that the laurel, the palms, and the paean are due to go to the publicity-agents of the Faith, without protest. The large and enduring success of the Propaganda through the ages is an object-lesson to show how great is the efficacy of *ipse disix* when it is put over with due perseverance and audacity. It also carries a broad suggestion as to what may be the practical limits eventually to be attained by commercial advertising in the way of capitalisable earning-capacity.

Commercial sales-publicity of the secular sort evidently falls short, hitherto, in respect of the pitch and volume of make-believe which can be put over effectually and profitably. But it also falls short conspicuously at another critical point. It is of the nature of sales-publicity, to promise much and deliver a minimum. *Suppressio veri, suggestio falsi*. Worked out to its ideal finish, as in the promises and performance of the publicity-agents of the Faith, it should be the high good fortune of the perfect salesman in the secular field also to promise everything and deliver nothing.

Hitherto this climax of salesmanlike felicity has not been attained in the secular merchandising enterprise, except in a sporadic and dubious fashion. On the other hand, hitherto the publicity-agents of the Faith have habitually promised much and have delivered substantially none of the material advertised, and have "come through" with none of the tangible performances promised by their advertising matter. All that has been delivered hitherto has — perhaps all for the use of more pointedly menacing language; but it has always been more language, with a moratorium on the liquidation of the promises to pay, and a penalty on any expressed doubt of the solvency of the concern. There have of course, from time to time, been staged certain sketchy prodigies, in the nature of what the secular outdoor advertisers would call "spectacular displays," apparently designed to demonstrate the nature and merits of the goods kept in stock. These have not infrequently been highly ingenious, and also quite convincing to such persons as are fit to be convinced by them. They have carried conviction to those persons whose habitual beliefs are of a suitable kind. But as viewed objectively and as seen in any other than their own dim religious light, these admirable feats of manifestation have been after all essentially ephemeral and nugatory hitherto; very much of a class with those lunch-counter sample-packages that are designed to demonstrate the expansive powers of some noted baking-powder, in miniature and with precautions. They are after all in the nature of publicity-gestures, eloquent, no doubt, and graceful, but they are not the goods listed in the doctrinal pronouncements; no more than the wriggly gestures with which certain spear-headed manikins stab the nightly firmament over Times Square are an effectual delivery of chewing-gum. Bona-fide delivery of the listed goods would have to be a tangible performance of quite another complexion, inasmuch as the specifications call for Hell-fire and Kingdom of Heaven; to which the most heavily capitalised of these publicity concerns of the supernatural adds of broad margin of Purgatory.

There is, of course, no call and no inclination to take the publicity-agents of the Faith to task for failure to deliver the goods listed in their advertising matter. Quite otherwise, indeed. Since the sales-publicity from which these publicity-concerns derive their revenue plays on unreasoning fear and unreasoning aspiration, the output of goods listed in their advertising matter falls under the two general heads of Hell-fire and the Kingdom of Heaven; so that, on the whole, their failure to deliver the goods is perhaps fortunate rather than otherwise. Hell-fire is after all a commodity the punctual delivery of which is not desired by the ultimate consumers; and according to such descriptive matter as is available the Kingdom of Heaven, on the other hand, should not greatly appeal to persons of sensitive taste, being presumably something of a dubiously gaudy affair, something in the nature of three rings and a steam-calliope, perhaps. It might have been worse.

This failure to deliver the goods is brought up here only as an object-lesson which goes to show what and how great are the powers of sales-publicity at its best; as exemplified in a publicity enterprise which has over a long period of time very profitably employed a very large personnel and a very extensive and costly material equipment, coupled with no visible ability or intention to deliver any material part of the commodities advertised, or indeed to deliver anything else than a further continued volume of the same magisterial publicity that has procured a livelihood for its numerous personnel and floated its magnificent overhead charges in the past. In this lucrative enterprise the Propaganda of the Faith employs a larger and more expensive personnel and a larger equipment of material appliances, with larger running expenses and larger revenues, — not only larger than any given one line among the secular enterprises in sales-publicity, but larger than the total of all that goes into secular sales-publicity in all the nations of Christendom.

Notes

i "The needs of the market," of course, means "what the market will carry off at profitable prices."

ii Other items that enter into production-costs, as, e.g., the staple raw and structural materials and the power employed are scarcely amenable to manipulation from the side of the manufacturing business. It is, on the whole, a question of take it or leave it. The business concerns who dispose of the key industries and staple natural resources are massive bodies and occupy a secure position at the apex of the system, and those who deal what them find it unprofitable to kick against the pricks. Except for the somewhat special case of those manufacturing concerns which do business in farm products, there is small chance of practicing parsimony in production at the cost of any others than the hired man-power. And as a business proposition parsimony becomes a question of shifting production-cost to someone else.

On the other hand the provocation to parsimony in wages is insidious and speciously promising. The industrial man-power is voluminous, but it is scarcely compact enough to be called massive. Hitherto and for the time being it seems quite unlikely that these workmen can be drawn together in such massive formation as would enable them to make head against the business concerns which, between them, control the key industries and the maufacturers and transportation system. By force of circumstances the concerns that make up the great body of the business community work together, in effect, to a common end in their negotiations with the hired workmen; the common end being the defeat of the workmen and the consequent shifting upon them of so much of the production-costs as the traffic will bear. In this contest the employer-owners present a massive formation, at the same time that they habitually find themselves legally and morally in the right, resting their case on ancient principles of law and custom; so that any intervention from the side of the constituted authorities will have habitually work out to their profit. The bias of the established order and of its appointed keepers runs in favor of business; so that the keepers of law and order will, in effect, be the guardians of the business interests against all comers. And the same bias of principles still runs also throughout the body of hired workmen.

iii It is not to be overlooked, of course, that there are such phenomena as the Ford cars and the chain-stores and mail-order houses, which cut into the profitable traffic on a footing of quantity production and underbidding. But all men know these concerns to be disturbers of the peace and enemies of society, whom the business community at large would be glad to outlaw. They are the filibusters who drive a trade on the too trustful integrity of the business community at large and the too lenient justice of the nation's Business Administration.

iv As this matter was recently summed up at a staff conference of a certain noted advertising concern: "Blank has got the market; it is our problem to dislodge him."

v This is not said by way of aspersion. In these intimate matters of health and fabricated beauty and beneficent working of faith are manifest; if it should not rather be said that the manifest benefit derived from these many remedies, medicaments, lotions, unguents, pastes and pigments, is in the main a work of faith which acts tropismatically on the consumer's bodily frame, with little reference to the pharmaceutical composition of the contents of the purchased container, provided that they are not unduly deleterious. The case may, not without profit, be assimilated to certain of the more amiable prodigies wrought in the name of Holy Church, where it is well known that the curative efficacy of any given sainted object is something quite apart from its chemical constitution. Indeed, here as at many other points salesmanship touches the frontiers of the magical art; and no man will question that, as a business proposition, a magical efficacy is a good thing to sell.

vi All the while it appears on inquiry that the number of distinct articles — distinct in point of name and container — carried in stock under the head of "Toilet Goods" on the first floor of a well-known New York department store exceeds 10,000. So it also appears on the same inquiry that floor space so devoted to the distribution of these 10,000 yields larger net earnings per square foot than any other similar area of floor space employed by this prosperous business concern. Of course the 10,000 items are not all, or nearly all, containers of fabricated beauty, but even a cursory view of the premises will find such containers very much in evidence, and will also show that this particular case presents nothing exceptional.

vii This is, of course, to intended to say that the net effect of these things, apart from their beneficial effect on sales, is ordinarily of a serviceable character; but only that there are mitigating circumstances. Materially speaking, these things are in the nature of nuisances, but there is something to be said in abatement. There is commonly a variable, often negligible, fringe of serviceable information, and the like, attaching to their salesmanlike use. In their net effect, sign-boards, placards, carcards, posters, electrical blinkers, and the like devices, are a public nuisance, of course — *de facto, not de jure* — but to a variable, though fractional, extent their subsidiary and unintended effects may often be serviceable.

viii There are exceptional cases, perhaps more apparent than convincing, where old established merchant-houses have continued to do business in a modest but profitable way on a footing of clientele and goodwill coming down from the custom of past years. Indeed, such a house will have a substantial advantage so long as its clientele holds out, in that it incurs but a minimum of expense for publicity at the same time that it comes in for its volume of sales at the enhanced prices which the rising costs of publicity at large entail. Increased sales-costs entail rising prices and widening margins for the general body of competing concerns, while the old established firm, which rests its business on its ancient clientele, shares in the rising prices and widening margins without a proportionate share in the rising costs of publicity. So that a concern so placed will be in a position to maintain its volume of net earnings even while the volume of its custom is shrinking. The circumstance is perhaps best to be rated as a case of past salesmanship capitalized and carried over as intangible assets.

ix There is, of course, no actual fabrication of persons endowed with purchasing-power ad hoc, although much of the language employed by the publicity-agencies appears to promise something of that kind; nor is there even any importation of an unused supply of such customers from abroad, — the law does not allow it. Viewed in the large, what actually is effected is only a diversion of customers from one to another of the competing sellers, of course. But as seen from the isolated standpoint of any given selling-concern it foots up to a production of new customers or the upkeep of customers already in use by the given concern. So that this acquisition and repair of customers may fairly be reckoned at a stated production-cost per unit; and this operation lends itself to quantity production.

x The schools, on private foundation or at the public charge, are turning a greatly intensified and amplified attention to the needs of salesmanship and the propagation of salesmen, and they are turning out a rapidly swelling volume of graduates in this art of "putting it over." Indeed, this scholastic propagation of salesmen may fairly be cited as an example of quantity production; standardised both in its processes and in its output.

The production of customers by sales-publicity is evidently the same thing as a production of systematized illusions organised into serviceable "action patterns" — serviceable, that is, for the use of the seller on whose account and for whose profit the customer is being produced. It follows therefore that the technicians in charge of this work, as also the skilled personnel of the working-force, are by way of being experts and experimenters in applied psychology, with a workmanlike bent in the direction of what may be called creative psychiatry. Their day's work will necessarily run on the creative guidance of habit and bias, by recourse to shock effects, tropismatic reaction, animal orientation, forced movements, fixation of ideas, verbal intoxication. It is a trading on that range of human infirmities which blossom in devout observances and bear fruit in the psychopathic wards.

xi In strict accuracy and to avoid the appearance of oversight, it should be added that such a closed market, that is to say the volume of purchasing-power available, will be narrowed by approximately so much as these expenditures on salesmanship may amount to the aggregate.

xii There is the qualification, to be noted for what it may be worth, that the current, very urgent, sales-publicity may be presumed to divert a little something from savings to consumptive expenditures, and so may add that much of a margin of funds to the volume of purchasing-power currently available for expenditure on advertised goods. For what it may be worth, this unremitting impulsion to spend rather than save is to be counted in as a factor in the case.

xiii It has long been a commonplace among those who are interested in these matters that proprietary remedies, "patent medicines" and the like — what are sometimes called "nostrums" — can always be marketed with a good profit by use of a suitable kind and amount of publicity, somewhat irrespective of any inherent merit in the goods, — provided always that the seller-proprietor and his publicity-agent go about the business with the requisite lack of scruple. Something to the same effect holds true of sales-enterprise in many productions of commercialised art, which are plausibly alleged to be conductive to the prestige of the consumer; as e.g., grave-stones, lap-dogs, parlor-furniture, cosmetic pigments, fashionable dress and equipage generally.

xiv Of the secular order, as contrasted with the propaganda of the Faith; for it is to be remarked — and it carries a comfortable note of authentication for salesmanship at large — that the stupendous spiritual edifice of Holy Church also rests quite secure on this profitable gift of credulous and lasting fear stabilised with tireless publicity.

xv The fear of losing prestige has often been confused with personal vanity; a mistake due to incomplete analysis of the facts in the case. Closer attention to certain everyday facts, e.g., will satisfy any passably judicious bystander that the spirit which chiefly moves the young generation in these premises is not a boundless aspiration to out-bid and out-run all competitors and reach a preeminent notoriety for a splendid and colorful personal presence. Cosmetic pigments and preposterous garments are applied to the person with a view to avoid falling short of the blamelessly best, to avoid unfavorable notice rather than to achieve notoriety, to "keep up with the times," rather than to set the pace. And it is to this fear of derogatory notoriety that the expert advertisers of these ways and means of fabricated beauty address themselves and adapt the flow of their intoxicating verbiage. Even a cursory view of advertising matter bearing on this point will show that its dominant note is minatory; it runs, by constant suggestion, on the evil case of those foolish virgins who "get left" in the matter of personal prestige.

On any common-sense reflection it should seem highly improbable that anything but unreasoning fear would drive any person to the habitual use of these singular means of adornment. It is also known to ethnologists that practices of a similar nature and of somewhat the same aesthetic value among the peoples of the lower cultures — as, e.g., tattooing and scarification, tooth-filing, nose-boring, lip-buttons — rest directly and unequivocally on the fear of losing prestige. And at this point, as indeed at many others, it is profitable to call to mind that the hereditary human nature of these Europeans and their colonies is still the same as that of their savage forebears was in the Neolithic Age, some ten or twelve thousand years ago.

xvi Salesmanship which is not immediately concerned with merchandising is less closely bound up with these two standard ways and means; as, e.g., in the manoeuvres of salesmanship by which business is conducted in the key industries and in the money market. The more habitual recourse here is sabotage, an expert restriction of supply, though by no means to the entire neglect of publicity and bargaining. These lines of business will be considered in a later chapter.

xvii In its elements, of course, sales-publicity is nothing new but in its eventual working-out under absentee ownership it has disclosed a character and significance beyond anticipation and beyond ancient example. Yet much of the doctrinal matter that goes into print in behalf of yeast-cakes, "style-plus" clothing, lipsticks, face-creams, and the like, still reads not unlike that ancient achievement in publicity, the royal preamble to the Code of Hammurabi, said to date from the twenty-first century B.C. There is in both the same diligent attention to over-statement and the same unfailing avoidance of all that is to be said in abatement.

And as has already been indicated, the normal guide of sales-publicity is the old Latin formula: — *Suppressio veri, suggestio falsi.*

xviii The oldest existing advertising agency, according to figures supplied by the New York Council of the American Association of Advertising Agencies (know to the trade as A.A.A.A.) was founded in 1864. It is still one of the largest, most reliable and most successful. It has now a business turnover of something approaching $15,000,000, and has established branch offices in several of the larger American and European cities. The life-history of this corporation may fairly be taken as typical of the business. It has been successful from the outset and has done an increasing volume of business since its foundation, but its largest growth and most gratifying success lies within the past decade. Its business turnover for the current year runs in excess of that of any previous year; not even excepting 1920, when the Treasury decision to the effect that expenditures on advertising are exempt from the Income Tax led to an extraordinary increase in such expenditures.

xix Something may conveniently be said of the comparative merits, costs, volume, and present standing of these two chief divisions of sales-publicity. During the past year, e.g., at a conference of the well-informed men of the country, interested in these matters, the estimate was offered that "national" advertising (as distinguished from "local") in the newspapers of the country amounts at present to some $600,000,000, rather over than under. Well-informed persons within the body of conferences have held that $750,000,000 would be nearer the facts. The total expenditures for advertising in 1922, in newspapers and magazines, has been some $800,000,000; while estimates for 1923 run over $1,000,000,000.

Of outdoor advertising, Mr. E. O. Perrin, of the Media Department in the J. Walter Thompson Co., says that, "Until 1919 it amounted to about $5,000,000. Since then, the increase has been tremendous, and last year (1921) the total volume of outdoor advertising in the United States exceeded $30,000,000. — Prices vary greatly — according to size and location — some of the spectacular displays rent at extremely high figures. The big Wrigley (chewing-gum) electric sign at Times Square, New York, costs the advertiser $108,000 a year." — E. O. Perrin, "The Development of Outdoor Advertising," in *The J. Walter Thompson News*, February, 1922. At a conference of outdoor advertisers the previous year in Baltimore it was stated, on a deliberate estimate, that that year's expenditures on sign-boards alone — what are known in the trade jargon as "Bulletins" and "Posters" — were running over $60,000,000.

"In the city of Chicago ... it is possible to secure forty-eight painted walls and bulletins at a cost of $1,250 per month. The cost of a full page for one insertion in Chicago's largest newspaper is $1,708. In Kansas City, a display of one hundred standard twenty-four sheet posters costs $755.60 per month, as against $1,064 for one full page in the leading newspaper. A representative poster campaign covering the entire country and consisting of 17,169 posters would cost the advertiser about $140,000 per month." (The Same.)

xx It is, accordingly scarcely an over-statement to say that something like one half of the wood-pulp that goes through the papers mills, together with one-half the man-power and mechanical equipment engaged in the paper industry and the printing trades, is consumed in the making of competitive sales, the net effect of which is to raise the prices paid for goods by the consumers. The yearly consumption of newsprint paper in the United States and Canada is about 2,600,000 tons, according to figures submitted at a meeting of the Canadian Pulp and Paper Association.

As giving some indication of what the figures for expenditure on sales-publicity are like, in the periodical press outside of newspapers, it is reported on reliable authority that the total advertising revenues of 72 publications of this class for 1920 came to $132,414,799. This was the year immediately affected by the decision which exempts advertising expenditures from the income tax. The corresponding figures for 1919 were $97,208,791, those for 1918 $61,312,888. The corresponding total for "Color Copy" (1920) was $39,644,545. As a maximum value of advertising space in periodicals of this class, a single (preferred) page of a single issue of the presumed leader among them sold, in the winter of 1921, at the standard rate of $11,000; coupled with an engagement to buy the same space at the same rate in 13 issues during the year. This price does not cover the preparation of the illustration or the reading matter, which are supplied at the expense of the advertiser. - Cf. ITALAdvertising in National Publications 1914-1920/ITAL, Curtis Publishing Company, 1921. (For private circulation.) Expenditures for advertising in newspapers are said to run about seven times as high as what goes to the magazines.

xxi Outdoor displays have been classed under three standard forms: Bulletins ("Any outdoor sign which is hand painted in colors"); Poster ("A lithographed paper sign which is pasted on a metal panel"); and Spectacular displays ("An electric display built on a skeleton steel frame with flashing devices").

xxii "Big corporations with many branches have separate window display departments with a staff of men expert in various branches of the art, designing, color, and some even have a psychologist on the staff to decide whether the finished effect will prove alluring to the public. "The great amount of material used in these windows has already made itself felt in several industries, the Copper and Brass Association figuring that 2,000,000 pounds of copper will be consumed during 1922."

12

The Larger Uses of Credit

The pivotal factor in the business enterprise of this new era is the larger use of credit which has come into action during the last few decades; larger in absolute scale and volume as well as in the ration which it bears to those underlying tangible assets on which it is conceived to rest. This volume of credit is more widely detached from all material objects and operation, and increasingly so.

The business men of the nineteenth century, too, habitually conducted their affairs on a basis of credit, with slight, infrequent and inconsequential recourse to transactions in cash or in kind; increasingly so as the century advanced and as the credit system progressively matured into something like the stability and self-sufficiency which it now has attained. Prices ran on a credit basis, as a workday matter of course and of convenience, and virtually no payments of any consequence were made or expected to be made in any other medium than credit-instruments; so that the price-system had already in the nineteenth century become, in effect, a system of credit-prices. The banknote currency employed was a volume of credit-instruments, to which the underlying specie-reserve stood in the relation of a contingent emergency fund and a base-line of inflation. The "deposit currency" which served as the chief medium of exchange and method of payment was somewhat more widely out of touch with any cash basis, being related to the underlying specie-reserve at the second remove only. At no time would the price-level decline to or near its cash base-line, except in a convulsive way in times of commercial crisis. At such times the familiar credit-instruments by use of which business was carried on would fall somewhat under suspicions, transiently, and the margin of price-inflation would then be greatly narrowed.[i]

So soon as business picked up again the brisk times returned after these periods of partial deflation, the habitual credit-inflation would regain any lost ground and would then ordinarily run to a slightly higher level than before. Through all this fluctuating price-inflation that so made hard times or prosperity there runs a certain air of irresponsibility or fortuity, particularly through the earlier half or three quarters of the century. The business community was still unable to control its necessary credit relations at all effectually. The country's credit relations were not ready to be organised on a reasonably compact and inclusive plan, such as would combine stability with a sufficiently flexible administration of details. They were therefore subject to ungoverned seasonal and local contingencies, which upset the balance between credits and debits from time to time and so spread derangement and consternation abroad through the business community.

The precise point of the difficulty appears to have been that there was no effectual concert of collusion governing the use of credit at large in that earlier time. The debits and credits on which business was kept afloat were not subject to effectual joint control; there was no effectual pooling of assets and liabilities. So that debtors and creditors, even those of the larger sort, were still somewhat at cross-purposes; with no effectual teamwork between those massive creditors and debtors, who, between them, make up the substantial core of the business community. The large debtors were not identified with their creditors in point of management and control, at least not in a degree sufficient to maintain a reasonably stable balance of things on a basis of community interest. In more concrete terms, the general run of the key industries had not been tied up with the larger banks.

A convenient point of departure for the rise of the new era in business enterprise may be found in the late nineties; and the new departure may be said to have been set afoot in the financiering of mergers and holding-companies during those years by the late J. Pierpoint Morgan and those others who presently followed his lead.

In that time the holding-company came to stand as the advanced and perfected type-form of corporate ownership and control as employed in the conduct of industrial business. It was a well-considered advance over the earlier methods of absentee ownership and absentee management. In point of form, the holding-company is of a more perfect order of absenteeism, in that by this device the lawful owner draws back farther by one remove from any personal relation with the property which he owns and from which he derives an income; whether the property in question be tangible assets or a vested usufruct. At the same time the owner's claim on and control over his property shift to a more impersonal and statistical footing, if possible; to a footing of standardised quantitative allotment in terms of perceptual units. His relation to the property and its use thereby comes to carry a slighter effectual responsibility for any action taken, or for any tangible outcome of such action taken by the corporate management to which he has in effect delegated his rights and powers. In the holding-company, even more obviously than in the ordinary corporation, the owner delegates the powers of ownership, and retains only its rights and immunities. So also it leaves him a correspondingly slighter chance of personally influencing any action taken by the management.

The holding-company has commonly been of a large size; and that fact has likewise had the effect of submerging the individual owner and his personal bias and initiative. The result is a pronounced degree of impersonality and standardised routine. So also, in the practical conduct of its affairs by the holding-company, the effectual control and management of any corporate business has passed into the hands of a relatively smaller minority of the ultimate owners, and at the same time the effectual control exercised by this relatively small minority of the owners has taken on a more unequivocally statistical character. So much so, indeed, that their effectual oversight and control will ordinarily touch nothing more tangible or more personal than certain figures supplied by the corporation's accountants; commonly numbers running to some half-a-dozen digits, having to do with certain price-totals.

The holding-company is no longer viewed with apprehension, as it once was; nor does it hold that dominant place in the business of credit and capitalisation which it held about the turn of the century. Not that it has gone out of use or out of mind. It has been proven and found good and has become a part of the standard apparatus of business, a commonplace formality of the routine. But at the outset, when the holding-company was coming into use, it was the effectual means of reorganising the business of the key industries on an enlarged, more elaborate and more manageable plan. It served to bring these industrial business concerns together into larger agglomerations than had been practicable up to that time, and it served also to detach the ownership of these concerns from their management more widely and effectually than before. By this move the whole apparatus and management of industrial business was placed on a foundation of credit in a more unqualified fashion than before, and thereby the management of the business was enabled to "trade on a thinner equity"[ii] than had been practicable in the past. Corporation finance was enabled to take on still more of the character of standardised routine. So that the holding-company has been an instrument and an exemplar of that drift of things in the conduct of business which has brought on the current state of things, and which has made the difference between the situation of the nineties and that of the present.

Much of the use which the holding-company has served has been that of standardising the routine of "big business" and familiarising the business community with that larger-scale and wider detachment that is characteristic of the ordinary use of credit and the ordinary duties of ownership in this later time. In a very passable fashion men have learned all that now, so that it is no longer beset with the distrust of the unknown, — which is said to be a nearly universal infirmity of sound business men. What the use of the holding-company once served to drive them to has now become a familiar matter of course.

Something to much the same effect is to be said for the use of "interlocking directorates," which also once loomed up in popular apprehension as a formidable, if not a menacing, innovation in the conduct of business. The interlocking directorate has also not passed out of use. It, too, is still a convenient arrangement for purposes of mutual understanding and support. But these purposes for which these devices were once resorted to as a means of constraint, have how become habitual matters of routine; and the devices therefore have ceased to claim that degree of attention which they were once presumed to merit. They are no longer of the essence of this case.

The late J. Pierpoint Morgan saw an opportunity and turned it to account. It is not likely, and it does not appear, that he rated himself as a path-finder or in any sense as the pioneer of a new era in business enterprise, or that he harbored any ambition or design to change the face of the business community. For all his large initiative and his large powers and responsibilities, he was a notably unassuming person; being apparently driven by nothing more spectacular than the habitual incentives of safe and sane business of the larger sort;[iii] although his larger initiative led him beyond his contemporaries and associates, and at times, indeed, led him close to the frontiers of sound business practice.

The undertakings which are associated with his memory at this point, and which played a typical part in leading over to the new era, may be described in general terms somewhat as follows. At that time (late nineties) there were a large number and variety of established business concerns doing business primarily in certain of the key industries, notably steel, ore, coal, and railways. Many of these concerns were in a moderately bad way financially, for one reason and another. They were, not uncommonly, unable to command such a volume of credit as was needed in the conduct of their business. They were commonly over-capitalised — in excess of their market value as going concerns and notably in excess of the value of their tangible assets. So they were carrying overhead charges somewhat in excess of what their current earnings would warrant; and their earnings were declining rather than otherwise.

This state of their affairs was due in some measure to a more or less pronounced obsolescence. It was in part an adolescence of their industrial plant, but with more critical effect these concerns also suffered from a rapidly growing obsolescence of locality, particularly as related to the means of transportation on which they depended for their supply of raw materials and for the delivery of the marketable output. In some instances their business facilities were also going out of date; their markets were in process of obsolescence, through a shifting of the population, through changes of custom and usage, through being cut under by other concerns doing business in the same market. There had been ceaseless change in the technique of these industries during the lifetime of these business concerns; and more particularly during the lifetime of the "underlying companies" and industrial plants on which these industrial business concerns were based; for the greater number of those concerns that are in question here were composite organisations, built up out of previously existing corporations and firms, by merger, purchase, and consolidation. And throughout this period of industrial growth, changes in the processes of industry and in the localisation of the various industries had been going forward; due in great part to the growth and redistribution of the population and to continued extensions and enlargement of the transportation systems. New natural resources also continued to be drawn into the industrial system and to be engrossed by certain of the larger owners. All of which conspired to put these business concerns out of date and out of joint with the conditions of the market. Perhaps the gravest of the factors which contributed to this obsolescence and perplexity of these industrial business concerns was the competitive character of their market, both for raw materials and labor and for disposal of the output; and this competitive market was all the more precarious because the productive capacity of the existing plants was already greater than the market would carry off at a profitable price, even within the shelter of a high protective tariff. The most embarrassing appears to have been the inconsiderate competitive position taken by those Carnegie properties which presently came to play so magisterial a role in precipitating the formation of the U.S. Steel Corporation.[iv]

Not infrequently the management of these previously established industrial business concerns was in the hands of elderly and opinionated owners, who had an old-fashioned sentimental interest each in his own corporation, as being his own creation, and whose occupation would be gone in case their own concern were to be merged with others or sunk in an inclusive holding-company. These survivors of an earlier business regime were by way of being "captains of industry" of the obsolete sort, in that they commonly combined some degree of technical training, experience, and aspiration, with a customary knowledge of the markets and of corporation finance. And they were commonly out of date in both respects, by force of what may be called obsolescence by displacement in technical practice and in financial usage. They were patriarchal holdovers, with much of the intolerance that will commonly invest the self-made patriarch. Things had been moving forward in matters of knowledge and practice during the lifetime of these elderly captains and their establishments, and among the forward changes were such as made imperatively for a larger scale and a more far-reaching teamwork in the processes of production, a larger use of credit, and for a more carefully guarded competition in the markets. And none of this fell in readily with the settled habits of these elderly captains or with the standing business relations among their several concerns.

These industrial business concerns, and their underlying companies and plants, had in their time been projected with a view to the traffic of a fairly open competitive market, and they had expanded by successive extensions and accretions, and so had grown to maturity under conditions which that traffic had created. With the progressive filling-out and closing-in of this market they found themselves, progressively, in the position of competitive producers for a closed market of variable volume. They were consequently somewhat overstocked with industrial plants of a fair productive capacity, which not unusually duplicated one another, and which had been placed somewhat hastily by rule of thumb in somewhat haphazard locations, and had grown from relatively small beginnings by a process of patchwork and extension. And all the while their combined productive capacity rather exceeded the capacity of their market — at any such price as would afford them a "reasonable profit" on their output. In this sense the market was closing in. It was becoming too narrow for a free run of output at the price-level at which these enterprises had been projected. The period of competitive business in the key industries was closing. So that continued open competition among them became "cutthroat competition"; such as to entail present and prospective decline of their earning-capacity. As one consequence of their situation, they were greatly in need of additional credits for use in their business, at a time when their credit capacity was falling off and their liabilities were already becoming distressingly burdensome.

When the affairs of the corporations in the key industries had reached this pass, the dean of the banking community saw his own occasion in the present needs and the dubious prospects of these industrial business concerns. Of course there were others, too, and not a few, who were ready to see the same opportunity and to profit by it so soon as it had been placed before them in an object-lesson. The conjuncture was essentially that of a sweeping transition and realignment, incident to the passing of the common run of the key industries from a footing of competitive business in an ample market to a footing of collusive traffic in a closed market too narrow for unguarded competitive production.[v]

As the event has taught, the executive use of the country's credit resources in a large way and on a reasoned plan was the appointed means by which the due reconstruction of the business was to be worked out, and also the means by which the needful running collusion in the further conduct of the business was to be enforced and regulated. The holding-company and the merger, together with the interlocking directorates, and presently the voting trust, were the ways and means by which the banking community took over the strategic regulation of the key industries, and by way of that avenue also the control of the industrial system at large. By this move the effectual discretion in all that concerns the business management of the key industries was taken out of the hands of corporation managers working in severalty and at cross-purposes, and has been lodged in the hands of that group of investment bankers who constitute in effect a General Staff of financial strategy and who between them command the general body of the country's credit resources. This general staff, or inner group, command the credit resources of the country at large; although it would presumably not do to say, at least not just yet, that they — the large business financiers and their banking-houses — own or comprise or constitute the credit resources of the country.

Out of this drift of things the "Investment Banker" has emerged, to serve as a powerful instrumental factor in working out the new alignment of ownership and industrial business, and presently to take his place as one of the essential workday institutions of the business community. It should perhaps be remarked that he is not yet in existence *de jure*, but only *de facto*. Just yet he is still in process of standardisation as regards his precise nature and uses; so that no sharply defied description of him and his work can be drawn, just yet, although there is some thing to be said of him and his functions.[vi] He is the source of the channel, as the case may be, of capitalisation and of corporation credit at large, — a source if he amounts to a banking-house of the first magnitude, a channel if his place in the economy of Nature is that of a subordinate. At the same time and in his appropriate degree his is the standard container of such credit and the standard repository, original or vicarious, of the larger intelligence and discretion in these fiscal matters. He initiates movement or pressure in the conduct of business, or he transmits initiative and pressure. In point of pedigree, considered as a institution, his formal line of descent out of the past traces back to the business of underwriting, as it ran in the time before the banking community had taken over the general initiative and foresight in the conduct of industrial business. But he is also rooted in the business of commercial banking and banks of issue, as well as in the trust-companies that have come up and grown great in his own time; and then there is about him, too, a broad hint of the bill-broker of earlier times. In point of form, he is affiliated with his client-corporations as creditor, underwriter, sponsor, banker, broker. In effect, he is the comptroller of their fiscal affairs and, within reason, the master of their solvency; being custodian of their absentee owners' interests at large.

Hitherto, and in so far as it has touched the larger contingencies of business, this work of initiative, discretion, foresight, and control, which has become incumbent on the country's investment bankers, has habitually taken effect by way of collusion or concerted action. This concert of action is of the essence of the case. It is by virtue of such concert among the larger and more responsible ones that they constitute in effect the General Staff of the business community — what may be called the One Big Union of the Interests. Under the surveillance of their general staff, it has become incumbent on the investment bankers as an organized body to deal with the run of business as an organic moving equilibrium. This highly responsible task enjoins a collusive sobriety, a collective and concerted moderation, such as is intended in the colloquial phrase, "sitting tight." The investment bankers collectively are the community custodians of absentee ownership at large, the general staff in charge of the pursuit of business. And since the conduct of industry is incidental to the pursuit of business, the state of industry and the rate, volume and balance of production also are dependent on this sagacity and goodwill. So that it is here, if anywhere, that responsibility of the country's material welfare may be said to rest.

In his time, the great pioneering creator of mergers and holding-companies came to stand as the chief of investment bankers and the dean of the congregation of corporation finance. And from that time on, the investment bankers have progressively taken over the control of industrial business in the large. Investment-banking as it is conducted now, owes its rise and character to the circumstances of that time, and it has continued to work out along much the same lines to which it was then brought by the experience of Morgan and his associates. This financial enterprise may therefore be said to have arisen out of the mobilization of those banking resources which were already employed in underwriting corporate capitalisations, and to have arisen as an enterprise in mergers, recapitalisations, and businesses; but it presently fell into settled lines as a standardised routine of investing funds and allocating credits. This standardised routine of investment and allocation is what engrosses the energies of the community of investment bankers. It is also the ways and means by which they, working together as a general staff of financial strategy, govern the country's business at large and so regulate the ordinary rate and volume of productive industry. In all this, the continued merging of old concerns and creation of new ones goes forward as a routine matter of administration incident to the allocation of credits. And the credits are — also as a routine matter-of-course — allocated with an eye single to the greater gain of the investment bankers who see to the allocation of them.

In its beginnings, in the nineties, this enterprise in mergers and recapitalisation was primarily concerned with bringing certain elderly units of the industrial business community to terms, by a persuasive use of financial pressure; to prevail upon them to surrender their several corporate powers and enter into some arrangement in the way of a merger, commonly under the form of a holding-company. By this means these concerns ceased to govern their own affairs individually, were drawn in under a centralised management, and so ceased to be effectual competitors in the market. In the main this reorganisation had to do with business concerns which were in the position of holdovers in the key industries, and more particularly such of them as were in financial straits, as a good proportion of them were.

In this connection it has also been believed, on circumstantial evidence, that the great financier, and after him also the lesser ones, would now and again take pains to maneouver such an embarrassed concern into financial extremities; such as would incline its management to surrender the controlling interest and to allow a suitable "bonus" to the captains of finance who managed to reorganise.

During the early years of the period it was this bonus that was the immediate object sought by the reorganising financier, and the chief incentive to the reorganisation. The bonus commonly took the form of a block of securities issued in the name of the new incorporation. And it was commonly quite a substantial bonus, so as to take up a very appreciable percentage of the new capitalisation. This bonus which the underwriter of the new corporation securities came in for appears to have been the valuable consideration sought by these financiers in undertaking these early mergers and recapitalisations. It does not appear that these financiers commonly set out with the purpose of taking over the management of the incorporations which they created. But the transactions which they entered into in their pursuit of the bonus entailed commitments and obligations which stood over after the initial transactions had been concluded. The recapitalisation and its endorsement at the hands of the financier, of investment banker, together with the practice of taking over his bonus in the form of a block of securities issued by the new incorporation, entailed a continued community of interest between the investment banker and the new incorporations which he had created. A community interest of a special sort, in that it committed the investment banker — the financier and his banking-house — to a continued responsibility for the success of the new incorporation; which in turn vested the banker with power to act, and lodged in his hands a virtually plenary discretion in the oversight and management of the new incorporation. The outcome has been that the banking-houses which have engaged in this enterprise have come in for an effectual controlling interest in the corporations whose financial affairs they administer. And it is this outcome that has proved to be the enduring and decisive factor in the new business situation created by this recourse to mergers and recapitalisations under the auspices of the investment bankers.

At least in some very consequential instances, the further course of events and the further manoeuvres and commitments in the way of recapitalisation and credit extensions, were also governed by the pressure of necessity bearing on the investment bankers in the case. The financiering bankers were involved in the affairs of their client corporations in such a critical fashion as to require a further move of coalition and recapitalisation, as a measure of safety. That consolidation of interests which resulted in the U. S. Steel Corporation, e.g., was precipitated by pressure of this kind. At the same time it is worth noting that the financier who, under pressure, carried out this consolidation of the steel interests came in for a bonus in the form of a block of the new corporation's securities bearing a face value of $50,000,000; in which sum the new corporation formally became indebted to its sponsor, as payment for his services. This bonus was in the nature of an addition to the corporation's capitalisation. And it may be added that in the end, after some further financial manoeuvres, the securities which made up this bonus came to be worth fully their face value.

The bonus which so lay at the root of these early reorganisations of industrial business habitually took the shape of a block of corporation securities representing new capital values added to the total capitalisation in the operation of recapitalising the underlying properties; the capitalised value — face value, book value — of these properties being thereby augmented by that much. Such as been the standard usage. It is in effect a matter of routine. The bonus which so entered into the total capitalisation represented no acquisition of new capital; in the sense that it added no new funds and no new tangible assets to the total; but only new liabilities, added to the total of the corporation securities that resulted from recapitalisation. That is to say, according to the standard routine in the matter, the total outstanding securities, representing the previous capitalisation of the underlying companies, were increased by that much without any corresponding increase of the underlying assets. It was a transaction in credit pure and simple, a creation of new credit values; or it was a redistribution of the old values under cover of a make-believe creation of new assets.

Also habitually, apart from any underwriter's bonus, in any such reorganisation the total capitalisation of the resulting collective holding-company is made somewhat larger than the sum of the outstanding capital securities of the underlying companies, and very appreciably larger than the aggregate market value of the underlying tangible assets. Habitually, as a matter of standard usage, the recapitalisation of industrial properties in this way has resulted in an increased volume of outstanding corporation securities, with or without, but commonly without, any increase in the underlying material assets. This addition to the volume of outstanding capital securities arising out of any such reincorporation may run to fifty per cent of the total previous capitalisation of the underlying companies, or to some such figure, more or less.

The outcome of successive reorganisations has accordingly been a series of successive recapitalisations at a successively higher figure, resulting in a progressively increased volume of outstanding credit instruments and involving a corresponding progressive revaluation of the underlying assets at a progressively enhanced figure. As a rule rather than as an exception, in the key industries, the operation has been repeated in several successive recapitalisations of the same properties into successively larger coalitions. In effect it has been a creation of new values by an extension of credit. And in the main this progressively increased valuation of these corporate assets has been justified by the event. Indeed, the assets of the larger coalitions which have been created in this way have habitually increased in value even apart from and in excess of any such credit operations designed to add something to the face value of the outstanding securities.[vii]

Such transactions in corporation finance were the outstanding feature of the business situation during the ten or a dozen years which overlapped the turn of the century, and the like transactions have continued to be an active factor in the conduct of industrial business since then; most notably and with the gravest consequences in the key industries. There has been a continued turn to consolidations with recapitalisation at a higher figure, and new incorporations with flotations of new securities. The visible purpose of them, as seen from the side of the investment bankers, and the presumptive aim of the transactions, as transactions in corporation finance, has been the creation of new capitalised wealth by new extensions of credit. The benefit of the newly created capitalisations has, in the main, inured to the investment-banking houses which have carried on this work. In great part, the gains which accrue from investment banking still are derived from transactions of this class.[viii]

Recapitalisation at an increased figure has been the standard practice in reorganising and merging industrial business concerns during this period. New incorporations on any reasonably large scale have followed the same general principle, in that the capitalisation has commonly exceeded the value of the underlying assets. And with a very fair degree of generality this inflation of the capital-values of corporations and their assets has proved to be sound; in the sense that the inflated corporations have presently, if not from the outset, approached or reached such an earning-capacity as to justify their inflated capitalisation. The assets so created by a transaction in credit have proved to be sound assets, good property.

The increased earning-capacity of such inflated recapitalisations had been conditioned on an advance of the price-level for the sales from which the earnings are drawn, or on keeping up the established price-level in the face of declining production-costs. To maintain or advance the level of prices in this way requires an effectual freedom from unguarded competition in the market, among the business concerns engaged in the traffic; and the most advantageous arrangement for the purpose will be a virtual absence of competition; such as has been the rule, e.g., in the steel business, and such as has come near being the rule in coal. This can be accomplished by a reasonable degree of collusion and concerted action. By this means the margin of earnings is enlarged, at the same time that the hazards of the business are greatly reduced or virtually eliminated.[ix]

The required degree of concerted action, or the needful reasonably collusive regulation of things, has not called for a close-knit organisation of the banking community in set form, or, indeed, for anything like a formally defined compact of joint action among the ruling captains of solvency in their underlying banking-houses. These latterday transactions in credit and capitalisation are of so transparently gainful a nature as to enjoin on all the parties in interest what amounts in effect to a collusive regulation of things, even in the absence of any provision for a formally concerted plan of action. The transactions which make the outcome are large, particularly such of them as are patently worth-while and worth bearing a hand in, and the business procedure in the case has already fallen into something of a standard routine, in pursuance of which this manner of large and lucrative transactions recur in a somewhat orderly succession; and the operations are of such a character as to make it plain to the meanest understanding that they will be carried through to a safe and lucrative conclusion only by such team-work among the several investment-concerns as will obviate all cross-purposes, and will at the same time provide a broad collective reserve of credit resources and eliminate all hazard of unforeseen contingencies. And bankers are imbued with a reasonably conservative spirit, such as will conduce to safe and sane business of this kind.

Any member of the banking community who might so far exceed the limits of conventionally blameless cupidity as to be led into cross-purposes and fall short of reasonable team-work at a critical juncture, would expect to be counted out of the game at the next turn. He would lose that most essential item among his own intangible assets, the goodwill of his fellow bankers, deprived of which he would no longer come in for the steady run of workday business that makes the broad foundation of his earnings. At the same time he would, in effect, cease to be an investment banker. Such is the turn which things have taken. In effect, whether it runs to commercial banking or in the field of investment, banking is essentially now a competitive business, except collectively as against the underlying population. And investment banking in an eminent degree is a line of enterprise in which it is incumbent on all the parties in interest to take hands and help, in which one good turn deserves another, and in which there can be no tolerance for men who wantonly disregard the rules of the game. Any flotation of securities, but more particularly any major operation of such a character as to promise large and easy gains, is in practical effect an occasion for mutual support among the makers of credit, and for faithful team-work throughout an extensive network of banking-concerns, who are bound in an orderly system of correspondence and through whose hands the credit instruments that are to be marketed will have to pass on their way to those investors who may be called the ultimate consumers of this product. For any bank or banker it is the part of wisdom faithfully to "stand in" and in all sobriety to take an equitable share in the margin of profit that is to be derived from these sales of credit.

This bond of union and concert that so holds the investment bankers to a profitable routine of team-work in disposing of this running output of credit instruments is greatly strengthened by the fact that the country's commercial banking is already established on the same lines of team-work and joint interest; it is taken care of by the same community of bankers, governed by alike routine of equitable give and take, in pursuance of which also all excesses and delinquencies are penalised with automatic punctuality. In the business of commercial banking, too, the superior discretion and initiative are perforce vested in the massive financial concerns that inhabit the country's financial metropolis, and whose massive resources enable them to create credit somewhat at will, and to regulate its expansion and allocations. By force of circumstances these banking concerns of the first magnitude make up the living nucleus of the banking community, and by force of circumstances it is the part of wisdom as well as of professional ethics for the lesser and outlying members of the craft to wait faithfully on the motions of these masters of solvency, who by force of circumstances constitute the General Staff of the banking community.[x]

The investment banker, severally and collectively, is custodian of the credit-interests of his own banking-house and of his clients. He is a custodian with plenary discretion, *de facto*; the exigencies of absentee ownership make him so. In the nature of the case these interests are the interests of absentee ownership, like other credit interests, and in the nature of the case their custody takes effect in the way of an absentee control over that business and industry out of which the gains of these absentee owners arise. In effect, absentee ownership is a claim on free income to be drawn from the property owned; so that the property is necessarily of the nature of assets in so far as it is held in absentee ownership; and "assets" is a financial category. Also in the nature of the case, the resulting absentee government of current business and industry, which so if vested in these custodians of credit, is in the nature of a fiscal administration, a strategic regimentation of assets, essentially a running allocation of credit allowances; which can take effect only by way of withholding needed credit extensions from doubtful and undesirable enterprises, — doubtful or undesirable in their bearing on the "income stream" that goes to the bankers and their clients. So that the powers and sanctions commanded by these custodians are of a permissive sort. That is to say, their strategy and administration are necessarily of a negative, quiescent, sedative character, something in the way of a provisional veto power, a contingent check on untoward undertakings and excursions, a fiscal disallowance of such projects in business and industry as do not manifestly promote the advantage of those absentee interests that are taken care of by the given investment banker or group of bankers, in effect a species of fiscal sabotage.

Crudely and in general terms the working-out of this absentee government of business and industry by this general staff of solvency may be described as follows. It works by way of an allocation of credit allowances among the clients of these custodians of solvency, preferentially and particularly among those corporate concerns that are clients of those larger captains of solvency who are effective members of the general staff, — concerns which are bound to these captains by a community interest of a businesslike sort. The credit resources of the country, the main body and dominant mass of which are under the hands of this general staff of solvency, may be, and by pressure of ordinary businesslike cupidity they will be, employed productively in the creation of new wealth in the way of intangible assets, after the fashion already explained in an earlier passage. In ordinary times this expansive creation of intangible wealth goes forward in a cumulative fashion, by routine; it is part of the ordinary day's work of the banking community. This newly, progressively, created wealth is in the nature of capitalised overhead charges on current business and industry.

In practical effect, the rate at which such new assets will be created is determined by two main factors: (a) the volume of credit obligations already outstanding and assimilated into the routine of business ratings and transactions, and (b) what may be called the tensile strength of the business community's temper as regards new commitments in the way of liabilities and capitalisation. The latter is often spoken of loosely as "public confidence." Neither of these two factors which condition the rate of output of intangible wealth is a constant quantity; as one might say, neither has a constant coefficient of efficiency. And neither can be measured and reduced to a quite satisfactory statistical statement in objective terms. They are, therefore, not fully amenable to control by statistical computation or by an apparatus of bookkeeping. Accordingly the rate of production of intangibles and overhead charges is not a constant one, nor can it or its fluctuations be quite safely calculated beforehand. There is still in all this traffic a substantial margin of contingencies, which leaves a certain elbowroom for the personal equation of the captains for sagacity and rule-of-thumb. The personal equation of these captains runs to "safety first"; at least so they say. Accordingly that element of uncertainty and hazard which still enters into the case will greatly further a faithful collusion among the sound captains of solvency.

When all due allowance has been made, therefore, the rate of production of intangibles will still be a rate which may be estimated with a very fair degree of approximation by those persons who are conversant with the credit business and its resources. And barring accident, this ordinary rate of production of intangibles should evidently rise progressively higher as the outstanding "digested" mass of obligations on which it is conditioned grows progressively larger; so that under ordinary circumstances the rate of output of these capitalised liabilities will be subject to a cumulative acceleration, although no definite coefficient of acceleration can be assigned.[xi]

Credit is extended by the keepers of the credit resources in the form of current credit-accounts — typically "deposits" — as well as in the flotation of new securities; it is extended to such business concerns of a sizable magnitude as prove themselves worthy. Those are eligible who can be depended on duly to pay over to their creditors such fixed charges as are borne by the credit instruments so created. They are worthy, of course, because and in the measure in which they continue to yield a secure net in coke to the dispensers of credit and to the absentee owners whose guardians the dispensers are. Directly or indirectly, the resulting credit instruments go to swell the volume of collateral on which the fabric of credit is erected and on which further extensions are negotiated. These credit extensions in this way enable the concerns in question to trade on a thinner equity. That is to say, such business concerns are thereby enabled to enter into larger commitments and undertake outlays that are more largely in excess of their tangible assets than before; to go into the market with a purchasing-power expanded by that much — or a little something more — beyond their available possessions, tangible and intangible. Which goes to enlarge the effective purchasing-power in the market without enlarging the supply of vendible goods in the market; which will act to raise or maintain the level of prices, and will therefore enlarge the total of the community's wealth as rated in money-values, independently of any increase of tangible possessions; all of which is "good for trade."

Any business concern which is in this way enabled to trade on a thinner equity will, by so much, be placed at an advantage as against the rest, provided that the rest do not come in for a similar advantage by a similar recourse to credit. Any advantage so gained is of a competitive or differential character, in that it presupposes that the rest will not make use of the same expedient, and it will immediately be offset and neutralized if and in so far as the like recourse to credit is adopted by the rest. From which it follows that all those who are to be saved, in the business sense, will go and do likewise. The practical outcome, as all men know, has been that the generality of such business concerns will habitually make such use of their borrowing capacity as they can, on pain of failure. From which it follows that such recourse to credit brings no net advantage to them, either as a differential or in the aggregate.

But it also follows that by this competitive recourse to credit these business concerns, commercial and industrial, all and several become clients of the dispensers of credit, are loaded approximately to capacity with suitable overhead charges payable to the absentee holders of their paper, whether in the form of commercial credits or of corporation debentures. Whereby the business community at large, being made up of such business concerns doing business on such a credit basis, comes to be dependent on these dispensers of credit for the means of commercial subsistence and salvation, — in the degree in which this "credit economy" prevails.[xii]

To commercial and industrial business as a whole no net aggregate gain accrues from this traffic in credits. But to the lenders there accrues a differential gain which is offset by a corresponding loss to the rest of the community; a net aggregate gain equal to the aggregate overhead charges borne by the resulting obligations, less the cost of carrying on the traffic in credits.[xiii] Therefore, the fuller the utilisation of credit and the greater its stability, the thinner will be the equity on which business is carried on; the larger will be the aggregate of overhead charges to be paid over to the trustees and owners of the credit resources; and the closer will the conduct of business and industry be bound up with the measures taken, for their own profit, by those captains of solvency who command the credit resources of the country.

Such would be the upshot of the matter, "other things remaining the same." And if such were the whole of the case, the futility of it should presently become patent even to the business men who are immersed in this expansive credit and who (proximately) pay the cost. But other things do not remain the same, and among these other things is the price-level; which rises and continues to rise to meet the rising volume of purchasing-power that is thrown loose on the market at large by the current ubiquitous recourse to credit.

And like other persons, the business men are creatures of habit. By unbroken habit, prices are the substance of things in the working conceptions of the business men. Therefore their habitual frame of mind enables them to believe, or effectually to make believe, that they are gainers by as much as the prices advance; because they are enabled to foot up their assets and their net receipts in so much larger a number of smaller units of value. Such is the force of habit. The business man faithfully views the dollar *sub specie aeternitatis*, even when he knows better. In extenuation of this businesslike imbecility it should also be noted that the men who do business are kept from reflecting on this state of the case by the fact that the cost of it all does not fall on them, finally and visibly, but on that underlying population with whom they deal, also called "the ultimate consumer."

As a further consequence, which is more immediately to the point here, by force of this endless network of credit that ties up the business concerns of the country in an interdependence of fiscal give the take, they are at the same time, each of his degree, large and small, tied in under the paramount fiscal jurisdiction of these keepers of the country's credit resources, as clients whose fortunes are forever in the balance and whose continued good fortune is conditioned on their continuing to be lucrative clients.

The key industries, it is true, occupy a special position in this regard, and the argument will return to their case presently. Smaller and outlying industrial and commercial concerns may be touched only at the second remove, by the other ramifications of the fiscal organisation, but they are all caught in the network of credit which serves the workday needs of all those who do business. And inasmuch as the country's industry is in the hands of the business men and is carried on as a business enterprise, it follows also that any question of industrial employment and of the rate and volume of production is likewise and perforce referred back to the same fiscal grounds and incentives, at any point that involves a question of initiative or eventual control. So that the industrial system, too, the productive use of the country's man-power and industrial plant, likewise waits on the collusive fiscal strategy of the same custodians of absentee credit. Whereby the livelihood of the underlying population becomes, in the language of mathematics, a function of the state of mind of the investment bankers, whose abiding precept is: When in doubt, don't.

Progressively, indeed at a cumulative rate, as the credit resources have been drawn together under a wide-reaching routine of profitable give and take, under the responsible surveillance of half-a-dozen massive credit institutions at the financial metropolis, the whole business of making credits and regulating them has gained in expedition and security; so that it has now reached an admirable footing of stability and swift execution. Stability, greater security from unforeseen or undesigned contingencies, will enable trading in credits and capitalisation on a thinner equity; which signifies a larger volume of fixed charges payable to the makers of credit, on the resultant increased volume of outstanding obligations; which means that the custodians of credit are enabled to take over the assets of the business community with increasingly greater expedition; which in turn will increase the stability of the business as well as the measure of control exercised by the keepers of credit over the conduct of business and industry at large. Eventually, therefore, the country's assets should, at a progressively accelerated rate, gravitate into the ownership, or at least into the control, of the banking community at large; and within the banking community ownership and control should gravitate into the hands of the massive credit institution that stands at the fiscal center of all things.

The stability of this fabric of credit, as well as the facility and effect with which its control of business and industry will be brought to bear, is greatly promoted by the inner concatenations of the system; particularly by the working arrangements and bonds of common interest that gather about the nucleus of credit institutions at the fiscal center. These concatenations are of such a nature that, in great part, the chief banking-houses and their chief clients are now identical in point of their business interest; to a very appreciable extent identical in point of ownership. So that the same "Interest" — that is to say the same group of absentee owners working together as a team in pursuit of gain — will not infrequently be found to be the dominant owners on both the debit and the credit side of given account; both within a given financial banking-house or group of affiliated banks and in the greater ones of the corporations whose credit and securities are taken care of by the given banking-house and its affiliated banks.[xiv]

Such an arrangement will conduce in a marked degree to the stability of all suitable credit-extensions, capitalisations, and flotations; suitable, i.e., for the purposes of those who make up the general staff of solvency. At the same time it affords a ready means of discountenancing or disallowing ill-advised and adventurous projects, such as do lend themselves to profitable capitalisation under the same auspices. Such, in effect, is the lie of the land in the domain of credit.

Any given one of these massive Interests will be the dominant factor in a number of corporate enterprises of the larger sort, each of which will do a large credit business with several of the greater banking-houses and their affiliated banks. It is a matter of common notoriety, if not of record, that the great Interests have been gaining ground of this sort at a progressively accelerated rate; gaining both in point of mass and financial consequence and in the reach and variety of the ramifications of their ownership throughout the business community. And it is fairly to be expected that their progress will continue unabated on somewhat the same lines in the calculable future. There results an intimate linking-up of client and custodian, a community interest between creditor and debtor, such as should virtually preclude any consequential derangement of the equilibrium of debits and credits except by mutual consent. In practical effect, the outcome is a pooling of credits and debits, within the financial sweep of the Interests. In practical effect, therefore, the preponderant mass of outstanding obligations and intangibles has come to rest in stable equilibrium, not to be upset except by choice of the interested parties, in pursuit of their joint gain, at the cost of the rest of the business community.[xv]

This assured stability of the general fabric of credit serves greatly to augment the tensile strength of the business men's endurance in the face of new commitments. So that their goodwill and tolerance become available for capitalisation on behalf of the investment bankers at a higher coefficient than before. Whereby the output of new credit extensions and new capitalisations is enabled safely to expand at an unexampled rate.

So far, the argument has run to the effect that this American "credit economy,"[xvi] organised in this way, will work unremittingly to draw the assets of the business community in under the ownership of those massive Interests whose captains constitute the general staff of solvency, in the manner already described. Such is countless the main drift of the forces engaged. But if the proposition were left standing in this unqualified form it would be too bald to serve as a sufficient description of what is actually taking place or of what is immediately in prospect. The main drift and its convolutions do not make it so simple a tableau. It is necessary to note that the Interests and their captains and custodians do not appear to drive at all consistently and with a single mind toward such an undivided ownership of the assets engaged; nor does such an outcome habitually follow from their management of affairs, as a formal outcome, *de jure*.

It appears that, at least for the present and in great part, what is actually sought and obtained by their manoeuvres is an effectual usufruct of these resources, rather than a formal acquisition and tenure of them in strict ownership. Formally of the purpose of continued gain, such an effectual usufruct of the country's resources will serve as well as their formal ownership, at the same time that it can be administered quite as readily and profitably under the existing forms of law, and is less likely to irritate the public sensibilities. In effect, through the due working of this traffic in credit and capitalisation, the Interests and their custodians come in for the formal ownership of a progressively increasing share of these assets; and at the same time and by force of the same traffic they also come in for a progressively larger and more secure usufruct in the assets which still continue formally in the ownership of those concerns that have become their clients and that are dependent on their continued good will for indispensable credits by means of which to do business.

The case of the common run of these business concerns — that is to say, of the business community at large — as it is taking shape during these last years under the perfected credit economy, has a notable and instructive parallel and analogue in the plight of the prairie farmers, who have fallen into a state of something like effectual clientship and usufruct at the call of the implement makers, commission men, warehouse men, millers, packers, and railways. *De facto*, by drift of circumstances and sound business methods, these large business concerns which deal with the farmers and deal in their produce and their supplies have now come in for a reasonably secure and inclusive usufruct in the work and output of this farm population. The country bankers and country merchants, of course, also come in for their equitable share. Throughout this farming community there is a fairly steady drift of ownership into the hands of these business concerns with which the farm population does business; which takes effect in great part through the use of credit in the way of book accounts and deferred payments. But apart from absentee ownership of tenant farms and a certain, quite appreciable, volume of farm indebtedness, there is habitually no formal title of ownership, actual or contingent, covering the farmers or their work and output and vesting in the usufructuaries. The more substantial and more profitable source of gain to these concerns and Interests that make up the farmer's markets is doubtless their *de facto* vested right to do business with the farm population on their own terms.[xvii]

The current relation of usufruct between the packers, millers, warehouse men, and railroads, on the one side, e.g., and their underlying farm population on the other side, has no existence *de jure*, of course; the principles of jurisprudence which touch these matters being of an earlier date and not covering these features. It is only that as a practical matter of fact these Interests are in a position to make the terms on which the prairie farmers will go on with their work, if any; all the while that the farmers are left quite free to take or leave the terms offered, but with the reservation that their livelihood is contingent on their taking them. By this businesslike arrangement the farm population comes in for a very tolerable subsistence, to be had and for steady work; while the railroads, packers, millers, etc., come in for a capitalised usufruct of the farm population and its work and for a steady run of earnings, — such a run of earnings as the traffic will bear.

In much the same fashion those major Interests on the financial plane, whose custodians are in command of the credit resources of the country at large, are enabled, informally and by a standard routine of management, to take over a reasonably complete usufruct in the run of business carried on by the business community at large. All the while this arrangement need involve no formal tenure of ownership of the underlying business traffic on their part. It may quite practically be done, as it is being done and as the circumstances entail that it must be done, by informal concert of action among those major Interests which are massive enough to make their pretensions good, and by a disciplinary "rationing" of the lesser business units in the allowance of credits with which to carry on their business. The packers, millers, etc., who do business with the farm population on a footing of usufruct may be entitled to rank among these major Interests that serve as custodians of the country's solvency, or they may belong among the lesser order of clients through whom the income-stream runs; — all that is a question of detail and personalities, which does not materially touch the general sweep and balance of the credit system and its appointed work.

Its appointed work, appointed by the drift of circumstances, is the due tutelage of the business concerns of the country and the governance of their conduct of the country's business and industry, with an eye single to the largest procurable net gains for those aggregations of absentee ownership that are spoken of as the Interests.

The procurable net gain in which the Interests are interested is counted in terms of the money-unit, of course; and it is invariably rated, received, accumulated, carried forward, disbursed, and accounted for, by way of a credit-instrument of some sort, book-account or transferable paper. Material wealth, metallic money, does not pass from hand to hand in this business traffic, except in transactions so small as to call for the use of what the economists call "token-money"; which is, in effect, another form of credit-instrument. The nearest approach to the material realities in the handling of these elements of income and disbursement is the use of banknotes; which is in the main confined to minor transactions. In ordinary times banknotes are presumed to outrun their specie basis by something over 500 per cent; of late years they have fluctuated within an interval of perhaps twice that amplitude. It is in units of this fiduciary currency that the gains of business are valued and accounted for, and that the earning-capacity of any given business concern will be capitalised.

The increasing centralisation and cooperative spirit of the banking community, helped out by the good offices of the Federal Reserve, have been adding materially to the security of the outstanding note-issues. So that this increased volume of paper money commands an increased measure of public confidence. That is to say, the paper money business is enabled to trade on a thinner equity. The note-issues have been enabled to depart somewhat more widely from the specie basis on which they are, at least ostensibly, hypothecated. In effect, these credit-instruments which serve as the habitual measure of values are less exposed to the hazard of being called to account, at the same time that they are more widely detached from any material base.

It is this fiduciary currency that serves as the workday ground of reality in the pursuit of business, transactions being concluded in its terms and gains being "realised" in its units. Evidently, this fiduciary currency is of the nature of certified make-believe, in the main; being a volume of intangibles hypothecated on the sound sense of the banking community and the Federal Reserve Board. The tutelage and governance exercised by these custodians of solvency over the conduct of business, therefore, has come to rest on this groundwork of outstanding liabilities which so are shielded from any ordinary hazard of liquidation, and their manoeuvres of guidance and management are confined to a give and take between credit-instruments of one description and another. The work is carried on by a systematic rationing of credit allowances.

The purpose and end of the traffic so carried on by the keepers of solvency is the up-keep and enlargement of the run of gains that will be credited to the party of the first part. As has already been noted in an earlier passage, the gains which so are to be credited to the creditors are drawn from the receipts of the underlying business traffic, as an overhead charge of the working assets engaged in business. To enable such an augmented overhead charge to be carried by the underlying business traffic — and to be carried at a net profit — the gross receipts of this business traffic must also be enlarged by the same move and in a corresponding measure. The safe and sane procedure by which to bring receipts up to a practical maximum in any business enterprise is to limit the supply of vendible goods of services out of the sale-price of which the receipts arise, and thereby to advance the price per unit of supply up to the limit of what the traffic will bear, as has also been explained already. In ordinary times the supply and the sale-price will already have been adjusted, within reason, to what the traffic will bear, regard being had to the current level of prices and the available volume of purchasing-power. Therefore, to enlarge the receipts of the underlying business traffic and so enable it to carry an enlarged overhead charge, it will be necessary to raise the limit of what the traffic will bear; which it accomplished automatically by the increase of purchasing-power that is thrown on the market in the creation of the new credits which impose this new overhead charge, in that the new purchasing-power granted in these credits will go to raise the price per unit of vendible things and so will go to swell the aggregate price-receipts of the traffic by that much.

As a proposition in business and accountancy the outcome of these manoeuvres is quite admirable; as a proposition in industry and livelihood it will stand somewhat different. It brings an increase to aggregate wealth and income as counted in money-values, independently of any increase of tangible possessions. But as a business proposition that is just as good, if not better. Such creation of new credits has much the same effect as the production of new gold used to have under the old dispensation;[xviii] but with the difference that the expansion of prices created by credit rests on the tensile strength of the popular credulity instead of the output of gold. Yet this later ground of price-inflation is presumably quite as secure as the earlier, more particularly by grace of the Federal Reserve Board's vigilant stabilisation of note-issues and commercial rediscounts.

It will be seen that the argument on this head runs on a progressive, automatic, and presumably interminable inflation of money-values; or on a continued depreciation of the effectual money-unit; according as one may choose to view it. Under the old dispensation of unconcerted banking, in so far as the money-unit was eventually accountable to an impersonal specie basis, such an inflation would be riding for an eventual fall, whereof there were repeated demonstrations. But under the new dispensation, since and so far as the price-level has become accountable to the sound business sense of the Federal Reserve Board and the keepers of the credit resources, no such sinister eventuality need be apprehended. The general staff of solvency have the situation in hand, and their interest in its maintenance may be counted on to endure.

The secure upward trend of the price-level, and its buoyant endurance under difficulties during the last few years, should sufficiently demonstrate the superior stability of a price-inflation which rests on constituted authority and businesslike commonsense. Provided that the price-level continues to rise at a reasonable rate, such a temperate rate as will not greatly jar the popular credulity and such as the sound business principles of its guardians may reasonably be counted on to dictate, then there should be no reason to apprehend that this price-level may not safely be advanced indefinitely, to the continued gain of those who stand to gain by it.

To any footloose observer it will be evident that the general price-level has been rising, without serious break or abatement, during the past quarter-century. The new gold has had something to do with this movement, more particularly during the earlier part of this period, and the new credit facilities have had more to do with it, particularly in later years. In a very appreciable degree this movement of price-inflation has been masked by the continued advance in the industrial arts, which has run along without abatement over the same period and has greatly increased the productive capacity of the country's industry, and which so has acted powerfully and unremittingly to lower the cost of production of the output, and thereby to depress prices of vendible goods and services.

In the face of a steadfast resistance from the side of safe and sane business, particularly from the financial section of the business community, the continued new growth of the technology of physics and chemistry has continued to insinuate a progressively heightened productive efficiency into the industrial system, cumulatively and ubiquitously, and with a particularly stubborn drive along the lines of quantity production; such as to depress the costs and enlarge the scope and rate in the quantity production of vendible goods and services. If these improvements in the ways and means of industry had been given a free run through this period, and if prices had not at the same time been inflated by use of credit, the higher potential of production of which these technological improvements have enabled the industrial system to do its work should in the course of this period have lowered production-costs at large to such a level as would have brought general prices down to an inconspicuous fraction of the current figures.

But such a free run of production, such as the technicians would be ready to set afoot if they were given a free hand, would mean a full employment of the available forces of industry, regardless of what the traffic would bear in point of net profit from sales; it would bring on such an inordinate output of vendible goods and services as to glut the market and precipitate an irretrievable decline of the price-level, and consequently also a fatal decline of earnings and default and liquidation of capitalised earning-capacity, — a disastrous liquidation of capitalised intangibles. Therefore such a free run of production has not been had nor aimed at; nor is it at all expedient, as a business proposition, that anything of the kind should be allowed.

Still, under all that handicap of cautious businesslike retardation which sound business principles have entailed, the continued growth of the mechanical technology has taken effect in cheapened production in so large a measure as to have greatly masked that progressive inflation of prices which the larger use of credit has brought on and carried forward during the same interval. With the partial exception of the crude products of the soil, there is no one of the major lines of production that has not been gravely affected by it. From time to time the technological advance has even been able to give the progressive inflation of prices the appearance of being no more than a stabilisation and maintenance of the price-level; although in the long run the cumulative expansion of credit, re-inforced with a resolute businesslike restriction of output all along the line, has proved to be the stronger, and has proved to be the determining factor in that parallelogram of economic forces the resultant of which has been a sustained upward trend of general prices and a cumulative capitalisation of intangibles.

Apart from scattered speculative gains which may come to shrewd outsiders here and there, those who stand to gain by this long run of expansion in money-values are the constituent members of the One Big Union of financial Interests. Between them they make up the party of the first part of that advancing press of credit transactions by which the expansion is made and maintained.[xix] This One Big Union is not precisely a trade-union of bankers; although it is on the ground of investment banking and by use of transactions in credit and capitalisation that the One Big Union's tutelage and regulation of business and industry go into effect. It is essentially a union of Interests, not of persons; at least not in a personal bearing; although it is through measures taken by those persons who are the appointed custodians of these Interests that those business principles by which they live have come to regulate these large matters, in point of tactics, scope and policy, not in point of detailed manoeuvres. There has been, hitherto, no such degree of organised responsibility and control as would permit this General Staff of custodians to dictate specific manoeuvres to their clients, except it be at a critical juncture, when the common good of the Interests is in the balance or when the fabric of credit and capitalisations is exposed to some imminent hazard. If the name be employed in such a loosely descriptive fashion, the One Big Union of the Interests will come to much the same thing as what is covered by the colloquial phrase, "Big Business," but with a particular reference to that community-interest and that solidarity of principles which is entailed by the common responsibilities and the common benefits of the larger absentee ownership.

These Interests which so are drawn together, by force of circumstances, into this inchoate One Big Union of absentee ownership are many and various; but they have at least one distinctive trait in common, viz. large absentee ownership. It is also a characteristic fact that the Interests, or their assets, are quite generally if not invariably engaged in two or more lines of business at the same time, and that each of these distinct lines of business engages these assets to their full amount. Two such lines of business carried on in this way simultaneously for the same Interest and by the sue of the same assets will touch and mutually re-inforce one another in respect of their solvency, although they will be quite distinct in respect of their corporate identity and the technical character of the business traffic carried on by each.

The one line will be financial, in the nature of investment banking, occupied with the creative use of credit resources, capitalisations and flotations; while the other line will be commercial or industrial business of the corporate sort, perhaps more frequently the latter, occupied with the output and sale of vendible goods or services. Few if any of these Interests, or blocks of absentee ownership, are not to be counted with in both of these bearings; particularly such of them as rise into a position of dominance in the business community. This type-form would be that which is shown by those well-known dominating Interests whose force of ownership is to be counted with equally in the banking community at the fiscal metropolis and in one or another of the key industries, as, e.g., steel, coal, oil, or railways. But of much the same value and effect, for the purpose of the present argument, are those other notable Interests which combine a metropolitan enterprise in solvency and capitalisations with large industrial undertakings that are not commonly classed as key industries; as, e.g., sugar-refining, meat-packing, flour-milling, the manufacture of explosives, or trolley lines. Illustrative instances will readily come to mind.

This characteristic bifurcation, or spread, of the Interests, or, if one prefers the expression, this conjugation of industrial and fiscal enterprises under the same block of absentee ownership, is by no means a casual or fortuitous occurrence. It is of the essence of the case and lies at the root of the current situation. It is not in any conclusive sense an effect of personal choice and inclination, for it is contained in that drift of circumstances out of which the whole situation arises, and which no personal bias or caprice can turn aside or defeat. The underlying and conclusive fact of the matter is that such procedure is profitable; which is conclusive for the pursuit of business.

Such double use of the available assets will yield double earnings; indeed, ordinarily something more. Sufficiently large assets engaged as corporate capital, say in one of the key industries, will at the same time and to their full amount, and without prejudice to their earning-capacity as corporation assets serve also to their full amount as assets of solvency in the fiscal enterprise of the metropolitan investment banking, provided always that the assets are held in sufficiently large blocks. Indeed, the more fully and profitably such assets are employed in such industrial business, especially if they are engaged on a large and dominant scale, the better will be their rating in the business community and the more securely and fully will they serve as the substance of that solvency on which the traffic in credit extensions and capitalisations is carried on. The larger the success, in point of earnings, and the more assured the prospective earning-capacity of any such block of assets, the larger and more assured will be its solvency and its funded carrying-power as a factor in the business of investment banking, and the more effectually, therefore, can it be mobilised for the creation of new credit extensions and new intangibles. Its effectual capital-value is enlarged by so much.[xx] For what they are worth, industrial assets of the larger sort have, therefore, such a secondary — or perhaps rather a primary — service to render their owners, or their constituted custodians, under the conditions inaugurated by this new order of business enterprise that runs on funded credits. The whole fabric of business is built on and about this double use of assets, and its movements are regulated by the circumstances which govern this double use.

Sound business principles — the principles of the main chance — will not allow the benefits of such double service of assets to be overlooked, nor will they let this fruitful duplication of earning-capacity go to waste. To lend itself most profitably to such double service, the parcel of assets in question should be of reasonably massive proportions, such as to place its owner or manager on a footing of some strategic independence and initiative among those large absentee owners on whose assets the country's credit system is erected and with whom he will have to negotiate for whatever share is coming to him out of the proceeds of that business. All the while it is also true, and it lies in the collusive nature of the fiscal system and its work, that many businesslike owners who command only relatively small and inconsequential parcels of assets will elbow their way into participation in the traffic, to come in for whatever margin of supernumerary profits they can touch while serving as outliers of the system and subsidiaries of the larger captains of duplication.

This is one of the prime considerations on the strength of which their banking operations are carried on by that multitude of minor and outlying banking concerns that do business as branches, subsidiaries, and correspondents, immediately or remotely dependent on the favorable attitude of the major concerns at the metropolitan center of solvency. These outliers are bound into the working system of credit by a bond of profitable compliance with the tactical dispositions made by its masters. On this ground do the ramifications of the system run. Without this faithful docility which characterises these outlying correspondents, the efficiency of the system as a generator of intangibles and incomes would be greatly curtailed, if indeed it could come to anything substantially lucrative at all in that case. By this double use of assets, and by help of this all-pervading give and take of profitable margins and commissions, the assets which are so employed are made to pay their way both going and coming, as one might say. The organisation is in the nature of a contrivance for killing two birds with one stone, or for making two overhead charges grow where one grew before, if one should prefer that form of the adage.

In the nature of the case, those massive aggregations of absentee ownership that are elected by circumstance to make up the One Big Union of the Interests, and to share in its counsels, revenues and perquisites, will necessarily take on such a duplex working formation; whatever may have been the underlying sources from which their assets have once been derived, or the employments in which they may once have been engaged during their growth and maturation. The earning capacities which enter into their composition as assets, and the personnel which administers them as Interests, may be of one derivation or another; they may, e.g., have come out of oil or out of commercial banking. But whether a given Interest has in its initial phase been identified with industrial business or with financial undertakings, its destiny under the circumstances which establish and regulate the new order of things in business will be to throw the full weight of its assets and prestige into both lines alike, so soon as it reaches the due measure of maturity in mass and in years of discretion.[xxi]

In respect of their financial commitments and their share in the guidance of the country's financial polity at large, these several Interests and their several custodians stand together on reasonably common ground; but the like is not to be said of their strategy and tactics as concerns engaged in industrial business. As financial Interests they are drawn together in team-work for their common good and are able to take measures in common, looking to their joint advantage and particularly to their mutual security, to the security of their several commitments and the maintenance of the level of capitalisation. Whereas in their capacity of industrial business Interests they are habitually somewhat at odds, if not at cross-purposes; being in the position of rival salesmen in a limited market. As industrial Interests, that is to say as business concerns which do business in an output of vendible products, they all are in some degree in the position of rivals in trade, sellers of alternative goods in a closed market, in which one tradesman misses what another takes of the available purchasing-power. In this bearing the most amicable contact which the circumstances of the case and the ethics of trade will admit among them is the watchful courtesy of a negotiated peace, — a peace negotiated for their mutual relief from "cutthroat competition" and for the common gain of the same Interests in their capacity of credit-brokers, investment bankers, creators of capitalised intangibles. It is, therefore, as massive parcels of funded solvency and formidable strategists in capitalisation that they come together as constituents of the One Big Union of the Interests; and it is as such that they safeguard that peace of moderation and mutual concessions that broods over the traffic of industrial business.

All the while, of course, it is the same Interests, the same parcels of assets and administered by the same responsible personnel, moved by the same incentive of net aggregate gain in terms of price, that do business in both connections. It is incumbent on these custodians and strategists of the Interests, collectively and severally, to regulate and administer affairs in a large way both in the traffic of industrial business and in the marketplace of credit and capital. But the seat of executive power as well as the high court of judicature, touching all the major issues of business traffic of whatever complexion, under this new order, are to be found on the financial ground, in the bailiwick of the high magistrates of solvency. Circumstances have taken such a turn.[xxii]

Chief among the circumstances which have given this turn to the pursuit of business, and which so have given rise to the new order of things and the sovereign powers of the larger credit, has been the circumstance that a businesslike competition in production and marketing was running loose among the major industries in the late nineties, at such an unguarded rate as to be a menace to the traffic; such as threatened to entail a grievous retrenchment of the outstanding capitalisations and jeopardise the fixed charges payable on outstanding debentures. The discord in the industrial business was rising to an intolerable pitch and volume, such as to threaten the continued earning-capacity of the business corporations that were caught in it. The new order of things has emerged from the remedial measures which that state of affairs invited, as has been explained in an earlier passage in describing the rise of the investment bankers. It lies in the nature of this industrial business, as conducted in a closed market by competitive business concerns, to breed dissension, distrust and cross-purposes among the Interests engaged in the traffic.[xxiii]

In due time, so soon as the corporate interests that were contending for the traffic had grown to formidable proportions and their market was closing in, this unhappy state of affairs became intolerable. So, under the spur of desperation, there has presently emerged the new order of collusive moderation under the administrative guidance of the One Big Union of the Interests. Concert and mutual accommodation in the conduct of this industrial business is effectually dictated not by the technical requirements of industry but by considerations of finance, with a view to mutual financial benefits, by financial concessions and alliances, under pressure of financial necessity.

Financial peace and stability is a matter of the first consequence to the Interests, and to all those who are concerned in the business of capitalised credits. The fabric of credit and capitalisation is essentially a fabric of concerned make-believe resting on the routine credulity of the business community at large. It is therefore conditioned on the continued preservation of this prevalent credulity in a state of unimpaired tensile strength, which calls for eternal vigilance on the part of its keepers. The fabric, therefore, is always in a state of unstable equilibrium, liable to derangement and extensive disintegration in case of an appreciable disturbance at any critical point, with unhappy consequences for the business of capitalisation and overhead charges. Hence the eminently wise and unremitting exhortation to retain or restore confidence, and to return to "normalcy" in case the popular credulity has suffered a lapse. This care is incumbent on the Interests on the One Big Union. So that it is incumbent on them to stand united and play safe, to avoid shock, to promote moderation and tranquility throughout the world of credit and capitalisation; for it is after all a confidence game — in the blameless sense of the phrase — and is to be played according to the rules governing games of that psychological nature. To this end these major

Interests, which in their financial entity make up the One Big Union, will use a reasonable degree of neighborly accommodation in pursuing their several advantages as special interests in the traffic of industrial and commercial business. And to the same salutary end the minor participants, subsidiaries, outliers and interlopers in the industrial business will be rationed in respect of their needful credit extensions, according to the same reasoned plan looking to the stability of price-levels and outstanding capitalisations.

The outcome of this régime of financial peace and stability is not that rivalry and sharp practice are eliminated from current industrial and commercial business, not even from industrial business of the larger sort which will generate a "Special Interest"; but only that the rivalry and competitive manoeuvring runs within reasonable and salutary bounds; that is to say, reasonable and salutary for the purposes of profitable financiering, as touches outstanding credits and the level of capitalisation. Reason and security in this bearing have to do with the maintenance and enlargement of earnings, of income and in terms of money, and of possessions in terms of price; not with the maintenance and enlargement of productive output or of livelihood. Competitive manoeuvres in industrial business under this régime, therefore, may without hazard run free in so far as they will not tend to impair the price-level. It is on the price-level that the level of capitalisation rests, at the same time that the volume of capitalisation determines the price-level, in the main and in the long run.

Competitive manoeuvres which will leave the price-level intact, or which will tend to raise it, will be manoeuvres of competitive salesmanship, not of competitive production, of course. Now and again such manoeuvres of salesmanship will involve an increased output of the line of goods or services to be sold, in case the manoeuvres enlarge the volume of sales. As an incident of the business, in such a case efficient salesmanship may provoke an increased production of the given line of goods. In a closed market, that is to say in a market which runs on a provisionally fixed volume of purchasing-power, such increased production and sale in any one given line of goods will be balanced (approximately) by an equivalent curtailment of output and sales in other lines which come in competition, directly or indirectly; or otherwise the price-level will be deranged. In effect and in the main it is a question of alternative purchases.[xxiv]

This state of the case leaves a fairly large scope for initiative and enterprise in salesmanship. And as is well known, a very large and steadily increasing expenditure of talents, funds, and apparatus has gone into this work in salesmanship in recent years. Even those major industrial Interests which would seem to be in a position to make their own terms, the terms on which they will buy their materials and on which they will dispose of their marketable output, have been going strong on this rivalry in salesmanship, as, e.g., the packers or the millers. They too are driving hard against these pliable but resilient barriers of competitive salesmanship in a closed market. The only ones among these industrial business enterprises which are passably exempt from the cares of salesmanlike rivalry are those which have to do immediately with one or another of the key industries. And even they are not wholly exempt, as may be seen, e.g., in the case of the oil business, whose sign-boards, advertisements, and decorated sales-booths are to be met at every turn; while their very reputable spokesmen continue to solicit the popular good-will with the most assiduously devout and humanitarian verbiage.

It is after all in the Key Industries — in coal, steel, oil, lumber, railways, waterpower — that the administrative center of this system of industrial business traffic lies; just as its executive center lies outside the industrial system proper, in the massive credit institutions of the fiscal metropolis. And it is on these key industries, in the main and primarily, that the dominant Interests of the One Big Union rest their weight of absentee ownership and pivot the sweep of their industrial dominion. The Key Industries are so called because the rest of the industrial system waits on their operations; so that they set the pace and govern the practicable rate and volume of employment and output for the industrial system at large, — practicable, that is, in point of business expediency.

The management of the key industries works out, in effect, as an administrative control of the industrial system at large; immediately through the mechanical industries, and indirectly also throughout the underlying industrial system. But all the while the management of the key industries is neither prompted nor guided by any such far-reaching administrative purpose, not is it biased by any sentiment of administrative responsibility in that connection. This guidance of industrial affairs is all, in a way, an undesigned and fortuitous by-product of the steadfast pursuit of their own advantage by those Interests that do business in the key industries. The measures taken by the Interests are directed to no such end. But such is the exacting balance and concatenation of the work and of its ways and means, under this mechanistic state of the industrial arts and under the price-system, that the operations of these key industries which turn out the primary output of coal, steel, oil, and transport, will unavoidably make the pace for the rest of the mechanical industries, whether by design or not.

As a matter of common sense and a fact of common notoriety, the key industries are managed on the businesslike principle of charging what the traffic will bear; that is to say, what will bring the largest net gain to their owners and managers. It is a simple, though sometime delicate, question of restricting the rate and volume of their output to such a figure as will yield the largest net return in terms of price, when the price is determined by this restriction of the output.[xxv]

Those other massive industrial undertakings that come into the same class with the key industries in respect of their dominant mass and reach and in the respect that they are concerned immediately with the price necessities of life, stand on much the same footing in this matter as the key industries proper; as, e.g., meat-packing, flour-milling, or sugar-refining. The management of these has the initiative in industrial business; that is to say, the initiative rests finally with the financial management of these concerns. Therefore, the Interests which have the financial custody and direction of these key industries are in a position to make the terms on which industrial production will be carried on, and it is for the management of the underlying industries in the system to take or leave the terms which are offered them.

The business men in charge of the key industries are able to use this discretion with a passably free hand, inasmuch as these industries stand at the apex of the industrial system, — the apex of growth and of industrial strategy. Their management is vested with the initiative in industrial matters. Their administrative policy consequently falls into relatively simple lines, in its general application. In its elements, it comes to the broad question of how large an output of these price ways and means of industry will yield the largest net aggregate price-return to the businessmen in charge and to their absentee owners. In its practical application this will foot up to a question of how far production had best be allowed to go, or how nearly full an employment of the available equipment and man-power will yield the largest net income, for the time being, to these owners and their managers; which may be restated as a question of how large a running margin of unemployment will best serve this purpose.

In ordinary times there is always such a running margin of unemployment, both in the key industries and in those underlying industries which depend on them for their necessary ways and means. And even in busy times few if any of these industries will ever come up to anything like the volume of production that would result from a free use of the same man-power and material resources under competent technical management with an eye single to production. Sound business considerations will not permit it. The businesslike duties of management turn constantly on sagacious restriction of output at the point of "balanced return," and on the many exacting details of speeding-up and slowing-down, of laying-off and taking-on, of hiring and firing, which arise out of this necessary strategy of balanced unemployment. Balanced Return involves Balanced Unemployment.

The gains of business enterprise, whether in the key industries or in the underlying industries of the system, are money-values and they are derived from the margin of sales-price over the cost of the output. The aim of business is to widen this margin and to come in for as large a share of it as may be. The margin may be widened by raising the sales-price or by lowering the cost of the output. And any given business concern may increase its share in this margin by more efficient salesmanship. These are the points to be covered by the strategy of industrial business management.

As has already been explained above, the price-level at large will rise progressively in response to that progressively enlarged volume of purchasing-power which arises out of the progressive creation of credits in the ordinary course of investment, merchandising, and corporation finance. This expansion is self-propagating. Each successive advance of the price-level calls for a corresponding increment of the working-capital of all those concerns that do business within its scope; which includes virtually all of the business community. The needful increase of working-capital is got by a creation of new credits; which goes to increase the volume of purchasing-power; which goes to raise the general level of prices, etc. It is a matter of workday routine, and is, in effect, to be broken into only by such a general liquidation of credits as is no longer to be apprehended, since the Federal Reserve and the One Big Union of the Interests have taken over the stabilisation of credits on a reasoned plan.

The major financial transactions of investment-banking work out to the same effect, these being also in the nature of a creation of credits, capitalisations, and overhead charges. So that the progressive rise of the price-level goes forward in an orderly, and conservative, way, as a secondary but unavoidable outcome of business-as-usual. By so much, industrial business enterprise at large is assured of a reasonable and progressively widening margin of money-values over the cost of its merchantable output, provided always that the (money) cost of the output does not also advance in the like measure.[xxvi]

[....], the business concerns of the underlying industrial system, the concerns that do business in commerce and manufactures, as these words are commonly understood, are engaged in competition among themselves for a share in the run of the market, — competitive management designed to increase each concern's share in the distribution of the available purchasing-power. Their market is a closed one, in a large way, in that the volume of purchasing-power available for distribution among them at any given time is a fixed quantity. Under current conditions the volume of purchasing-power will expand by a more or less orderly progression in the course of time and with the continued expansion of the outstanding volume of credit. But for the time being it is limited within fairly definite though not inflexible bounds. Salesmanship may divert given items and fractions of this outstanding volume of purchasing-power from one line of sales to another, but it does not in any appreciable degree enlarge the total volume of sales at any given time.[xxvii] Expenditure on sales-cost, taken as a whole, will therefore count as a deduction from the available margin of sales-price over cost or output. Yet continued and progressively increasing attention to salesmanship, and a continued and progressively increasing expenditure on sales-cost, are primary and essential to any reasonably large success in this field of business enterprise under the current conditions.[xxviii]

Again, inasmuch as the gains of business, the earnings of enterprise and invested capital, are always eventually to be drawn from the margin of sales-price over production-cost, it is incumbent on all business management to curtail production-cost so far as may be. The earnings of invested capital are of the nature of overhead charges, for the sake of which the business is carried on, and any curtailment of which will therefore foot up to so much of a defeat of the purpose for which business is carried on. It follows that any curtailment of production-cost which shall be reasonable, within the logic of business enterprise, must be curtailment in expenditures on those factors of production which are not capitalised or included among the rateable assets of the business community. Which comes to saying that the curtailment, if any, must take effect in those expenditures which go to the industrial man-power and the outlying farm population; these factors of the industrial system being not capitalised and, for the time being, not capitalisable, and so being not carried on the books as assets to which the business is bound over in the way of fixed charges.

In respect of their business interests, therefore, there results a division of cleavage of the people who live under this system of industrial business, whereby the business community, heading up in the Interests of the One Big Union, comes to stand over against the underlying population, which is taking articulate shape in the labor organisations and the sentimental swarming gyrations of the farmers. Quite generally these organisations and the projected movements among the underlying population run true to the "action-pattern" of business-as-usual, in that their consistent aim is to come in for an increasing share in the margin of sales-price over production-cost. This they endeavor to accomplish by bargain and sale, enforced by a well-considered limitation of their marketable supply, quite in the spirit of that larger financial business enterprise that administers the affairs of the capitalised manufactures, and that governs the rate and volume of the industrial output by a conscientious withdrawal of efficiency, as dictated by the law of balanced return. In these endeavors the fortunes of the underlying population are subject to ebb and flow; but in the nature of the case it is mostly ebb. The underlying population, it is true, is caught in the business system; but it is after all not an executive factor in the system; only a creative factor, which is quite another matter. It comes into the strategy of business enterprise at large in a more passive way, as man-power to be employed at discretion in the pursuit of earnings on capitalised industry, according to that law of balanced return, and as a body of ultimate consumers to be supplied at discretion in the pursuit of commercial gains, according to the principle of what the traffic will bear.

As organised industrial man-power, particularly as mobilised in the shape of standard labor-unions, these elements of the underlying population are consistently endeavoring, with a fluctuating measure of success, to enforce an indefinitely extensible claim in the way of better pay. But in the nature of the case these endeavors if successful will ordinarily come to nothing more than a running process of catching up. The better pay is better in terms of price. But in the nature of the case the general level of prices continues to rise under current conditions of credit, capitalisation, and salesmanship. And since these progressively better-paid workmen are at the same time ultimate consumers of the goods whose prices continue progressively to advance, they continue to lose in the higher cost of living whatever they gain in the advance of wages. With a change of phrase the same proposition applies to the farm population. And it should be noted in the same connection. As applying without much distinction to all classes and conditions of ultimate consumers, that all the while the ever-increasing personnel and proficiency employed in salesmanship continues to convert additional articles of superfluous consumption into items of morally necessary use; at the same time that the increasing expenditure on sales-costs goes unremittingly to raise the price of living.

The organised industrial man-power endeavors, with a fluctuating measure of success, to make good its claim to an enlarged allowance of livelihood. The ways and means employed in these endeavors foot up, invariably, to a standardised conscientious withdrawal of efficiency, designed to bring the Interests to terms by a punitive restriction of the industrial output. In effect, this is the sole purpose for which the industrial man-power has been organised. So also the farmers are aspiring to make head against the Interests and to reinstate themselves as "Independent Farmers," after the good old fashion of the day before yesterday. The Independent Farmer is one of the lost arts of the nineteenth century. They are hoping to contrive some sort of a businesslike plan of concerted action by which to put themselves collectively in line as a practicable Interest that shall be able to make terms and reshape the scheme of things nearer to the bucolic heart's desire. By and large, the remedial aspirations of these farmers appear to fall under three several heads: restriction of output; restraint of trade; and expansion of credits. Their great hope appears to center on an inflation of prices by a conscientious withdrawal of productive efficiency and an inflation of purchasing-power. By this means they hope to cover their outstanding liabilities and procure their needed working-capital. Their aspirations, at least, are businesslike.

Meantime the Interests, the One Big Union of the Major Interests and the network of minor concerns through which the business of credit and capitalisation runs, are engaged on a loosely collusive plan for bringing the industrial man-power to reasonable — that is to say profitable — terms by the punitive use of unemployment. At the same time the volume of outstanding capitalisation is being continuously augmented by a continued flow of securities, in great part representing recapitalisations of existing assets, and working-capital to be applied toward increased sales-costs. By and large, or "in principle," the Interests and the Federal Reserve take a position of prudent conservatism; in practical effect the drift of businesslike exigencies decides that, as a matter of transactions in detail, the continued issue of new capital-securities runs well up in the hundreds of millions weekly; while the physical aggregate of the capitalised assets appears on the whole to be declining in a moderate way, through uncovered wear and tear. More particularly will it be seen that the physical ways and means are falling short when it is considered that both the numbers of the population and the requirements per capita go on increasing, with no sensible net addition to the ways and means of life and production, while an increasing proportion of the available ways and means is spent on sales-costs.

As has been explained in earlier chapters, and as will readily be seen by any intelligent person who takes an interest in these matters, secular life among the peoples of Christendom is governed in recent times by three several systems of use and wont, sovereign action-patterns induced by the run of past habituation: — the mechanical system of industry; the price-system; and the national establishment. The existing industrial system is dominated by the technology of physics and chemistry, and is a product of recent times, a profoundly modified derivative of the handicraft industry. The current price-system is dominated by absentee ownership and is also a greatly altered outgrowth of the handicraft industry and its petty trade; its continued growth in recent times has, in effect, changed it into a credit-price system. The nation, considered as a habit of thought, is a residual form of the predatory dynastic State of Early modern times, superficially altered by suffusion of democratic and parliamentary institutions in recent times.

By continued growth of use and wont in recent times the price-system has in effect become a credit-price system; and driven by the same growth the system of ownership has to all intents and purposes become a system of absentee ownership, in all that concerns any effectual initiative and authority in the conduct of economic affairs. The effectual control of the economic situation, in business, industry, and civil life, rests on the control of credit. Therefore the effectual exercise of initiative, discretion, and authority is perforce vested in those massive aggregations of absentee ownership that make up the Interests. Within certain wide limits of tolerance, therefore, the rest of the community, the industrial system and the underlying population, are at the disposal of the Interests, as ways and means of business, to be managed in a temperate spirit of usufruct of the continued and cumulative benefit of the major Interests and their absentee owners. The nation, both as a habit of thought and as a governmental going concern, comes into the case, in effect and in the main, as an auxiliary agency the function of which is to safeguard, extend and facilitate this work of surveillance and usufruct which has by drift of circumstances become incumbent on the Interests.

Such appears to be the state of the case, in the large and in so far as the forces engaged have yet fallen into definite lines and groupings, in those respects which come in question here.

It will be seen, accordingly, that the current economic situation is drawn on lines of a two-sided division of its forces or elements: — the Interests; and the underlying population. Such is the situation, typically, in the case of America; and such is also the state of things in the other civilised countries, in much the same measure in which they are civilised according to the same pattern. The Interests, properly speaking, are made up of those blocks of absentee ownership which are sufficiently massive to come into the counsels of the One Big Union of the Interests. Associated with these in their work, as copartners, auxiliaries, subsidiaries, extensions, purveyors of traffic, are the minor Interests and the business community at large; primarily the banking community. The work which they have in hand is to do business for a profit by use of the industrial system and the underlying population has two uses: — as industrial man-power; and as ultimate consumers, — that is to say as ultimate purchasers, since the business interest does not extend beyond the ultimate sale of the goods.

To do a profitable business one should buy cheap and sell dear, as all reasonable men know. In its dealings with the underlying population the business community buys their man-power and sells them their livelihood. So it is incumbent on the business men in the case to buy the industrial man-power as cheap as may be, and to sell the means of living to the ultimate consumer as dear as may be. All of which is a platitudinous matter of course.

The source of profits is the margin of sales-price over production-cost (or purchase-cost). [...] it has already been explained how this margin is widened by raising the level of sales-prices; both by efficient salesmanship in the merchandising trades and by a continued expansion of the outstanding volume of purchasing power through a continued creation of credits at the hands of the investment bankers and similar credit-establishments. In the same connection something has also been said of the service which the agencies of government render, in the way of enhancing prices by contributing to the security of this expanded volume of credit and so helping to make it indefinitely expansible without risk.

On the side of costs the underlying population comes into the case as being the industrial man-power that is to be bought, including the skill and technical knowledge that makes up the state of the industrial arts. On this side this population comes in as vendors of the ways and means of production. For the present purpose they may be classed loosely under two heads: — the industrial workmen; and the farmers. Also loosely and with a negligible fringe of exceptions it may be said that both of these groups of industrial man-power come into the negotiations on a businesslike footing, governed by the principles of the price-system and aiming to sell as dear as may be.

In these endeavors to sell dear the farmers have hitherto met with no measurable success, apparently for want of effectual collusion. In effect and in the common run the farm population and its work and livelihood are a species of natural resources which the business community holds in usufruct, in the nature of inert materials exposed to the drift of circumstances over which they have no control, somewhat after the analogy of bacteria employed in fermentation.

Notes

i The ordinary width of this margin of inflation is a matter of conjecture rather than computation. It varied appreciably even in ordinary times, and it grew gradually wider on the whole as the century advanced. Toward the close of the century a reasonable estimate would perhaps make it something between 500 per cent and 1000 per cent of what the price level might conceivably have been in the absence of bank credit. But since substantially no business was conducted on any other than a credit basis there are no data on which to base a secure opinion.

ii The expression, "trading on the equity," as employed in this connection, is borrowed from W.H. Lyon, *Capitalisation*, where a very competent discussion of this principle is to be found in chapter ii.

iii As is related of Jakob Fugger, "Er wollte verdienen dieweil er könnte."

iv For descriptions and argument on this movement in the nineties and after, cf. the testimony of various witnesses before the U. S. Industrial Commission, in the Commission's *Report*, vols. I, IX and XIII. So also W. Z. Rilpley, *Trusts, Pools and Corporations*; E. S. Meade, *Trust Finance*, and *Corporation Finance*; W. S. Stevens, *Industrial Combinations and Trusts*; C. W. Gerstenberg, *Materials of Corporation Finance*; A. S. Dewing, *Corporate Promotions and Reorganization*.

v There is, of course, no sharp date-line to be drawn in such a case, but 1897 will serve to mark this turn of affairs as well as any.

vi Cf. A. S. Dewing. *The Financial Policy of Corporations*, vol. II, ch. ii and vii. In the same connection see also The Same, vol. III, ch. ix, on the Voting Trust. Also Hastings Lyon, *Corporation Finance*, Part II, ch. ii and iii.

vii So, e.g., the market value of the securities of the U.S. Steel Corporation, or of the various Standard Oil subsidiaries, has persistently gone over par, even when large issues of stock-dividends have been set afloat.

viii It has not been customary to describe transactions of this class in precisely these terms. It is even doubtful if writers on corporation finance and investment banking would accept what has been said above as a faithful description of the relevant facts. Habitually, the point of view of such writers, and more particularly their point of attention, has been somewhat different from the perspective which governs the present argument. It has been customary to discuss transactions in corporation finance from the side of the tangible assets and their use, rather than from the side of investment and valuation. The argument here is concerned with the workday uses of credit in transactions of capitalisation.

When new incorporations or reorganisations, involving new and larger flotations of securities, are here spoken of as transactions looking to the creation of capitalised wealth by new extensions of credit, it is not intended to say that such new extensions of credit will enlarge the existing volume of "productive goods." It is not intended to say that such addition to the outstanding credit obligations will create material assets, or will in any way directly add to or augment the country's tangible possessions, or enhance the tangible performance of the country's productive industry. As a matter of tradition, it has been customary to believe that some such effect will commonly follow indirectly from such new and increased capitalisation, but that is a question with which the argument is not concerned at this point. Immediately and traceably, the creative effect which these transactions have is altogether in the nature of a creation of intangible assets. Indirectly and presumptively, by what may be called a repercussion of optimism, there may also result something in the way of increased industrial activity and an enlargement of industrial plant; but all that lies outside the immediate operations of investment banking or corporation finance. Such tangible facts are not of the same order of things as an issue of fiduciary paper.

Intangible assets may be created by a suitable extension of credit embodied in corporation securities, as has been abundantly shown by the run of things during the past quarter-century. To their owners these intangible assets will be an effectual item of capitalised wealth, as is likewise shown by the experience of the same years. It is true, such intangible assets constitute no part of the country's material possessions and have no creative part in the tangible performance of the country's industrial forces. They are wholly in the nature of an absentee claim to a share in the country's income; in the last analysis, of course, a claim on the product of industry, to which all the while they have contributed nothing. By and large, intangible assets constitute a valid claim to get something for nothing; and such a claim may be created by an extension of credit; and to its owner it is wealth to the amount of what it is worth. It is also a marketable commodity, and it may be employed as collateral by means of which to procure a further extension of credit, which may be turned to account in the same way and with the like ulterior effect.

These intangible assets, capitalisations of usufruct, which so are created and added to the existing book-values of the country's wealth, constitute a new claim on the existing volume of income; therefore they constitute a substraction form the body of income which would otherwise go to other, earlier claimants. The owners of these newly created intangibles, therefore, come in for the effectual value of their newly acquired assets at the cost of a corresponding loss to the general body of owners. By force of these transactions, in credit and capitalisation, the existing property owners and workmen lose as much as the owners of the new assets gain, plus the cost of the operations. The loss which so falls on the general body of owners (and workmen) is a loss only in the material respect, by weight and tale of the things which their incomes will purchase, not a loss in respect of the book-values of their assets. The credit extension which goes to the creation of these new assets will mask the confiscatory character of the transaction by adding the face value of the new assets — and ordinarily something more — to the outstanding volume of market values. The new credits go into the market as an addition to the current volume of purchasing-power; thereby correspondingly lowering the purchasing-power of the money unit. It foots up to an inflation of the total volume of wealth in hand as rated in terms of price, with no corresponding increase of tangible possessions; whereby the investment bankers and their clients come in for an increased share of the wealth in hand, at the cost of the general body of owners and workmen. — CF. also *Theory of Business Enterprise*, ch. iii, pp. 99—132, ch. iv, pp. 148—168, 174—176.

ix By "sound business management," proceeding on such a reasonable understanding among themselves, the investment bankers who command the credit resources of the country are enabled to trade on a progressively thinner equity; so that they are able to enlarge the volume of outstanding credit, indefinitely, by means of a progressive creation of intangible assets on which to base a further extension of credit, etc.

x In due time this force of circumstances, which so has drawn the banking community together in a centralised ramification of equitable give and take under the collusive surveillance of the great credit houses of the metropolis, has been given a local habitation and a name, by act of a businesslike Congress, in the installation of the Federal Reserve Board. The working-out of this measure appears to have been wholly salutary and to have fallen quite neatly in with the drift of circumstances that has shaped the men and structure of Big Business. It is true, the surveillance and disciplinary powers formally vested in the Board neither derive from nor devolve upon the massive banking-houses of the metropolis; nor, on the other hand, do they extend by specification to anything beyond commercial banking and the issuance of fiduciary currency. But it is the same concatenation of banking concerns, bound in the same inclusive system of financial correspondence, by which the commercial paper and the paper currency are taken care of, that also takes care of the country's credit resources and their allocation and distribution throughout the channels of investment banking; and the work is carried on by the same personnel, at the same time, through the same channels, and by use of a solvency resting on the same assets. The creative use of credit in generating and floating corporations securities is, after all, no more than another branch of that business of issuing, endorsing, and transferring fiduciary paper, that has to do with bank-notes and commercial banking. The transactions are of the same general kind. The banker's incentive in both cases is also the same margin of gain to be got for letting someone else go to work, whether it takes the form of a bonus of commission for the flotation of corporation securities, or a rediscount, or an excess of note-issues over the legal reserve; the method of earning this margin of profits is the same trading on the confidence of clients and customers; and the ulterior effect of the traffic is the same expansion of money-values through depreciation of the unit of purchasing-power. — Cf. H. L. Reed, *The Development of Federal Reserve Policy*.

xi The standard manuals of economic theory make no reference to any such cumulative acceleration in the ordinary rate of output of capitalisation of liabilities, as a factor in the economic system with which their speculations are occupied, although writers on corporation finance have called attention to the practice from time to time. Economists habitually have seen the whole matter in another light. Economic theories have habitually been standardised in forms which would meet the requirements of that earlier "cash economy" that has been falling out of the scheme of things in recent times. Under the old order the use of credit was a matter of "deferred payments," rather than an instrumentality of absentee ownership. So economists have not been in the habit of looking to the volume of outstanding obligation and intangibles — capitalised overhead charges — as a creative factor in the continued expansion of liabilities and capitalisation; particularly not the certified economists of the ancient line. (Cf., e.g., J. Laurence Laughlin, *The Principles of Money*, chapters on Credit and on the Refined

System of Barter). Their perspective has been somewhat faithfully foreshortened to fit the legal formalities of incorporation and the stipulations of economic doctrine as drawn up in the middle nineteenth century; at a time when it was still passably true in practice, or at least in the established tradition, that any extension of credit would be presumed to be secured by tangible assets available as collateral, in the case of negotiable securities, or by an available reserve or specie in the case of paper money. That was under the old order of business practice and the still older order of legal and theoretical conceptions. There is no call to take exception, or to call ungraceful attention to that ever-widening fringe of intangibles which was by that time progressively enveloping the nineteenth-century fabric of cash assets, and which eventually has overrun and surmounted it.

All that was under the old order, or under the rigorous tradition of it; while the slow-dying presumption still held its ground, that "assets" mean "tangible property"; that corporate capital is measured by the initial cash cost of the corporation's plant; and that intangibles can be capitalised only by subreption, by making believe that they are transferable objects of use and have a rateable cost of production — as, e.g., patented processes and contrivances — and so entering them on the books along with the tangible properties and writing them into the capitalised assets at a make-believe purchase price. Except *de jure*, all that has changed and passed, progressively with the passage of time and the accumulation of new usages and conceptions. In effect, assets are now capitalised on their earning-capacity regardless of cost or tangibility; the corporation is rated and capitalised at its value as a business concern, and among its valued and rateable possessions is its ability to borrow. An industrial corporation is necessarily rated on the sales-capacity of its industrial plant; that is to say, the prime factor in capitalisation is now in the nature of an intangible. Things have taken such a turn.

In the further course of capitalisation the capitalised intangibles, duly covered with negotiable securities, serve as collateral on which to secure an extension of credit, to be capitalised and covered with securities, which will be acceptable collateral so soon as they are "digested," etc. There is no question of the main fact; it is only a question of the rate of cumulative progression. It should also be noted that such liabilities may also serve as a creative factor in the progressive expansion of credit values without being formally capitalised in the shape of corporation securities conveying title to alleged assets. This is well shown by the case of government bonds or treasury notes and certificates, which are quite unexceptionable collateral at the same time that they neither represent tangible assets nor enter into the capital account of a corporation.

xii This outcome follows in so far as business comes to be conducted on a credit basis. It is the working-out of a progressively improved stability of credits and improved facilities for their expeditious negotiation. The greater the ease with which credit extensions are negotiated, and the greater the security of outstanding obligations, the more will the use of credit become an everyday necessity and the more urgent will be the inducement to make full use of one's borrowing capacity; and the larger will be the volume of outstanding obligations and the resultant aggregate of overhead charges falling on business and industry. And evidently no net gain accrues from this traffic, except what goes to the dispensers of credit; which is evidently of the nature of a differential gain at the cost of the business community at large.

xiii What amount is to be deducted as net eventual loss on the score of this cost of operation may be estimated, with a degree of approximation, from the total cost of carrying on the country's banking business, which is chiefly occupied with just this work; a reasonable allowance being made for other services rendered by the banks. What then remains of the sum of the cost of the traffic may be set down as paid to the bankers and their creditor clients for having enabled the country's business concerns, one with another, to inflate the figures of their receipts and disbursements.

xiv So, e.g., the same "Interest" which dominates the corporate business and industry in oil will at the same time dominate the leading banking establishment with which this oil business has to do, as well as its extensive retinue of affiliated banks. Among those business men who do business in oil it is a matter of course that the very extensive network of affiliated banks that are dominated by the Standard Oil Interest will faithfully serve that Interest in its endeavors to engross the oil resources of the country. Much the same disposition of forces is to be found in steel and railroads, of course. It is in no way obnoxious, either to the law or to business ethics.

xv It is always conceivable, of course, that this American pool of solvency, or some one of more of the major Interests comprised in it, may under urgent pressure enter into hazardously extensive commitments toward the outside, — e.g., toward insolvent European clients. This may give rise to contingencies of so grave a nature as would eventually leave the pool at loose ends, derange the team-work of the Interests, and precipitate an unadvised and unmanaged liquidation. In view of the known European commitments of certain American Interests, it has been believed by apprehensive persons that the current situation in Europe is likely to contain the elements of such an eventuality. It is known that there is such an element of hazard for the American Interests in the case, but no person outside the American General Staff of Solvency, as already spoken of before, is in a position to hold a reasoned opinion on the complexion and the magnitude of that hazard; and those persons who so are in a position to speak are maintaining a large and salutary reticence.

xvi As students will recognise, this term is borrowed from Knies and Hildebrand, who brought it into use in a somewhat wider application.

xvii To avoid dispute and exception, it may be as well to admit and note that such rights of usufruct have doubtless been capitalised in the capitalisation of these concerns that do business with the farm population, and that so they have been covered with corporation securities and incorporated in the assets of the corporations in question. In this way they doubtless make a very substantial mass of capitalised intangibles in the aggregate, and constitute a valuable body of assets; in the case of many such business concerns presumably these are the chief elements in their capitalisation. In so far, of course, this relation of usufruct has been given a formally legal existence, being capitalised and covered with negotiable corporation securities.

xviii See chapter vii, Section iv.

xix *De jure!* there is no such One Big Union of the Interests, of course. It is perhaps needless to say so. This descriptive phrase applies only *de facto*. And even *de facto* the One Big Union of the Interests appears, hitherto, scarcely to have had a settled local habitation and a name. Only in respect of the One Big Union's surveillance of note issues and rediscounts can it be said the Federal Reserve has given its membership a "Central" — if on may take a metaphor from the usage of the telephone. The One Big Union, hitherto, has no corporate existence. It foots up to a concert of action and policy enforced by the drift of circumstances, rather than by deliberation and reasoned plan looking to the long run. But by drift of circumstances — the drift of sound business principles and a common solicitude — their several movements result, in effect, in such a convergence of forces and such a concert of policy and action as to merit the name.

xx Such enlargement of effectual capital-value of given assets by the proven earning-capacity of an industrial business concern is well shown, e.g., in the case of the Standard Oil securities that were outstanding in some years ago; when the market value, and the consequent value as collateral, of the common stock advanced by steady growth of earnings till it reached some 700 per cent. over its face value. As an element of solvency and a credit-bearing asset that parcel of securities then counted at their market value, of course, not at their face value; as was also seen and turned to account presently in the issuance of stock dividends of some 700 per cent. Substantially the same operation has been repeated by the various Standard Oil properties during the past year (1922).

xxi Consider, e.g., two such typical credit institutions of the first rank as J. Pierpont Morgan & Co. and the National City Bank, which have come into the business from widely different beginnings and antecedents, but which now count at their full weight both in industrial enterprise and as banking houses.

It is also interesting to note that the dates from which the two take their departure as prime-movers in this twofold pursuit of gain, coincide in a loose way with the period out of which the new order of credit and capitalisation took its rise.

xxii There is a singular, but presumably idle, coincidence of dates and characteristics between this *de facto* magistracy of solvency, its scope and powers, on the one side, and the rise and scope of the Injunction as applied in American court practice on the other side. Both are unprecedented, both have grown out of inconspicuous beginnings and have come to their present sovereign powers within the same general period of time: The same period during which the large-scale industrial business and the free capitalisation of credits have also come into bearing, and have in time come to dominate the country's industrial system and its scheme of life. Both serve the ends of the larger absentee ownership, in the main and *de facto*. Both combine judiciary with executive powers, and the powers of both are of an inhibitory sort; essentially powers of retardation and inertia, powers which take effect by way of penalising activities that are not otherwise obnoxious to law or morals. It appears also that, in practical effect, the two mutually befriend and sustain one another.

xxiii This description of the case, as necessarily running to distrust, cross-purposes, and sharp practice, applies to the conduct of the business, not to the mechanics of production. It is a proposition concerning business principles and practice, not concerning the technique of industry. It remains true all the while, of course, that in point of workmanship, in point of efficient tangible performance, as contrasted with the strategy of salesmanship, the industries are always and everywhere best observed by a cordial and calculated cooperation between the various industrial units that make up the industrial system. The maximum net production is to be reached only along that line. But business enterprise is a pursuit of maximum net gain in terms of price, not of maximum production in terms of goods. It is an enterprise in salesmanship, whether the trading is done in material goods or in the credit instruments.

In the technological respect, as a proposition in workmanship and tangible performance, the industries of the country are bound together in an orderly network of interlocking processes of production; but in respect of the business interests engaged as a proposition in salesmanship and sales-profits, in their capacity of business concerns, these many parcels of industrial property are at cross-purposes, being in the position of competing bidders for custom. The strategy of salesmanship and net gain brings with it into the industrial system that defects of its own qualities, and among these defects is an inveterate bias of distrust and sharp practice.

xxiv So, e.g., increased sales of yeast-cakes, cosmetics, Red Cross doles, furs, or rubber tires — wares which have of late been selling very notably increased quantities as a result of large and persistent advertising — will be offset by a shrinkage of sales in other, alternative lines, as, e.g., fruits, flannels, alcoholic beverages, savings-bank accounts, or butcher's-meats.

The current situation of this business community at large, which so does business in commercial and industrial traffic within the bounds appointed by the massive Interests of the One Big Union, is a situation of much the same complexion as that which has prevailed in the country towns of the Middle West, [...]. The traffic runs on the same general lines of reserved and evasive rivalry within and of sturdy solidarity toward the outside, toward the underlying population; very much as the local community of retailers carries on the business traffic of a typical country town. Except for its larger dimensions it is much the same thing over again, both as regards the manner and the degree in which the cost of it all falls on the underlying population. In both cases it is an enterprise in usufruct carried on under a loosely defined code of Live and Let Live, designed to safeguard the joint advantage of the usufructuaries.

xxv The net aggregate price-return is a product of two variables; one of which — the output — varies at the discretion of the businesslike management, and the second of which — the price per unit — is a function of the first. "What the traffic will bear" is that volume of output which will give the largest product when multiplied into the price per unit. Hence the need of a vigilant restraint on production.

The principle of restraint which so comes to govern the business of what the traffic will bear has been spoken of as the "law of balanced return"; as being a principle which determines the expedient maximum of output in any given case, and which therefore also determines what will be the expedient size of an industrial business unit in any given line of production and sale. — Cf. A.S. Dewing, *The Financial Polity of Corporations*, vol. iv, ch. ii.

xxvi It will be seen that the current situation in this respect has much in common with the interval of prosperity, inflation, or speculative advance, that make up the rising segment of such a business cycle as the experience of the nineteenth century and the discussions of the nineteenth-century economists have made familiar; but with a difference. There is in the current situation an element of sobriety and a factor of salutary reserve that were lacking in the nineteenth century. Prosperity ran somewhat headlong in those days, and came, in the ordinary course, to a headlong liquidation, ending in panic, crisis and depression. Under the conservative surveillance of the Federal Reserve and the One Big Union of the Interests in the twentieth century the prosperity of business — that is to say the inflation of capital and prices — does not run riot. It is an orderly advance, in the course of which the progressive creations of credit and capital are duly stabilised and "digested," distributed and consolidated under the aegis of the Interests, with such effect as to make them a secure ground on which to hypothecate further creations of the same character, in indefinite progression. And no undesigned liquidation need be apprehended in this case, since the major debits and credits are pooled, in effect, by being drawn in under the custody of these major Interests that informally make up the One Big Union. Both the need of credits and the progressive creation of them are indefinitely extensible.

xxvii The "market" as here used is the volume of effective demand for things to be bought at the current level of prices, and it may be taken to mean the national market of the international market at large, according to the context of the argument. In either case it is a "closed market," in the sense that the available purchasing-power which constitutes the demand in this market falls short of the productive capacity of the industrial system, at the ruling level of prices. Hence attention and expenditure in this field of business enterprise have been converging on salesmanship rather than on increased production, with the result that total sales-costs have gained largely and progressively, at the same time that the rate and volume of output have remained relatively stationary on the whole.

xxviii One of the secondary consequences of this imperative recourse to salesmanship and enhanced sales-cost is to be noted in this connection. In great part salesmanship takes effect by way of establishing a conventional need for articles which have previously been superfluities, shifting given articles of consumption from the footing of superfluities to that of necessary articles of livelihood, necessities by conviction of morals and decency rather than by requirement of subsistence of physical comfort. By so much the necessities of life for the consumers will be enlarged, and by so much the (moral) subsistence minimum to be provided for out of wages will be raised, without a corresponding increase in the workmanlike efficiency of the wage-earners; which acts in its degree to increase the labor cost per unit of the marketable output of industry, and therefore also to narrow the margin of sales-price over production-cost. E.g., the moral necessity of consuming furs, cosmetics, or high heels.

Bibliography

Adams, Henry ([1900] 1983) "The Dynamo and the Virgin", pp. 1068—75 in *The Education of Henry Adams*/ITAL. New York: Viking.

Ahmed, Akbar (1992) *Postmodernism and Islam*. London: Routledge.

Bauman, Zygmunt (1992) *Intimations of Postmodernity*. London: Routledge.

Blaug, Mark (1992) *Thorstein Veblen 1857—1929*. Brookfield, VT: Edward Elgar Publishing.

Diggins, John P. (1978) *The Bard of Savagery*. New York: Seabury Press.

Dorfman, Joseph (1934) *Thorstein Veblen and His America*. New York: Viking.

Dowd, Douglas (1966) *Thorstein Veblen*. New York: Washington Square Press.

Frisby, David (1992) *Sociological Impressionism: A Reassessment of Simmel's Social Theory*. London: Routledge.

Giddens, Anthony (1990) *The Consequences of Modernity*. Stanford, CA: Stanford University Press.

Gilligan, Carol (1982) *In a Different Voice*. Cambridge, MA: Harvard University Press.

Lasch, Christopher (1970) *The Culture of Narcissism*. New York: Basic Books.

Mestrovic, Stjepan (1997) *Postemotional Society*. London: Sage.

Moynihan, Daniel Patrick (1993) *Pandaemonium*. New York: Oxford University Press.

Orwell, George ([1937] 1958) *The Road to Wigan Pier*. New York: Harcourt Brace.

Parsons, Talcott (1937) *The Structure of Social Action*. New York: Free Press.

Ritzer, George. (1992) *The McDonaldization of Society*. London: Sage.

Ritzer, George (1995) *Expressing America: A Critique of the Global Credit Card Society*. Thousand Oaks, CA: Pine Forge Press.

Rojek, Chris (1994) *Ways of Escape: Modern Transformations in Leisure*. Lanham, MD: Rowman and Littlefield.

Tilman, Rick (1985) *Thorstein Veblen: A Reference Guide*. Boston: G.K. Hall and Co.

Tilman, Rick (1992) *Thorstein Veblen and His Critics, 1891—1963*. Princeton, NJ: Princeton University Press.

Tilman, Rick (1996) *The Intellectual Legacy of Thorstein Veblen*. Westport, CT: Greenwood Press.

Veblen, Thorstein ([1899] 1969) *The Theory of the Leisure Class*. New York: Penguin.

Veblen, Thorstein (1904) *The Theory of Business Enterprise*. New York: Macmillan.

Veblen, Thorstein (1914) *The Instinct of Workmanship*. New York: Macmillan

Veblen, Thorstein (1919) *The Place of Science in Modern Civilisation and Other Essays*. New York: B.W. Huebsch.

Veblen, Thorstein (1921) *The Engineers and the Price System*. New York: Viking.

Veblen, Thorstein (1934) *Essays in Our Changing Order*. New York: Viking.

Veblen, Thorstein (1939) *Imperial Germany and the Industrial Revolution*. New York: Macmillan.

Veblen, Thorstein (1973) *Essays, Reviews and Reports: Previously Uncollected Writings*. Clifton, NJ: A.M. Kelley

Widiger, Thomas A., Mangine Steve, Corbitt Elizabeth M, Ellis Cynthia G., and Thomas, Glenn V. (1995) *Personality Disorder Interview-IV*. Odessa, FL: Psychological Assessment Resources.

Index

absentee ownership
advertising 141, 142
holding-companies 153
investment bankers and credit 163–70, 173–4, 179–80, 184
postmodernism 13
accountancy, universities 14, 73–7, 79–82
Adams, Henry 2
adornment 120–1, 125
Adorno, Theodor 1
advertising 2, 4, 14, 137–46
agency
advertising 14
instincts 20–1
splitting 11
agriculture
credit 169–70, 182–5
sabotage 133–4
Ahmed, Akbar 11
altruism 10
American Legion 131
anarchists 47–8
animism 21, 24, 115
anomie 10
anthropomorphism 21, 24, 25
apparel 120–6
art 18–19
authority, patriotism 105–9

banking, credit 153, 156–81
banknotes 170
barbarian cultures
patriotism 99–100, 103–5
predatory life 111–19
universities 68–70, 71
women 111–19
barbarism
advertising 2
law 16
narcissism 3, 5, 9–10
nationalism 15–16
postmodernism 12–13
war 5–6
West 15
Baudrillard, Jean 1, 13
belief 28–36
Bolsheviks 131
bureaucracy, universities 73–82

business
credit 152–191
manufacturing 133–51
narcissism 6–7
patriotism 96
professional schools 72–3
sabotage 85–93, 133–4
universities 53, 54–5, 66–7, 73–7, 82
war and peace 6

capital, sabotage 88–9
causation 24–5
censorship 14, 93, 130–1
ceremony, marriage 114–15
chaos, modernity 12
children, dress 126
citizenship 61, 96
civilisation, science 18–26
clothing 120
collective consciousness, narcissism 5–6, 9
colleges 61–4, 78–82
common good 103–5
commonwealth 47
communication, sabotage 92–3
communism 10, 131
community solidarity 103–5
competition
credit 154–6, 176–9
holding–companies 159
mergers 161–2
patriotism 6, 95
salesmanship 2, 135–44, 178–9
conscientious objectors 129, 131
conspicuous consumption 1
Germany 44–5
narcissism 3, 8
women's dress 121–6
conspicuous leisure 1, 3, 8
conspicuous waste 1
Germany 44–5
narcissism 3, 8
consumerism 16–17
consumption
advertising 14, 137–44
Germany 44–5
narcissism 3
postmodernism 1

consumption *cont.*
sabotage 88–90
women's dress 121–6
control, sabotage 87–91
cooperation, narcissism 9–10
cosmology 22–3
cosmopolitianism, patriotism 98–9
credit 13, 14, 152–191
credulity, publicity 141, 144
custom 28–36
patriotism 102
traditional societies 39–40

Darwin, Charles 10
Darwinianism 37–8
dementia praecox 127–32
disembeddedness 13
dislocation 13
dissociation 3
dog ownership, narcissism 5
dress, women 120–6
dualisms 9, 10
dynastic state, Germany 41–50

economics
credit 13, 14, 152–191
Germany 42–7
women's dress 120–6
education
barbarism 16
Germany 49
higher learning 52–84
modern civilisation and science 20
efficiency
credit 182–3
division of labour 111
over–production 172–3
patriotism 98–9
sabotage 14, 85–93, 133–4
universities 75–6, 78–9
women's dress 123
egoism 10
engineers 16, 33
envy 2
fashion 8
narcissism 3–5, 13
traditional cultures 11
university 14–15
equity, patriotism 96–8
esoteric knowledge 52–84
Europe
patriotism and heredity 99–105
World War I 127–9
excise, sabotage 91–2

farming
credit 169–70, 182–5
sabotage 133–4
fashion 7–8, 123–4
fear, publicity 141, 144
Federal Reserve Board 171–2, 181, 183
feminism 16
France 128
Freud, S. 11

gender, narcissism 9
Germany 41–50
babarism 15
narcissism 5–6
patriotism 96, 107
sabotage 93
World War I 127–8
Giddens, Anthony 1, 3, 10–11, 13, 15
Gilligan, Carol 16
globalism
nationalism 16
sabotage 14
gold 171, 172
government, sabotage 91–3
group heredity 37–8

habits 3, 28–36, 39–40, 52–5
heredity 37–8
patriotism 99–104
UK 47–8
higher education 52–84
holding–companies 153–60
hybrids, patriotism 100–2

ideal types 6–7
idle curiosity 8, 9–10, 16
intelligence 21
modernity 24
postmodernism 14–15
traditional societies 21–4
universities 54–5, 56, 65, 69–71
Imperialism, Germany 41–4, 48
imponderables 31–2, 33
industry
advertising 14
credit 152–191
Germany 41, 42–8
higher learning 54–5
manufacturing 133–51
marriage as ownership 116, 118–19
patriotism 98–9, 103–5
primative societies 111
sabotage 85–93, 133–4
technology 37–40
infirmity, barbarian culture 112
inflation 171–3

information, sabotage 14, 92–3
initiation, marriage 115
inner-directed type 1
inquiry, universities 59–61, 65–6, 70
instinct for workmanship 8–9, 10, 24–5
  higher learning 54–5
  machine system 9
  sabotage 14
  salesmanship 137
  women 16
instincts 20–1
insubordination 47–8
intelligence 20–1
Interests, One Big Union of 158, 167, 173–84
Internet 14
intolerance, US 129–31
investment bankers 13, 156–81
I.W.W. 131

Japan 5–6, 15
justice, patriotism 96–7

Key Industries 179–80
knowledge
  higher learning 52–84
  instability of 28–36
  science 18–26
  technology 37
Ku-Klux-Klan 131

labour, sabotage 85–6
Lasch, Christopher 4, 5
law, universities 71
law of efficient causes 24
laws, instability of 28–36
lawyers 6–7, 16
learning 52–84
legends 21, 22
leisure 1–2, 4
lockouts, sabotage 86–7
Loeb, Jacques 20
Lusk Committee 130–1

McDonaldization 12, 13
machine system 2, 10, 33
  advertising 14
  Germany 41
  higher learning 55–6
  modernity 2
  narcissism 9
  over-production 87–8, 133
  postmodernism 11, 12–13, 16–17
  publicity 139–40, 141–2
  science 25–6
  traditional cultures 11

McDonaldization *cont.*
  universities 73–7, 78–82
  university 14–15
  western civilisation and science 18
manufacturing 133–51
marginal differentiation 1
marriage, as ownership 114–19, 121–2
Marx, Karl 10
mastery 22–3
  over women 113–19
  patriotism 105–9
matriarchal culture 8, 9, 116–18
matter-of-fact knowledge 18–20, 55–8
medicine, universities 71
men
  dementia praecox 132
  marriage as ownership 114–19
  warlike prowess 112–14, 115–16
  women's dress 121–2
Mendelian units of character 99–102
mergers 153–60
military service 45, 48–9, 131
modern civilisation, science 18–26
modern culture
  heredity 103
  marriage as ownership 116, 118–19
  patriotism 98
  women's dress 121–5
modernity
  belief 28–36
  higher learning 55–6
  idle curiosity 24
  knowledge 28–36
  machine system 2, 11
  narcissism 3–10
  order and chaos 12
  self–reflexivity 10–11
money 170
morality
  instability of 28–36
  marriage as ownership 114
  patriotism 96–8, 102–3
Morgan, J. Pierpoint 153, 154–5, 158–9
myths 21

narcissism 3–10, 12–16, 17
national prestige, patriotism 94–7
nationalism
  Germany 43–4, 48
  narcissism 15–16
  patriotism 99–110
natural laws 23, 25
news, sabotage 92–3
news–print publicity 2, 142–3

One Big Union of Interests 158, 173–84

ornament 120–1
Orwell, George 2
other-directed type 1
other-directedness 1, 3
over-production 87–91, 133–4, 155–6, 172–3, 182–3
ownership 39–40
  marriage as 114–19
  patriotism 105–6
  traditional societies 39–40
  women's dress 121–2
  see also absentee ownership

pacifists 129, 131
packaging 2, 137–9
passive resistance, sabotage 85
passivity, splitting 11
patriarchy
  marriage as ownership 115–19
  narcissism 9
  women's dress 121–2
patriotism 6, 94–110
  Germany 42, 48, 49
  higher learning 58
  narcissism 9
  US 131
pay 182–3
peace
  narcissism 5–6, 8, 9–10
  patriotism 97, 107
pecuniary system
  narcissism 9
  sabotage 14
  universities 14–15, 54–5, 75, 78
pedigree 37–8
philosophy, universities 70–1
polygamy 116
postmodernism 1, 11–17, 33
poverty, patriotism 105–8
power 1
  Germany 42–5
  World War I 127–8
pragmatism
  barbarian cultures 23, 68–70
  knowledge 20–2
predatory culture
  advertising 14
  barbarian societies 111–14, 115–19
  knowledge 22–3
  technology 37–40
prestige
  barbarian cultures 104, 105
  national 94–5
  patriotism 106–7, 108–10
prices
  competition 161–2, 178
prices *cont.*
  credit 152, 166, 171–3, 178, 179–85
  over-production 172–3
  sabotage 86–91, 133–4
  salesmanship 136–7, 138–9, 142
  women's dress 122, 125
primative societies, industry 111
principles, instability of 28–36
production
  over-production 133–4, 155–6, 172–3, 180
  prices 172–3
  sabotage 87–91, 133–4
professional schools 60, 61, 64–8, 71–3
profit, sabotage 86–90
Propaganda of the Faith 143–6
property rights see ownership rights
psychiatry, narcissism 4, 5
psychology
  advertising 138, 141
  learning and knowledge 20
publicity 137–46

race 38, 99–104
rationality 10, 12
re-embeddedness 13
religion
  patriotism 96
  publicity 143–6
  universities 70–1
  US 129–30, 131, 132
research, universities 59–61, 65–6
restraint of trade
  patriotism 106
  sabotage 91–3
  trade unions 135
Riesman, David 1, 3, 6, 8
Ritzer, George 2, 12, 13
Rojek, Chris 1, 12
Romanticism, Germany 41, 48

sabotage 13–14, 85–93, 133–4, 163
sales-price 181–2
salesmanship 133–51
  competition 178–9, 181–3
  postmodernism 13
  sabotage 14
scholasticism 19, 23–4, 55
science 18–26, 33
  Germany and warfare 49–50
  higher learning 53, 55
  patriotism 98
  religion 129–30
  universities 59–61, 64–6
  warlike ambitions 58

Secret Service 131
self-made man/woman 7
self-reflexivity 10–11, 15
selling-cost 138–40, 141–3
servitude 22–3, 105–8
shame, publicity 141
social action theory 10–11
social Darwinism 10
socialism, machine system 10
sovereign, patriotism 107, 109
specialisation, publicity 142
Spencer, Herbert 10
splitting 3, 8–11, 12, 13
sports 45, 95
standardization
    modernity 2
    publicity 142
    universities 14, 73–7, 78–82
status
    barbarian cultures 111–14, 115–19
    narcissism 3, 4, 5
    postmodernism and credit 13
    university 15
    women in barbarian societies
115–19
    women's dress 121–6
strikes, sabotage 86–7
subsidies, sabotage 91
Sunday, Rev. Billy 130
superstition 129–30

tariffs
    Germany 43–4
    patriotism 106
    sabotage 91–2
    US 134
taxation 44, 91–2
technical schools 60, 61, 64–8, 71–3
technology 33
    Germany 46–7, 49–50
    higher learning 54–6
    over-production 172–3
    patriotism 103–5
    predatory culture 37–40
    science 26
theology, universities 70–1
Tilman, Rick 2
trade, patriotism 96–7
trade unions 135–6, 182–3
traditional cultures 10
    knowledge 21–4
    machine system 11
    narcissism 9
    ownership 39–40
    technology 38–40
    university and idle curiosity 15
    see also barbarian cultures
training, universities 59, 61–6, 71–3
tutelage, Germany 45–6

unemployment 87–8, 133, 180, 183
United Kingdom
    conspicuous consumption 44
    institutions 47–8
    sports 45
United States of America
    babarism 15
    censorship 14, 130–1
    dementia praecox 129–32
    narcissism 4
    patriotism 58, 131
    religion 129–30, 131, 132
    sabotage and censorship 93
    self-made man 7
    tariffs 134
    universities 61–4, 73–82
    World War I 6, 127–32
universities 16, 52–84
    business principles 7
    Germany 49
    higher learning 58–84
    narcissism and postmodernism
14–15
upward mobility, narcissism 4, 5
U.S. Steel Corporation 156, 160
utilitarianism 66–7, 68–71, 75

vocational training, universities 59,
61–8

wages 134
war
    barbarian societies and women
111–14, 115–17
    Germany 42–5, 48–50, 127–8
    higher learning 58
    narcissism 4, 5–6, 9
    patriotism 95, 106–7
    sabotage 88–90, 92
waste
    fashion 8
    Germany 44–5
    narcissism 3
    nationalism 15
    postmodernism 17
    women's dress 122–6
wealth
    patriotism 105–9
    traditional societies 39–40
    women's dress 121–6
Weber, Max 10
western civilisation, science 18–26

Widiger, Thomas A. 4
women
    barbarian status 111–19
    dress 120–6
    feminism 16
    narcissism 9
    professions 16
working classes, Germany 45–6
workmanship 24–5
    see also instinct for workmanship
workmen
    sabotage 85–6
    salesmanship 134–6
    technology 37
    unemployment 87, 88
World War I 5, 6, 34–5, 127–32
worldly wisdom 65
Wright Mills, C. 1